Stuart Stevens is a political consultant and writer, whose first book, *Night Train to Turkistan*, was a well-received travelogue. In 1984 he became the first person to race the complete Worldloppet International ski circuit in one year, a story told in the National Geographic television documentary *Marathon Winter*. His articles and stories have appeared in *The New Republic*, *Washington Monthly*, *Skiing*, *Esquire* and the *International Herald Tribune*.

'Reads like a sprightly comic novel featuring the author himself as a bumbling, put-upon hero . . . Mr Stevens emerges not only as an engaging picaresque hero, but as a clever and observant writer' *New York Times*

D1054851

Stuart Stevens

MALARIA DREAMS

An African Adventure

An Abacus Book

First published in Great Britain by Simon & Schuster Ltd 1990
Published in Abacus by Sphere Books Ltd 1992

ISBN 0 349 10211 2

Printed and bound in Great Britain by
Cox & Wyman Ltd, Reading, Berkshire

Sphere Books Ltd
A Division of
Macdonald & Co (Publishers) Ltd
165 Great Dover Street
London SE1 4YA
A member of Maxwell Macmillan Publishing Corporation

IN MEMORY OF

Tom Hairston, Cooper Neill, Bruce Studders—

OLD FRIENDS.

Malaria
Dreams

Preface

Just looking at the books made me feel better. They were piled in the adjacent airline seat, reassuring in their bulk. Each of the titles had an appealing no-nonsense quality. *Africa Overland* and *Sahara Handbook* were the thickest volumes, but my favorite was a skinny pamphlet called *Stay Alive in the Desert.* I liked the author's imperative tone. None of this "how-to" stuff, just a simple command: Stay alive, dammit!

I opened *Africa Overland.* "Nowadays one can read of travellers getting lost," the introduction began, "and into trouble, or even dying in the attempt to cross Africa, but the reasons for these tragedies are simple and there for anyone to see. The first and most important reason is insufficient planning."

This was somewhat unsettling. My planning had mostly consisted of one trip to Hatchard's bookstore to buy the books that evidently were now going to enumerate all the preparations I had not made.

"Such a trip must not be undertaken lightly, and should be planned on an expedition basis with the whole of the planning for the trip spread over a period of at least one year."

This suggested further problems. I had decided to travel across Africa about three weeks ago.

"Prospective travellers should not listen to rumours and hear-say of crime, muggings, abductions and other bad reports of happenings in African countries."

I read on, anxious to find out exactly *why* one shouldn't listen to these reports. Unfortunately, further explanation seemed to be missing. I skipped ahead to the section headed "Travelling Companions."

"The choice of persons or person to accompany you is of paramount importance and the success or failure of the whole trip can depend upon your choice."

I thought about this for a while, staring out the plane window at the red and orange bands of the sinking sun. We were over the Sahara.

The author elaborated on the proper characteristics of a trans-African companion. Or companions, really, as he made it clear that it was entirely unwise to consider such a journey without a proper "team."

"Physical fitness is an important factor in selecting your travelling companions, as there will be some extremes of temperature to contend with, and times when everybody will be required to push and heave when a vehicle becomes stuck, or to lift when it comes to changing a wheel. . . . Most important, at least one member of your group should be a professional motor mechanic or have sound mechanical knowledge."

I put the book down. Across the aisle my "team" was engrossed in *Breakfast at Tiffany's*. She was twenty-three years old, 5'5", 110 pounds, and possibly the only person ever to transfer from Bryn Mawr to the University of Oklahoma. In all likelihood Ann knew more about mechanics than I did, but I doubt I've ever met anyone who didn't. She was nibbling from a can of pheasant pâté. She'd acquired this treat at the airport in Marseilles when I had suggested she buy us some sandwiches while I held our place in the check-in line. She'd returned some time later quite pleased.

"What's that?" I asked.

"Pâté. Pheasant pâté."

"What happened to the sandwiches?"

"They looked yucky. All they had was ham and stuff like that."

"Ham."

As the plane began to descend, I finished the introduction to

Africa Overland. "It must be emphasized that the trans-African trip will not be a holiday. If you are able to accept this, you will lose completely the worries and inhibitions associated with the dull confines of civilization."

Chapter One

This is a story about Africa that began in a Thai restaurant. I was there with my friend Lucien.

"I've got this Land Rover, you know," he began.

"Yes." I was concentrating on the great heap of noodles and shrimp the waiter was delivering.

"It's in Bangui. The Land Rover is. Have you ever been there?"

"I've never heard of it."

"You'd like it. It's on the banks of the Ubangi River."

"Lucien, what continent are we talking about?"

He looked shocked and mildly disappointed, as if I'd committed a grievous faux pas at one of his dinner parties. Lucien and his wife were famous for their dinner parties.

"Africa," he said after a while. "The CAR."

"Right." I debated if I should let him know that, like Bangui, I had never heard of the CAR either or just let the matter drop. Lucien had certain esoteric interests that he could, if prompted, ramble on about for a very long time. Actually, he could do this without prompting as well.

"The CAR," he repeated imploringly. "The Central African Republic."

To my surprise, I realized I had heard of the country. "Bokassa's empire," I said. "The fellow who made himself emperor and ate all those schoolchildren."

"That's never really been documented," Lucien said firmly.

Later, too much later, this surfaced in my memory as a most suspect response.

"I spent a good bit of time in the CAR last year," Lucien explained.

I nodded, methodically working my way through a bundle of saté skewers. Lucien was always going off to obscure corners of Africa. No one seemed to know what he did or why, though supposedly it had something to do with gold and diamonds. This was something else I thought about a lot later on.

"Ongoing project . . .," Lucien continued, fluttering his hand over the table as if clearing smoke. "But I've got this Land Rover down there and I'd rather like to get it back." Lucien had learned English from a governess of Sloane Ranger origins.

"What I was wondering is"—he leaned forward and cocked an eyebrow—"if perhaps you would be interested in driving my vehicle back to Paris."

I had been in Bangui less than ten minutes when I was robbed for the first time. This proved to be very fortunate. Muggings, rape and murder, I quickly discovered, were the pillars of conversation among the white community, and my introductory theft gave me something to talk about on the party circuit.

It was early October. The season was a factor in the robbery as it had been cold and rainy in Europe and I had arrived at the Bangui airport carrying a heavy raincoat. It was a new coat, recently purchased in England. I liked it.

Bangui International Airport looks like a cross between a ruined Roman temple and a Quonset hut. The crumbling stone dates from the early days of French rule; the sheet-metal additions are part of the current government's modernization program.

Françoise Vidal met us. She was a slight, pretty blond mostly buried beneath a milling mob outside the customs shed. With one hand struggling to keep aloft a sign with my name on it and another vainly warding off the hordes, she looked even more lost than we did. I wondered how a woman so apparently fragile could survive in the middle of Africa.

"This is Ann Bradley; Ann, Françoise Vidal." We shook hands all around, our palms slick with sweat. I'd already explained to Ann that Françoise was the wife of Lucien's best friend in the CAR.

Françoise led us outside. It was night and there were no lights in the mud parking lot. Black figures rushed out of the darkness toward us, shouting. Instinctively, I drew back. Françoise hoisted up her skirt and propped one foot on the fender of an old Renault and thundered in French. "Goddamn, get away! What do you think you're doing? Stay back. Dammit!"

Like recruits before a drill sergeant, the crowd calmed. Then, in a lower but still forceful voice, Françoise directed the baggage porters to load our bags in the Renault.

This took a long time. We had an appalling amount of luggage. In addition to a small auto-parts store of Land Rover pieces, I had brought camping equipment and my book collection. Later, I realized I'd also packed an outlandish number of flashlights. Ann carried a big duffel bag and a hard-shelled suitcase larger than the Renault's trunk.

Françoise let out a piercing whistle. "Taxi!" she bellowed. Instantly five cars tore though the crowd. Several bystanders were flung up on hoods without apparent damage. People laughed. The drivers besieged Françoise, who quickly enforced order. "We must have a taxi for the luggage," she told Ann and me in a soft, charming voice, then proceeded to pit one driver against another in a vicious bidding war. "Too much, too much!" she scolded one. "He will do it for less." This evoked fresh pleadings and a chorus of wailing.

A deal was struck. We loaded the chosen taxi. Even with the two cars it was a tight fit. It made me glad Lucien's Land Rover was a Series 110, the long-wheelbase model designed for expedition loads.

Françoise pressed a wad of bills into my hand. She knew I

wouldn't have any Central African francs as there was no change bureau in the airport. "Ann and I go in my car, you follow in the taxi."

As soon as Françoise pulled away, the crowd surged forward, hands outstretched. "What? What?" I mumbled, drawing back toward the open door of the taxi. *"Patron!* Money! *Cadeaux! Patron!"* they shouted.

Some of these people had helped us carry the luggage, but Françoise had paid them, I was sure of it. I paused for a moment at the car door, glancing down at the sweaty bills in my fist. I wanted to be fair; maybe someone hadn't been paid.

My hesitation launched a fresh surge of bodies. Strong hands reached out and grabbed my arm, trying to pry my fingers open to get to the money. More hands thrust down into my pockets. I shouted without effect.

With one violent tug, the taxi driver jerked me into the car. A dozen hands shot through the open window. I reached for the window handle but it was sheared off. The driver started the car and screeched forward. A pair of children, no more than ten years old, flattened themselves against the windshield and pressed their faces to the glass. Their crazy, distorted features looked like smiles. Giggling, the driver slammed on the brakes and the kids bounced off.

"These children should be more careful," he said, frowning. "That is very dangerous. They could get hurt."

Halfway to the hotel I realized my coat, which I'd thrown on the back seat, was missing.

Chapter
Two

The news came the next morning over breakfast.

"There is a slight problem," Henri Vidal said. We were outside on the terrace of the Sofitel Hotel. A few feet away, the Ubangi River stretched a muddy half mile to Zaire. Waiters in white jackets brought us café au lait. I thought about the airport and the near riot, the children splayed across the windshield.

Henri, Françoise's husband, ran a coffee plantation in the western part of the country, shuttling back and forth to Bangui, where Françoise worked in the French embassy. He'd arrived last night about 2:00 A.M. from the "bush," as he called it, but seemed fresh and quite upbeat.

"Problem?"

"With the Land Rover. Lucien's Land Rover."

"Lucien did mention something about a possible technicality that needed to be cleared up."

"Yes? So then it is already understood?" Henri smiled, relieved.

"He said we might need to get some export document."

"Oh." Henri slumped in his chair and took a long sip of café au lait. "I think perhaps it is not understood so well after all."

I nodded. In the middle of the river big hunks of grass floated down the swift current. Fishermen worked the water in hollowed-out log pirogues, narrow and tilting upward at both ends.

"Lucien's Land Rover," Henri continued, "it is very nice, no?"

"That's what I hear."

"There are not so many nice cars in Bangui. Most have broken. Everything is very expensive."

I nodded, not understanding why I was hearing this.

"There is an official. In the Ministry of Mines. He has decided to like Lucien's Land Rover."

"Yes . . ."

"And he has taken the car."

"Taken it? Taken it where?"

Henri looked puzzled.

"Where is the car now?" I asked.

"Here. In Bangui. I think the official, he likes very much to drive this car."

"You mean he has seized the car?"

"*Seized?* What is *seized?*" Henri asked.

"He will not give us the car?"

A flock of white egrets swooped down into the reeds along the riverbank.

"Why?" My voice, I thought, sounded unnaturally high.

"It is very complicated." Henri shrugged and smiled. "Africa."

"But can't we just go to the head of the Ministry of Mines—"

"You mean the minister of mines—"

"Okay, go to the minister and tell him one of his officials has taken Lucien's car?"

Henri frowned. "But it is the minister who has seized the car."

"The minister of mines is driving *my* Land Rover?"

Henri shrugged again. "Africa. Perhaps, I think, you will grow used to it."

"But I didn't come here to get used to it. I came to drive a Land Rover back to Paris."

"Yes, that is why we have a problem."

Henri left after breakfast to fly to Cameroon for three days. Though I'd known him only about an hour, my spirits sank as I watched him leave. He seemed very competent, knew his way around Bangui and was clearly willing to help.

He was also the only person I knew in Africa. Except for his wife. And Ann.

I found Ann in back of the Sofitel by the pool. It was on a jetty jutting out into the Ubangi. She wore a bathing suit with a large number 7 on it and was reading a five-pound Italian *Vogue*, another Marseilles acquisition, surrounded by a half dozen very pale young men.

"They're Jaguar pilots," she told me. Somewhere behind her sunglasses and the red St. Louis Cardinals hat pulled down low, I caught a trace of a smile.

I thought about this for a moment trying to figure out what she meant, but the image of these earnest boys propelling animals through the sky confounded me.

"Jaguars are French fighter planes," Ann explained peevishly.

"Oh. Fighter jocks." Now it was my turn to smile. Ann's boyfriend back in Oklahoma was a fighter pilot. "A generic preference?" I inquired. Before she could respond, I explained to her what Henri had told me.

"So what do we do?" she asked, apparently delighted at the thought that we had traveled a few thousand miles to pick up a car that, at least for the moment, might as well not have existed.

"Cry for help," I said.

We spent the rest of the day barricaded in the room, trying to reach people by phone. Lucien had given me a short list of people he knew in Bangui, "just in case you run into difficulties," as he'd blithely put it.

There are telephones in Bangui and, surprisingly, they work rather well. My main target was a German named Rolph Kneeper, who worked as a lawyer for the CAR government. Lucien had assured me that he was intimately familiar with the Land Rover and, as a lawyer and government insider, could quickly solve any of the "technicalities" we might encounter.

We tried all day by phone to reach Kneeper, and another fellow named Amphoux, who was supposed to be Lucien's accountant, and three or four other people who worked in the CAR government. Each office told us our subject was out but assured us he would return momentarily. No one ever did.

"Maybe these people really don't exist," Ann suggested. I was afraid she might be on to something.

The next morning we set out on foot to find Kneeper.

"You can't do that," the desk clerk of the Sofitel, a Frenchman, told us as we were leaving.

"What?"

"Walk. Around town."

"Why?"

"You will die!" He threw up his hands dramatically.

"Oh, that," Ann said. She was not one to take such things very seriously.

"If you insist on walking," he asserted, "then I must ask you to settle your account before leaving."

"Now just a minute—," I blustered. This seemed to be carrying things a bit far.

"You have a credit card slip," Ann pointed out. "That should handle it."

"In that case, everything is in order."

Ann scribbled down something on a piece of paper and handed it to him. "This is my family's address. To ship the body."

"You were joking, right?" I asked her when we were outside. "Right?"

She pulled her Cardinals hat down and kept walking.

The Sofitel Hotel is on the edge of Bangui, a twenty-minute walk from the center of town. The road runs beside the Ubangi River, passing the customs shed for the boat traffic back and forth to Zaire. Though alert for ambush, we were accosted only by friendly vendors selling Coca-Cola and Coastal beer. Barechested men unloaded sacks of grain from a flotilla of pirogues. A line of women in wrap skirts carried great bundles of wood

balanced on their heads to the pirogues for the return trip to
Zaire. A dozen soldiers with automatic weapons watched the
women, laughing.

We were looking for the Ministry of Planning, where Rolph
Kneeper was rumored to have an office. It was touted as an easy
place to find, "just near the presidential palace." The latter is an
imposing structure of pink stone surrounded by a high wall, razor
wire and troops less sleepy-looking than most. Oddly, no one
seems to know what happens inside the walls. Bokassa had used
it as a sometime residence, one of his many palaces, and now
President Kolingba has an office inside. But everyone maintained
the current president was never there. "It's just his office," I was
told repeatedly, as if that explained everything. Of course, in a
town in which only a few years ago schoolchildren were not only
whacked to death but eaten by a president—or emperor, as
Bokassa crowned himself—it's understandable that no one ap-
pears too eager to ask the chief executive awkward questions.

The streets of Bangui are dirt, with just enough asphalt to
make them impossible to level with a grader. The potholes are
immense and even the lightest of rains makes the town look like
the setting for a Somerset Maugham tropical story.

On the day we searched for the Ministry of Planning, it had
not rained for some time and red dust floated in the air with every
passing Land Cruiser or Land Rover. These big vehicles belong to
the myriad of foreign organizations working in Bangui. They
cruise the streets like a benevolent occupying army. It is difficult
to comprehend, but in this small country of about two and a half
million, there are American, French, German, Dutch, Japanese—
even Chinese—agencies toiling, in theory at least, to improve the
life of Central Africans. With an annual per capita income of
under three hundred dollars and an average life expectancy of
only forty-four years, the challenge is formidable.

Many of the aid projects work with one particular agency of
the government and—the relationship is more than coinciden-
tal—the government of the CAR has a staggering number of
agencies. Foreign aid is to the CAR what cocaine is to Colombia.

Most of these agencies, we discovered, have offices near the presidential palace. In our search for Kneeper's office, we passed the Ministry of Education, the Ministry of Schools (apparently the two are not connected), the Ministry of Governmental Affairs (sort of a Ministry of Ministries), the Ministry of Water; I lost count at twenty. Each was in a little house with a tin roof, a stand of banana plants out front and a rickety plank bridging the drainage ditch paralleling the road.

The Ministry of Planning was just such a building, distinguished only by the newish Mercedes four-wheel-drive vehicle parked in the dirt yard.

We found Kneeper in his office standing in front of an air conditioner.

Tall, with bright eyes and a bushy mustache, he had wildly curly hair and, as did most of the European officials in town, wore casual clothes—an open sport shirt and pleated khakis. Only the Africans seemed to wear business suits in Bangui.

Kneeper greeted us warmly. He also had no idea who we were.

"Lucien didn't tell you I'd be coming to pick up his car?" I asked.

"What car?" he responded.

In my pocket I had Lucien's list of contacts in the CAR. Next to Kneeper's name he'd written: "Key player. Knows all about the Land Rover."

"Lucien's Land Rover," I mumbled. "A Series 110, diesel."

"Ahh," Kneeper said, settling down in a chair behind his large desk. "The Land Rover."

"Yes!"

He paused for a moment. I felt we were on the edge of a breakthrough.

"I really don't know a thing about that Land Rover," he finally said.

"Not a thing?" I pleaded. I was now willing to accept any smidgen of news. "Nothing?"

Kneeper shook his head. But he was willing to help. Leaning

back in his chair and toying with his thick Montblanc pen, he thought for a moment then launched into a flurry of phone calls in French.

Hanging up the phone, he stood and said, "Come, we go see the fabled Land Rover."

Bouncing around in Kneeper's Mercedes jeep, we searched for the Ministry of Mines. Kneeper had lived in Bangui seven years but, as he said, "there are so many of these things. You're not really anything in the government until you have your own agency."

We crisscrossed back and forth over the grid of streets near the presidential palace, finally driving up a hill in back of the palace. It took four-wheel drive to mount the steep slope with ruts large enough to swallow a Honda.

"Over there," Kneeper said casually as we topped the hill.

Under a shady mango tree, a green Land Rover sat looking forlorn. A pair of Africans in folding metal chairs leaned against the tree.

Kneeper greeted them and asked if the Land Rover was working. It was in very good shape, they responded, driven just this morning.

"Well, at least that's good news," I said, desperate for a bit of this apparently elusive commodity.

"Oh, no," Kneeper countered. "On the contrary. That is very bad news indeed."

Ann and I stared at him blankly.

"If it weren't working, the odds of getting it back would be much better. Particularly if it needed some hard-to-get part. Then it would be no good to them."

We nodded. It made a terrible kind of sense.

"Of course, most parts are hard to get for a Land Rover," Kneeper added. "It really is a piece of junk, you know." He patted his Mercedes and smiled.

We followed Kneeper inside a one-story pink stucco building. A soldier in sandals and camouflage fatigues saluted; Kneeper, looking amused, returned the salute.

We entered a small office adjoining an open breezeway. A French officer in khakis rose and saluted us. This time Ann returned the gesture. There seemed to be an awful lot of saluting going on.

"Capitaine Follope!" Kneeper motioned dramatically. The two men grinned at each other.

We sat down, four of us squeezed into the tiny office, and Kneeper explained who we were and why we were here. An air conditioner labored in one corner and a fan whirled at full force. The effect was like being in a loud wind tunnel.

The problem with the Land Rover was really quite simple, Capitaine Follope—whom Kneeper addressed as *"mon capitaine"*—explained. There were some fees that had not been paid on mineral leases Lucien had acquired from the government. The vehicle had been seized as collateral against future payment.

"The amount in question is very small," Follope said reassuringly.

"How much?"

"Half a million Central African francs."

It sounded like a lot of money to me. I tried to calculate quickly: 270 Central African francs, or CFA, to the dollar. It was a little less than $2,000. Not a small amount but certainly cheaper than buying a new car. Lucien, I figured, would gladly pay if he understood it was the only way to see his Land Rover again.

"Tell me," Follope asked casually, "how well do you know your friend Lucien?"

This was something I hadn't given much thought. I shrugged. "Fairly well, I suppose."

"And you are a friend, not a business associate?"

"Just a friend. Why?"

Follope waved his hand dismissively.

Just as we were leaving, Follope—a big man with a sizable chest—put his hand on my shoulder and asked, "Why doesn't Lucien come back himself? It's his Land Rover."

I laughed and said something about his being lazy. Follope looked at me, his eyes open and clear and curious.

Chapter Three

Walking back from Kneeper's office, a taxi passed us, then stopped and reversed back toward us in a cloud of dust.

Ann yelled as both of us jumped clear, along with a man who was urinating by the side of the road.

The taxi driver got out and came forward, hand extended. He reached down to us in the drainage ditch where we had landed to shake hands. The man who had been urinating lay on his back, staring, his penis dangling from his pants.

"It is very nice to see you again," the taxi driver said. "How do you like Bangui?" He was wearing a tee shirt that read "I'm a Girl Watcher!"

We crawled out of the ditch.

"The coat," he said pleasantly. "We must talk about the coat."

"Who are you?" I finally asked.

"My taxi. You do not recognize my taxi?" he asked, sounding a bit hurt. The driver gestured toward his car, which looked, as far as I could tell, like every other beat-up yellow Peugeot 504 in Bangui. "The airport?" He suggested.

I remembered. He was the driver from the airport.

"I have information," he murmured mysteriously, "about your coat."

This made me happy. What sort of information?

"I think I know where it is."

This was even better news. I suggested he take me to it.

"Yes, but first we must discuss price."

It was, apparently, a ransom situation. "How much do they want?" I asked.

"Fifty thousand CFA."

That was almost two hundred dollars, far too much. We negotiated for some time. Finally we agreed on five thousand CFA.

The driver held out his hand for the gentle handshake that seemed to be the African norm.

I got in the car. The driver looked puzzled.

"You can take us to the coat, right?" Ann asked.

He nodded, walked around to the trunk and pulled out my raincoat.

"Here!" he said proudly.

That afternoon we went looking for Monsieur Amphoux, Lucien's accountant. His office was just off the main square of town in an apartment building full of Peace Corps volunteers. It was three-thirty but his doors were locked; business hours in Bangui were a matter of personal taste.

Next door at the Tropicana Bar and Restaurant we waited for Amphoux to return. With ceiling fans and wicker chairs, the Tropicana looked like a Saint-Tropez beach bar. I expected top-less girls to wander in from plage de Tahiti. We drank Coastal beer while a young Lebanese detailed how he had spent the previous evening.

"With knives, they came," he said, still looking shaky. "Five of them. I was walking home from the bakery and it wasn't even late, only nine o'clock."

He took a long sip of beer and continued in a hushed tone. "One in the back, around the neck he grabbed me." The Lebanese jerked his neck backward, as if garroted with an invisible wire. "Another took my feet and then I am like this." He flailed around like a scarecrow in a stiff wind. Two French soldiers in shorts looked up from their card game.

"Three colleagues did the job. My wallet, my necklace, my shoes."

"Your shoes?" I asked.

He nodded. "And my pants half off when a soldier ran up."

"A French soldier or an African?"

He cocked his head. "You are new here, I can tell. A French soldier."

We drank for a while in silence, staring at the bar. The femur of an elephant hung over the rows of gin and whiskey. It looked exactly like a giant dog bone.

"If you resist," the man, whose name was David, continued in a melancholy voice, "it is *fini*." He drew a finger across his throat.

David's family ran a bakery and grocery store. "We came from Beirut ten years ago. For our country, it is over now. Here, Lebanese run everything. All the stores, the shops."

It seemed to be true. Every store we'd seen had a Lebanese behind the counter, assisted by Africans.

"And the French?" Ann asked.

David smiled. "They have the restaurants and the military." He shrugged and whispered, "We make the money. Us and the Muslims. But tell me, why are you here?"

We explained that we were waiting for Amphoux to return from lunch.

"Amphoux? That Amphoux?"

He gestured over to a far corner where a tall man with a de Gaulle mustache was hunched over a golf club. He putted across the floor into a little silver practice hole, raising his arm in silent triumph when the ball clanked home.

We introduced ourselves and the accountant hustled us into his office next door. He had a brisk, pigeon-toed walk; carrying his putter tucked under one arm and a small black purse in the other hand, he looked like a general hurrying off to review the troops. His tan safari suit aided this effect.

"Ridiculous!" he shouted when we told him what Capitaine Follope had said. "Those fees have been paid months ago."

Would he happen to have a receipt?

"Come!" he boomed. Ann and I looked at each other.

A small black man opened the door separating Amphoux's office from the spacious outer area. Amphoux ordered the man to find a receipt. *"Oui, patron, oui patron,"* the clerk mumbled, nodding and quietly shutting the door.

Amphoux propped his feet up on his desk and sighted down his putter at Ann. "Have you ever been to the Masters?" he asked pleasantly.

While Ann and he talked about Augusta and the weaknesses in Greg Norman's short game—something Ann, apparently, had considered in depth—I got up to go to the bathroom. It was located at the end of a narrow hall lined with hundreds of files piled in collapsing stacks. Amphoux's African assistant was bent over, sorting through the papers. *"Patron,"* he said softly, standing up so I could squeeze past. Our eyes met as our bodies brushed.

"They steal everything!" Amphoux was telling Ann when I came back in the room. "Just last month. I am on the telephone to Paris, behind my desk, facing this way"—he swiveled in his chair so that his back was to the door—"and when I turn around, I see my adding machine moving across the floor!"

Amphoux leaped from his chair and began to crawl around the room. His safari suit bunched up around his stomach, revealing expanses of white flesh.

"He sneaked in the door," Amphoux cried, "and crept across the floor." He demonstrated while Ann and I watched. "And then lifted the machine right off my desk! While I'm on the phone!"

As Amphoux was on his knees, bent over to lift the heavy black adding machine, his African assistant returned with a file.

"Patron?" he asked. His grin was almost invisible.

Henri Vidal returned a few days later from Cameroon. It was my birthday, the twenty-second of October. He and Françoise came by the Sofitel in the evening. I had just finished heating a very large can of paella on my little camping stove. The paella came from Bangui's one European-stocked grocery store; that I was having a dinner of canned food on my birthday reflected my rapid introduction to one of the more appalling aspects of Central African life: the price of food.

It was staggering. This was a town where hamburgers—bad hamburgers—cost twenty-five dollars, omelets were fifteen, a simple sandwich went for twelve. This was bar food; if you wanted to eat at a real restaurant—of which there were three or four—the tab would inevitably top seventy-five dollars a person. What baffled me was that there appeared to be no middle ground; either one paid these prices or one ate roots. Manioc root ground into flour was the nation's staple.

At the grocery store, a can of corn sold for five dollars, a package of spaghetti for six. The French housewives bought fresh cheeses flown in from France and seemed to think nothing of the prices. I watched one woman lay out over a hundred dollars for a handful of hors d'oeuvres.

The only bargains in town were little bottles of premixed gin and tonic that were sold everywhere like Cokes at about the same price—less than a dollar. Ann and I took to these in a big way. We drank several waiting for the paella to boil. The can of rice and chicken had cost about twelve dollars, but we were very excited about it; the artwork on the label was a masterpiece of gastronomic packaging.

I stared down at the bubbling mixture in a gin daze, attempting to reconcile what I saw with the pretty pictures on the package. Beneath me was a revolting mix of half-plucked chicken fat and bones with a few sad grains of rice.

"Happy birthday," Ann said, giggling.

The phone rang. It was Henri and Françoise down in the lobby insisting we join them for dinner. "Thank God," I said, quickly cutting off the stove.

"Thank God," Ann agreed, throwing a towel over the offending fare we'd been spared.

We crammed into the Vidals' Renault and negotiated the dark streets toward the center of town. Bangui demands a particular driving skill akin to that of a good slalom racer; deep holes—crevasses really—render lanes meaningless, and vehicles weave crazily. Near misses and collisions are the norm. There are stoplights but none work. Policemen or soldiers stand at every main intersection with absolutely no interest in directing traffic. "Money, money, money, it is all they think of," Henri said, explaining his preference for back streets. "They are paid practically nothing and their only salary is what they take from drivers. 'Oh,' " he mimicked, " 'your headlight goes the wrong direction. Five thousand francs please.' " He laughed. "It is like the superhighways in France. You must pay to drive."

Henri stopped at a little concrete building under a battered wooden sign proclaiming: Pizzeria. Typically, there was an enclosed parking compound with a black guard to watch the cars. It had rained, and we picked our way around thick mud to reach the heavy metal security doors of the restaurant. Crickets shrieked loudly.

We stepped inside to a French bistro. The scene was perfect: wine bottles with dripping candles, red checkered tablecloths, a little bar with espresso machines and copies of *Paris Match* lying around. A pretty French woman and a handsome African greeted us. There was much kissing of cheeks and hands.

"A simple little place," Henri said. "Just a pizza, a little salad." The pizzas were forty-five dollars each.

I explained to Henri what had happened with Follope and Amphoux.

"I can see what is next, I think," he interrupted.

"You can?"

"You took this receipt to Follope. He said to you, 'Thank you,' but now, several days pass, nothing has changed."

This was precisely what had transpired.

"You see," Henri explained, "the CAR has a very precise, formal legal system, one of the many gifts of my gracious country. Ahh . . ."

The pizzas arrived. They looked good but quite like eight-dollar pizzas in New York.

"But as far as I can determine," Henri continued, "this wonderful legal framework we French have constructed has nothing to do with what happens in this country. Nothing at all. Nothing."

The way to get anything done in the CAR, Henri explained, was through back channels. This person who is a friend of another person who has a cousin in this office, that's what counted. "Family, friends and"—he smiled—"of course, money."

"But this is your birthday," Françoise insisted, "we talk about business later." She poured around an excellent Beaujolais.

At the bar there was a young, very pretty white woman we'd seen on the flight from France. She'd been carrying a black baby, and I asked Henri and Françoise if they knew her.

"Oh, yes," Françoise said, "everyone knows everyone in Bangui. She met her husband while he was a student in Paris. They fell in love, married and came back here to live. He beats her regularly."

This was delivered not in a catty, gossipy way but as a simple statement of fact, like "The pizza is good."

"It's very common," Henri assured Ann and me. I suppose we looked as if we needed assuring.

"I do not even think," Françoise said, "that it has anything to do with meanness or anger. It is always done, so they do it."

"How quaint," Ann observed.

Henri looked over at the woman at the bar. "The white wives of Africans do not strike me as the happiest people in the world."

When the bill came, Henri insisted on paying. I made protesting noises that became gasps when I caught a glimpse of the total: $210.00.

"A little pizza is always good," Françoise said as we were leaving.

"Now I show you where the smart set goes in Bangui," Henri proclaimed, swerving carefully through the dark, cratered streets.

Not far from the presidential palace, we stopped in front of a club called Sango Nights. Inside, the Bee Gees blasted through the cavernous empty room lit by a hanging crystal ball reflecting

crazy splinters of colored lights. "Too early," Françoise said. It
was eleven o'clock.

"Or perhaps the smart set still recovers from last night's
ball," Henri suggested. He was smiling.

"Was there a ball last night?" Ann asked.

Henri laughed and ordered champagne before pulling Françoise onto the empty dance floor.

Ann and I talked with the tall, attractive woman bartender.
She was not, to our surprise, French. "Russian," she insisted, but
when we looked unconvinced, she relented. "Czechoslovakian,"
she admitted, as if that would make her presence completely
logical. "I married an African student studying at university."

"Does he beat you?" Ann asked.

I looked over at her, trying to recall how much Beaujolais
she'd downed at dinner.

"What?" the Czech bartender asked. The music roared.

"Does he beat you?" Ann yelled, slapping the bar a few
times for effect.

"What?"

"Beat you!"

The bartender laughed. "We are divorced now," she cried. "I
am a free woman in Bangui!"

Several stunning black women joined Henri and Françoise
on the dance floor, moving seductively in a private rhythm.

Later, when the champagne was gone, we moved on to another club, called Equator. On the edge of the city center, where
the houses disappeared and the shacks began, it was jammed with
white men dancing with black women.

"The pride of France!" Henri exclaimed, gesturing out over
the steamy club floor. The men all had short hair and wore the
preppy outfits that apparently were the norm for French men in
Africa; topsiders and bright Lacoste shirts, khaki pants and alliga-
tor belts.

"This is what the men in *Beau Geste* were fighting for," Henri
said. "Vive l'Afrique!" He ordered another bottle of champagne.

A group of large men quickly surrounded Ann. They looked

different from the others, not just bigger but put together with more right angles and sharp corners. Each wore jeans with a walkie-talkie strapped to his belt.

Shouting something about meeting "a few good men," Ann pulled me into the center of her admirers. Surrounded by the hulking bodies, I felt as if I had stepped into a football huddle.

We shook hands. "I need a beer," I announced. The club was unbelievably hot. "Who needs one?" Everyone eagerly accepted the offer. The largest marine, a six-and-a-half-footer named Ernie, helped clear a path to the bar. He was from California and looked it: blond and tanned. He also wore sunglasses.

"Look," he said, "you don't have to do this."

"What?"

"Buy these beers."

I waved my hand dismissively and ordered six Coastal beers.

"They only have Heineken," Ernie told me in a pained voice. "Let me tell you, these beers—"

"Here." I handed him several cold Heinekens.

"They cost—"

He stopped while the woman bartender handed me a bill. With a familiar feeling of fiscal panic, I frantically tried to calculate it in dollars. Ernie took a look and said flatly, "About sixty-five dollars. I tried to warn you."

"No problem," I mumbled, thinking back fondly to the bargain price of living on Manhattan's Upper East Side.

"The only thing cheap in this country," Ernie told me while we worked our way back over to the marine huddle, "is women, but then you got to figure most of them come with the gift that keeps on giving."

"What?" I had no idea what he was talking about.

"AIDS, man." He slapped me on the back. "You join the Marine Corps, you flat learn about that stuff. What you got here"—he gestured out over the dance floor crowded with white men and black women—"is one great hunk of AIDS. Right here is where it all started."

"Some of these French guys," another marine pronounced,

"I think they might have got it on with that first monkey started all this stuff."

"Hey." Ernie wrapped his big arm around my shoulder. "This girl Ann, she your girlfriend, or what?"

Later we went outside to watch two French soldiers in a desultory fight. The marines were unimpressed. "For the love of God, will you look at those fairies. Are they in love or fighting?"

The ranking marine, a sergeant who, in his late twenties, was the oldest of the group, steered his men toward a Land Cruiser where a black chauffeur was asleep. "Leaving E. Club," the sergeant barked into his crackling radio.

"Hey, look," Ernie told Ann and me, though mostly he was looking at Ann, "you guys got to come over to the marine house. We got a great cook."

"You have a cook?" Ann asked. She had a great interest in all things culinary.

"Hell, yes. Chauffeur too. Ain't life great?"

Ann agreed and asked if she should dress for dinner.

Chapter Four

We left Bangui for Berbérati six days later.

It was all Henri's doing. He insisted we come with him to visit his coffee operation. "It will be good for you," he asserted. "Get out of Bangui, take your mind off the Land Rover. There is nothing for you to do now for the car. You must wait."

The latter certainly seemed to be true. With Henri in the lead, we'd pressed our case relentlessly through Bangui's political back channels, shuttling back and forth among local power brokers like Henry Kissingers.

The Rock Club was our command post. It was a former French army officers' club converted to country club for the Bangui social set. Almost directly across the street from the French embassy—no coincidence there—it had the accoutrements of better clubs everywhere: a huge pool where sleek teenagers flirted, a bar that was never empty, rooms for dancing and rooms for card playing and movie watching, even squash courts and a small gym. At the Rock Club, it was easy to forget one was in Africa—which was, of course, the whole idea—until you turned south and peered across the Ubangi River, where pirogues ferried trade to Zaire and occasional hippos rolled like boulders shuddering downstream.

We met Kneeper here along with an African from the Ivory Coast who worked at the U.S. embassy. The two were in the same aerobics class (as Henri pointed out, "We are not a racist club, merely elitist; rich blacks are most welcome"). Chevron Thompson, the embassy employee, had a good friend who was inspector general in the Central African government, a position equivalent to attorney general in the U.S. Chevron was handsome, wore Vuarnet sunglasses and exuded an air of competence. One of the American Foreign Service officers confided in me that "Chevron really runs this damn place; he gets us cars, knows where to find freon when the air conditioner breaks and even plays a mean center field on the softball team."

Our war conference with Kneeper, Chevron and Henri convened by the Rock Club pool after the evening aerobics class. Kneeper wore a flowing white *bou-bou,* the long gown favored by African men, and sandals; Chevron had on a Jane Fonda Works Out! tee shirt and blue stretch tights. As usual, Henri dressed like a French nightclub owner on his day off: black loafers, no socks, elegant black silk shirt and slacks.

Kneeper related how Follope had forwarded the receipt furnished by Amphoux to the minister of mines, who in turn had forwarded it to the minister of justice. He was busy with a World Bank delegation visiting from Washington and had not looked at it.

"Which World Bank delegation?" Chevron asked. It seems there were at least two, and some people thought there were three groups from the World Bank in town. Every afternoon the Sofitel pool was jammed; after careful study, I'd determined that the World Bank people wore more modest bathing suits than the Jaguar pilots and drank gin rather than beer.

Henri suggested a two-pronged attack—Kneeper pursuing the minister of mines and the minister of justice while Chevron tried to initiate an inquiry in the inspector general's office.

A bribe, I asked, why couldn't we just bribe the Land Rover out?

This evoked a long explanation of the finer points of bribery.

"It is not good to just march in and give the money," Henri lectured in a somewhat shocked voice.

"Oh, no," Kneeper agreed.

"You must create the proper environment for the transaction."

"Environment?" I asked.

"Critical," Kneeper said. "There must be a fiction sustained that the official is really doing *you* a favor by solving this problem. He is doing so not for something crass like money."

"Heaven forbid." Henri shook his head.

"But out of the goodness of his heart. The money is merely a gesture of your goodwill and appreciation."

"You see, it is really a favor to you," Henri explained.

"Taking the money?"

"Yes, it is true. It's a favor to you so that you shall not feel quite so badly that this person has done so much for you and you've done so little for him. The African must feel that he acts not out of greed but of kindness."

But regardless of the proper climate, Kneeper felt a bribe in this case wouldn't work. "The problem is that the Land Rover is very large. Everyone has seen it. If it is to suddenly disappear, this fact will be noted. And the minister of mines has two very ambitious undersecretaries. They would be sure to raise a stink."

"It is unfortunate," Henri noted as we adjourned to watch the evening movie feature, *The Terminator,* "that the American ambassador cannot do more."

We all nodded gravely.

The American ambassador. Our meeting had been unsettling. Not that he wasn't pleasant or forthcoming; in truth he'd proven a delightful, intriguing man, a Foreign Service pro (as opposed to a Reagan appointee dunce) with twenty years in Africa.

It was what he had to say about my friend Lucien that troubled me. Or rather, not so much what he said but the look he gave me when I explained what I was doing in the CAR.

"Lucien. Yes, we all know Lucien."

That was all he said. And then he cocked his head and fixed me with a gaze that made it clear that this was a subject not worth pursuing.

\\\

On the drive to Berbérati, the owls sat in the middle of the dirt track, scores of them in a row. They looked plump and confident; their eyes flashing in the headlights of Henri's Renault. Not until they rose up—always at the very last instant before a crash—and those outlandish wings spread wider than the Renault, did you realize what truly significant, sizable beasts they were. Henri chuckled as I ducked for the first one and ducked for the last one, certain that *this* one was headed right through the windshield.

It is four hundred kilometers from Bangui to Berbérati. "The best road in the country," Henri reassured us, "the main route to Cameroon." This was, of course, before I understood what African roads are like.

Just getting out of town wasn't easy. A police roadblock sits on the outskirts; its primary purpose is to block people from entering Bangui, since 40 percent of the population already lives in the capital. But the gendarmes in their olive uniforms and black paratroop boots are curious as well about anyone leaving.

Henri, Ann, myself and Joseph were in the little Renault 12 station wagon. "He is my chauffeur," Henri explained when he introduced us to Joseph, a quiet African in his early twenties. Later, when Ann asked why Joseph wasn't driving, Henri seemed surprised. "But it is always I who drives."

We stopped about fifty yards short of the roadblock; Henri gave Joseph his identity card and an official-looking paper granting permission to travel back and forth to Berbérati. Ever quiet, Joseph nodded and walked to the shack that served as command post. While we waited, a dozen young boys besieged the car selling baguettes, little boxes of pasteurized cheese and yogurt. The cheese and yogurt were made locally, the only good cheap food—not counting the bottled gin and tonic—we'd discovered.

Soldiers roamed everywhere; several stood under a mango tree hurling metal tear gas canisters to dislodge the heavy fruit. "If the soldiers come," Henri said casually, peeling the foil off a square of cheese, "you must let me talk to them. Even if they ask you something directly, let me answer.

"Technically, this is illegal," Henri continued, "you traveling with me. My documents are good only for coffee company employees. If the authorities," he trilled the word mockingly, "know you are American, it will be a problem. Not a big problem but perhaps an expensive problem, and a time problem definitely. It could take hours."

We watched the soldiers attack the mangoes, ate our bread and yogurt, and waited. It was very hot in the car; the windows were rolled up in defense against the marauding peddler children, the only way to keep them from thrusting their hands and, as much as possible, their bodies into the Renault.

After a half hour Joseph returned, handed the papers to Henri with a soft, *"Oui, patron,"* and climbed in the back seat. When he opened the door, several kids tried to jump in the car until Joseph bashed them over the head with a long baguette, yelling fervent oaths in Sango.

There are less than two hundred kilometers of paved roads in the CAR, a country about the size of Texas, half of that due west of Bangui on the highway to Berbérati and Cameroon. It was the most terrifying automobile experience of my life.

As soon as we passed the roadblock, Henri pressed the accelerator to the floor. There it remained for the next hundred kilometers as the Renault—not a car built for speed—shuddered through one little village after another, over narrow bridges of loose planks, banging into ruts and clanking bottom on sudden dips.

Rounding a bend, we came to a herd of sharp-horned cattle crowding the thin stretch of tarmac, and at once I knew death was nigh. While Henri whistled *Carmen* (he loved opera) and spun the wheel wildly, I contemplated the woefully predictable results of the impending crash: the dull thud as a one-ton beast reshaped the front end of the Renault into a crude horseshoe, a horn spearing the windshield while Henri and I launched through the broken glass, Joseph and Ann tumbling with the jerricans of gas and water in a mad destructive jumble.

Somehow we missed. The Muslim cattle drivers in their white gowns flailed the beasts with long sticks, Henri bounced the Renault off the road, the planets were aligned properly and disaster was avoided. When the pavement turned into gravel and dirt, Henri stopped for a quick cup of coffee from a thermos. "We must be careful now," he said. "With the road not so good, driving can be tricky."

The end of the pavement marked the beginning of cattle-breeding territory. "These people are all Muslims," Henri explained, pointing to a little village of mud brick huts surrounded by cattle grazing in the long grass. "They are from further west, places like Burkina Faso and Mali. They are not Central Africans. It is like your Wild West; they drive cattle here to eat from the grasses and to sell. They are the new masters, these Muslims. Soon they will control this country as the French once did."

I asked how the Muslims were gaining control, what made them different.

Henri grew very serious. "They are great traders, quite sophisticated, with a sense of international finance. They bring the cattle here so they can escape taxes in Mali or Cameroon. And they work hard; their religion helps them succeed—not drinking, the strength of the family. And their wives."

Their wives?

"As Muslims, they can have as many wives as they can afford. What happens is, they buy wives from the local villages, say that village, perhaps." He pointed to a group of three or four huts. Under an open canopy of thatched leaves, a family sat watching the road. They wore tattered Western clothes; none had on the white bou-bou or skullcaps of the Muslims. "They buy a wife from her family and she then becomes Muslim and she has children and of course the children are Muslim. It continues on and on.

"For a family, it is very good if a daughter marries a Muslim. They get cattle and a little money and they know the daughter will be taken care of. The African Muslims and the Lebanese, they are the new masters of West Africa. It is finished for my people."

This was said without bitterness, in a relieved, almost cheerful voice.

"Can you see that?" Henri pointed to a crude wooden stand along the road, topped with an overflowing bowl of white powder. "That is the extent of business development in the CAR for most Africans. It's ground manioc root, and they grow it, grind it and sell it. And they sell some charcoal and occasionally a bed or chair, like there." We passed several woven bamboo beds along the road. "In all the years we French were here, we never developed African businesses. How these people live, it is not very different from one hundred, two hundred years ago. Is that good or bad?" He shrugged.

I thought back to a conversation with an American embassy DCM, Fred LaHor. He'd estimated there were fewer than five Central African businessmen in the entire country. We'd talked about the different approaches the French and English had taken to governing their colonies, how the English tried to integrate the indigenous peoples into their colonial governments while the French ruled from above through a loyal puppet leader.

And today, I'd asked; is it different now?

LaHor smiled. "No one thinks the French don't control President Kolingba behind the scenes. They flew in troops when Bokassa became too much of an embarrassment. This is still, in many ways, a colony. What's different now is that the French aren't taking very much money out of the CAR. They have a reserve base for the war in Chad and considerable uranium reserves, but none of this can justify the money—over forty million dollars annually—and manpower they pump into this country. It's a hard concept for Americans to grasp, but the French are deeply sentimental about the notion of spreading French culture. In part, the French are still in Africa for the same reason there is an Alliance Française office in San Francisco and Dallas."

At dusk we stopped in Yaloke, which Henri pronounced "Yellowcake." It was near the turnoff to Berbérati, where we would leave the main Cameroon road and head south. "It's not a good road like this one," Henri said, and though Ann and I laughed, he wasn't joking.

With a market and a single gas pump, Yaloke was a substantial place. We bought gas and Fanta orange drinks and ate slices of beef stripped from a haunch cooking over an oil drum stove. The chef, a tall man with jagged tribal scars across his cheekbones, wrapped the meat in a banana leaf with a little pile of fierce red pepper on the side. It was tough, fatty and delicious.

The sun collapsed behind rolling hills, and in the growing darkness I saw fires burning in the bush. A radio propped on the counter of a little store blared "Surfin' Safari" by the Beach Boys.

"It's close to here that Lucien looked for his diamonds," Henri said, leaning against the Renault and watching a teenager work the hand pump drawing gas from a fifty-gallon drum. "This is diamond country. That is one of the reasons," he grinned, "you see Muslims driving cars like that." He nodded to a newish Toyota Land Cruiser behind us waiting for gas.

"You mean they find diamonds?" I asked.

"I mean they buy diamonds from Africans. But mostly they smuggle."

Just outside Yaloke, beyond the twin rows of poplars planted fifty years ago by the French that make the road, if only for an instant, look like Avignon, a police roadblock stopped all traffic. Again Joseph took them the papers and Henri, a bit more on edge, cautioned us to remain silent. A soldier returned with Joseph and peered into the car, shining a light—it was almost dark—in each of our faces. Then abruptly he shook hands with Henri and waved us on.

"Diamonds," Henri muttered, just as the first owl burst skyward under our headlights.

Chapter
Five

Berbérati is the second-largest town in the CAR. This is very hard to believe.

There is not an inch of pavement, no bank (though one is rumored to be opening), no electricity after 6:00 P.M., and the one medical facility—not counting the leper colony—frequently lacks penicillin.

But I found it a hard place not to like.

Berbérati had an unfinished, outpostlike quality of another era. Henri was the most reliable source of mail delivery for the town. Each time he returned from Bangui, he brought a satchel with letters for the Catholic mission, the leper colony, the Peace Corps contingent, the Alliance Progrès French doctor, the Swedish missionaries and the Syrian store owner who also sold cars from Nigeria on the side.

Our first morning in town, we made the rounds with him. I have never seen anyone welcomed so warmly. "Pony Express," he'd announce, getting out of his battered Renault as the happy recipient rushed to greet him. Henri watched many old American movies on his VCR, giving him an endearing and unlikely knowledge of colloquialisms, such as "sheriff's posse" and "dance hall girl." "Stick 'em up" was also a favorite.

"Henri, my savior!" The Catholic nun shouted, hugging him and plucking the letters all in one well-practiced motion. "Come in, you must tell me all the news of the city!"

It took me a moment to realize she meant Bangui.

The buildings of the mission created a courtyard ringed with palm trees. "We spread salt at the base," the nun told me when she noticed where I was looking. "That's why we get good coconuts." She smiled. "We trick them into believing they are by the sea. Berbérati by the sea! A nice thought."

At the center of the square stood an imposing stone church with Gothic windows filled not with stained glass but lattice patterns of stone. The sight of it was sudden and shocking, a beautiful piece of work in a town struggling to build roads and keep babies from dying.

The office of the mission had stone columns supporting a corrugated tin roof. A wide, cool porch circled the building, and behind it there was a one-story structure like a long barracks. I walked closer and heard high voices singing in French. Peering in a window, I realized it was the mission school. A black schoolmaster patrolled the center aisle swinging a long thin cane. I thought of the observation made by the great Kenyan Jomo Kenyatta: "When the missionaries arrived, the Africans had the land and missionaries had the Bible. They taught us to pray with our eyes closed. When we opened them, they had the land and we had the Bible."

The Berbérati hospital was our next stop. It was a collection of low orange buildings near the central (almost the only) intersection in town, where the main market street met the highway (everyone called it this) to Bangui. A huge mural dominated the hospital exterior. It featured a bare-breasted black woman in shorts wielding a red lightning bolt spear against a horrible crab figure with threatening pincers. The woman was labeled "Prosperity," the spear "Hygiene" and the crab "Cholera."

A young French doctor ran the hospital. Reaching the end of his two-year assignment with Alliance Progrès, which doctors can enter in lieu of mandatory military service, he seemed to accept the limited resources. "Sometimes we have penicillin," he said, showing us his store of drugs, "mostly not."

"Is that all the medicine you have?" I asked, indicating a pile that was about the size a typical New York hypochondriac would have in his bathroom. The doctor smiled.

"Now you will ask me about AIDS, yes?"

He was right; I was about to ask.

"All Americans are obsessed with AIDS. In Bangui the hospital tests randomly for AIDS among blood donors." He paused for effect. "But if it is positive, they still use the blood."

He knew we would find this unbelievable.

"Here I don't bother. I'm sure we must be sentencing some people to death. But when we use blood, it is a case of the patient dying right now or maybe ten years later from AIDS." He shrugged. "This is a situation we don't study in school."

Henri suggested we go with him to visit a coffee outpost on the border of Cameroon. "It's not so far," he said. "You will enjoy the drive."

"How far?"

"Five or six hours." This, for Africa, was apparently just a jaunt.

We left in an old Peugeot pickup truck: Ann and I in the front with Henri driving; Joseph, the chauffeur, riding in the back. A few hundred yards past the leper colony, the dirt road deteriorated to a rutted track. We passed a Toyota Land Cruiser with a Rising Sun emblem on the side. "The Japanese gave it to the leper colony," Henri explained.

"That kind of foreign aid," he continued, "I guess it is not so bad. But most of it I am completely against. Like rice!" He gestured emphatically with one hand while the other held the steering wheel in a death grip. "They grew rice here once. Not so much but some; to grow any food crop is good for these people.

"But the Japanese decided Central Africans could do with more rice so they donated tons to the government. But of course the government didn't give it away; the president's family sold it. And since they hadn't paid anything for it, they could sell it cheaper than anybody else. So the Africans growing rice couldn't make any money and they quit. Eventually the Japanese heard the rice was being sold, so they stopped donating it and now there is no rice in the CAR. Foreign aid." He shook his head.

"It is the same for the clothes sold in the market. You've seen the secondhand clothes being sold, no?"

We nodded. It seemed to be a ubiquitous African feature: stalls of old clothes hawked usually by young men. Most, judging from the brands and the type—old Boy Scout shirts, college sweatshirts, McDonald's uniforms—were American.

"These clothes are donated by agencies, many from your country, thinking it will be distributed free to the poor natives. But the government sells it by the ton to the merchants."

The Peugeot slammed into a small boulder—the road seemed to be part streambed—bounced off and shuddered forward. "The Peugeot is a wonderful creature." Henri patted the dashboard. "I love her so very dearly. Like my very wife." He chuckled and then concentrated on driving.

At a small village, two men stood in the road waving their arms. We stopped, and after Henri conferred with them, a young woman ran out of one of the huts and climbed in the back of the pickup with Joseph. She had spiked hair tied with bright yarn and wore a wrap skirt printed with pictures of Madame Kolingba, the president's wife. By all accounts she was the Princess Di of Central Africa.

The cab grew intensely hot. Like a dog, I stuck my head out the window, mouth open, trying to suck up coolness.

On the drive from Bangui to Berbérati, each of the villages had looked alike: a cluster of mud and grass huts in a clearing of dirt hacked out of the bush. But now I began to discern differences. In this one the thatched roofs had yawning holes, and trash rotted in heaps; in that one freshly cut palms dried in the sun, readying for repair work. Some had groupings of sturdy chairs made from bamboo; others had no furniture and the inhabitants lay in the dirt. Occasionally metal water pumps—Peace Corps projects, most likely—gleamed proudly in the center of a village.

Three hours from Berbérati we turned off the dirt track through waist-high grass and scrub.

"What's wrong?" I asked.

"Wrong? Wrong with what?" Henri, who had been whistling *Madame Butterfly*, turned to look at me. He had a disturbing habit of insisting on eye contact in all conversations, a predilection unswayed by his role as driver.

"Why are we going through the woods?"

"Woods? What are woods?" Henri asked calmly.

"Okay! The bush. What are we doing here?"

"This is the road to my coffee station. Coffee tracks, we call them."

I started to say something but the Peugeot brushed a tree, slamming me against the door and impaling my leg on the window handle that had broken, forming a perfect spear. I cursed, Henri drove. Ann stared straight ahead, looking remarkably cool.

After a few kilometers, the road reemerged as a respectable dirt track. We crossed a series of rolling hills, and the Peugeot climbed with authority. Overhanging trees formed an arbor of green shade, and I had a strange, pleasant sensation of irresistible motion, like riding the rapids of a green and beautiful river.

Crossing an outcrop of rock, the Peugeot suddenly quivered and coasted to a stop. Joseph immediately hopped out of the rear to crawl under the car. He suggested that the clutch was broken. We dismounted and took turns peering under the vehicle, making appreciative grunting sounds. Joseph commenced to jack up the truck to remove the right rear tire. I was baffled as to what impact this course of action might have on the clutch, but it felt so good not to be bouncing in the truck that I welcomed the diversion.

Lying down in the track, back aching, I pondered enduring ten thousand kilometers—about the distance from Bangui to Europe—of this treatment. I wondered if the Land Rover was more comfortable than Henri's Peugeot, and then I started thinking what I would do if the Land Rover remained mired in the clutches of the Ministry of Mines. This made my head ache along with my back.

Joseph pulled on the right rear wheel for a while and then crawled under the car to look at the clutch. I joined him and marveled at what I saw: the clutch mechanism was held together, quite literally, with thick rubber bands.

"Henri, who does your maintenance?" I yelled from under the car.

"Preventive maintenance is a concept that has not yet reached the Central African Republic. When something breaks, somebody fixes it. However they can."

"I think," I said, sliding out from under the car, "that the last person had a fondness for rubber."

Ann took over. She reached under the car and jammed the gears into second—the gearshift on the steering column was useless—then directed us to push while she slid behind the wheel. Several African boys who appeared seemingly from nowhere joined the effort. The engine turned over, the Peugeot shuddered forward for a few feet then stopped. Ann got under the car and jammed the gears by hand and the process began again. This was repeated several times until we reached the base of a hill and could push no more.

I shook hands with our helpers and only then noticed that the most enthusiastic, a boy of about fourteen, had a deformed foot, twisted upward and grafted to his leg. The toes were webbed. He walked, or hobbled, on the stump formed by the upturned heel.

Henri and Joseph discussed our options. A military post lay ahead near the Cameroon border. No one knew how far, perhaps ten kilometers, maybe twenty. Henri thought they might have a radio and could contact either the coffee station or the Berbérati office. I offered to walk the distance.

"No," Henri insisted, "Joseph must do it. For you, a white man, to be wandering around near the border with the army nearby, it would not be good. Joseph doesn't mind."

There had been, as far as I could tell, no confirmation one way or the other from Joseph on this matter. He was, as always, quiet and expressionless.

Joseph left at four-thirty carrying a canteen. By ten o'clock we'd listened to the Voice of America's analysis of the rioting in Tibet and to a history of the B-side single on the *New Music USA* show. It was pleasant lying on the hood of the Peugeot, staring up at the stars.

At eleven Joseph appeared noiselessly from the darkness. *"Bonsoir, patron,"* he began his report, then continued in a mixture of French and Sango that neither Ann nor I could understand.

"This is not very good news, I think," Henri said quite chipperly. "No, I think not."

The story was that Joseph had lucked into borrowing a bicycle from an employee of the coffee company in the next village. He'd ridden fifteen or twenty kilometers to the military post. The army did indeed have a radio but transmitted only at fixed times—the next call was at 6:00 A.M.

There was nothing to do but wait. "It would be nicer, I believe," Henri suggested, sounding like a tour director, "to spend the night in the next village. We can maybe sleep inside, on a bed, and it is higher, away from this river." The Peugeot had died near a stream heavily populated by mosquitoes. They welcomed a new blood source enthusiastically.

"How far to the village?" Ann asked.

"Oh, just a few hundred meters, I think."

He was wrong. We walked a long time up the vague road. A dazzling moon rose in the east.

"It worries me, leaving Gladys," Henri said thoughtfully as we moved through the high saw grass.

"Gladys?"

"My cat. When I am gone, it is very dangerous for her. She is in peril as we speak."

"Why?" Ann asked.

"She may be eaten!"

"By what kind of animal?"

"Not an animal, a *domestique!* It is very dangerous for the kitty cat here in the CAR. Every time I must leave, I say to my *domestique*, 'There is a bonus for you when I return if my Gladys she

is well when I return.' " His voice dropped. "I had not long ago
two cats, you understand."

"Two?"

"And I return to Berbérati and voilà, only Gladys is there
still. I say to the *domestique,* "Now you must have only half a bonus
because I have only half so many cats. To think, my Cheryl,
eaten! A manioc side dish!

"It would be better for Gladys," he mused after we had
walked a while, "if I lived in Cameroon. There they eat dogs but
cats they are safe. Perhaps we should move before it is too late."

We passed a pair of huts, dark outlines illuminated by a low
fire. Voices murmured in the night.

I stopped, but Joseph, in the lead, motioned me on. A hundred yards more and we reached the village, a half dozen huts in
a line along the path. Fires smoldered and I could just make out
bodies lying near the coals. A man rose as we approached his hut.
He smiled shyly, offering his hand; other people quickly gathered. All offered their hands for the soft, gentle squeeze of Central Africans.

Joseph spoke Sango in a low voice, then motioned for us to
follow. He had become our leader. "We go to see the chief," he
said.

The chief was a short man wearing brightly striped pants cut
off below the knee and a tattered shirt without buttons. He
carried a furled umbrella as a swagger stick and greeted us in
French. Henri asked, quite formally, if we might be granted the
honor of spending the night in his village. The chief nodded
gravely and motioned with his umbrella, giving directions in
Sango.

Two broken bamboo chairs appeared and a low wooden
stool. The chief insisted we sit while a hut was prepared. Everyone in the village, about twenty people, gathered around.

The chief directed the installation of a pair of bamboo beds
in his hut. "They are looking for another one," Henri said, explaining the delay that followed. When I suggested he tell them

it didn't matter, that I would be happy to sleep on the ground or on one of the straw mats lying around, he answered, "But it is important to them. We are guests. We must allow them to give us the best of what they have or it will be shameful."

Eventually a teenager carried a bed from the first huts we had encountered down the path. With a certain grace, the chief motioned us to enter his hut.

It had two rooms, a dirt floor and thick mud walls. The three beds were grouped together in the first room, the bamboo slats covered with reed mats. A kerosene lamp gave off a soft, tentative light. Except for the door covered by a mat, there were no openings for air; it was very hot, with a layer of light smoke hanging like ground fog.

We lay down. The chief and his two wives and two young children moved into the other room, separated from us by a low mud wall. They spoke softly in Sango; somewhere outside a radio played the national station.

I woke in a slick sheen of sweat, coughing in the smoky room. The voices from the chief's quarters paused for a moment then continued. A soft laugh arose; the voices were peaceful and tangibly loving. Suddenly I missed my family, the comfort of familiar phrases; loneliness settled on me for the first time in Africa.

I staggered outside. The air felt almost cool and sharply clean. Around the smoldering fire in front of the hut, a family lay spread out on mats: four small children and a young mother and father. They were talking and I wondered if that was how it went all night, bouts of dozing and conversation, a gentle bit of laughter. Somewhere a radio played "Africa Unite."

In Bangui I had met a Peace Corps volunteer who explained with a little story his organization's reluctance to alter indigenous habits. In Mauritania some years ago, a Peace Corps volunteer, appalled by the smoky, unventilated huts in which the natives lived, proposed quite forcefully that a center chimney be added.

The huts were then free of smoke, with the result that mosquitoes no longer stayed away and the malaria rate soared.

I thought about this lying on the ground while whole squadrons of flying beasts launched saturation attacks on my body. Nodding to my neighbors, I moved between two children, inches from the smoldering, mosquito-banishing fire. A light, pleasant rain began to fall.

A dozen people were standing around staring at me when I drifted awake in the soft light of early morning. An infant, the only fat thing—animal or human—in the village, crouched near my head. He held out his hand. Feeling a bit Gulliverian, I shook his tiny, pudgy hand and fell back asleep.

On next awakening, I saw Henri sitting in one of the village's few chairs, legs primly crossed, reading *Paris Match.* "*Bonjour,*" he said blithely, as if we were spending the day at Saint-Tropez. He was, I noticed, wearing Gucci loafers, no socks.

"I have been thinking about your Land Rover," he began unexpectedly. For the first time since arriving in Africa, the Land Rover did not, at the moment anyway, seem very important.

"Yes?"

"What I cannot understand, if all Lucien has done wrong is not pay this fee on time, why do they make such a mess? Is that how you say, a mess?"

I thought for a moment. The fat child returned to place his face inches from mine.

"A stink, I think we would say. Why make such a stink?"

"Exactly," he said, as if I had proposed the idea. "Why?"

"Kneeper thinks the minister or Follope, the capitaine in the Brigade Minerale, is angry at Lucien. Maybe both."

Henri put down *Paris Match* and stroked an imaginary mustache. The fat child began to drool on me.

"I think," Henri finally decided, "that the minister thought he was going to make some money out of Lucien and our friend Lucien did not allow this to happen. Money must be involved somewhere."

"Where's Ann?" I asked, looking around.

"Or perhaps our friend Lucien, he does something that maybe he shouldn't. Perhaps he was a bad boy. She's playing with the gazelle." Henri mentioned offhandedly.

"Oh. But if Lucien did something wrong, why keep the Land Rover? And why not just come out and say it?" I thought for a moment, still waking up. "Gazelle?"

Ann appeared from behind the chief's hut. Cradled in her arms was a small, catlike creature with a sharp snout.

"This is Thompson," she announced. "Thompson the gazelle."

It looked more like an anteater to me than the sleek beasts I associated with the name.

Thompson had been found by a hunter in the village who had killed his mother. "We should take him back to Berbérati," Ann insisted.

"But it's bad to buy animals like this. It only encourages them to capture more to sell." I had read this somewhere and it sounded good.

"That may be true where there are tourists," Henri agreed. "Here I do not think it is a real problem."

I looked out at the thin dirt strip that connected the village to the world and had to agree.

"Anyway, it is a choice: If Ann takes the gazelle, it may live. If not, it dies." Henri shrugged and went back to *Paris Match*.

When by midmorning there was no sign of rescue, Henri decided we should start walking toward the coffee outpost. We said our goodbyes and took, at the chief's suggestion, a group picture of the entire village. The chief opened his umbrella for the photo. Henri presented him with a bottle of scotch he had intended for his employees. This seemed like a dubious idea to me, but Henri insisted it was the best present. "That way, everyone can enjoy it. They are not Muslims, these people. They like to drink."

We packed and left. At every step, scores of brilliant butterflies swarmed about our legs. Our procession had the look of a fable: Joseph in the lead carrying the wicker picnic basket packed with French cheese and sausage, Henri in his Guccis flipping through *Paris Match,* Ann nuzzling with the gazelle, and myself lugging a pack with the unlikely label "Himalayas."

Within the first mile we had to jump to avoid a Peugeot pickup hurtling down the track. It was our rescue mission, two men from Henri's company who had received radio contact from the army this morning.

We piled in the back and drove to Berbérati, leaving Joseph with the wounded vehicle. When I asked Henri what Joseph would eat—we were taking the sausage and cheese—he looked puzzled. "But there are Africans here, they will feed him. Manioc and bananas. You think Joseph is fond of Camembert?"

That night in Berbérati, we watched Fred Astaire and Ginger Rogers dancing cheek to cheek on Henri's VCR, powered by his personal generator. Afterwards, Henri played Cole Porter songs on his piano—"the only one in all this part of Africa"—while Ann fed Thompson drops of milk and I read James Hadley Chase.

To Henri's relief, Gladys the cat was safe.

Chapter Six

Over cocktails the next evening, it was decided that Ann and I should look around for a car in Berbérati—"just in case things do not go well in Bangui," Henri explained. "Difficult as that may be to imagine," he added, then giggled.

The little cocktail party was hosted by a friend of Henri's who ran the local tobacco company. Four French wines and ten liqueurs sat at the center of the round table on the front porch. A white-coated *domestique* hovered in the background. Gardens surrounded the porch; the scent reminded me of the American South but it was sharply sweeter, more pungent.

Henri's friend, Jacques, was strong and short, with a goatee he stroked like a method actor working into character; his bony knees jutted between khaki shorts and high white athletic socks. Little rubber bands held the socks in place. He had a highly developed tolerance for drink.

His black mistress sat across from him. She wore a simple white dress of the sort young girls wear on Easter Sunday. I thought she was nineteen or twenty but later Henri told me she was sixteen. She had been Jacques's mistress for several years. He had a wife in France, where he spent three months a year. When Jacques first came to Africa, twenty years ago, his wife had spent four or five months a year with him. Now she visited rarely. There were children in France, schools to attend, two houses to mind.

We left Jacques's house to see a man who knew cars in Berbérati. We found him in what looked like a junkyard, a metal shack on the main street surrounded by dead Land Rovers and disemboweled trucks. Henri informed me this was Berbérati's best garage. A jovial Syrian ran the place. He was a rather extraordinary-looking person, with large breasts and tiny eyes lodged behind smudged tortoiseshell glasses.

All car conversations, he informed us in the loud, excited voice he always employed, must be carried out over drinks. We must adjourn to his house to consider the matter in depth.

While we talked in the garage yard, a quick, cool breeze blew up and then all at once rain exploded. With the Syrian jiggling in the lead, we raced across Berbérati's main street, now a flash flood of red mud, to a small general store. Behind the single counter a florid blond woman dressed in a white caftan sold everything from Mon Afrique school notebooks to auto parts. I spotted a metal jerrican for sale at nineteen thousand CFA— seventy dollars; to make the trip north, I needed at least fifteen. As always when I thought of money in Africa—either how much I was spending or how much I might spend in the future—I quickly grew depressed. It seemed to violate some basic principle of traveler's rights that the Third World should cost significantly more than New York City.

"This is my wife," the Syrian announced, squeezing behind the counter to plant a passionate kiss on her powdered cheek. "Come." The Syrian motioned for us to enter a door to the side of the counter.

We passed through a small sitting room decorated with wedding photographs of the Syrian and his wife. Like the couple themselves, they were oversized. The groom wore a ruffled tux and sunglasses; the bride was wrapped in several acres of lace. A television and VCR sat on a metal bookcase, chained to the wall next to a stack of American porn films. *Blazing Mattresses* caught my eye.

The sitting room opened onto a pleasant courtyard roofed with translucent plastic, amplifying the thundering rain. Everyone raised his voice, except for the Syrian, who naturally spoke loud enough to compete with any environmental distractions. A middle-aged Frenchman, a friend of the Syrian's, appeared. He wore a greasy jumpsuit and had, I gathered, some official role in the Syrian's car dealings but said not a word.

Henri explained the situation of the Land Rover. The Syrian alternately nodded and laughed until Henri finished, and then he said, "Africa," with the requisite throb of fatalism. This was apparently a mandatory expression among non-Africans in Africa, though it seemed to make more sense coming from a Frenchman than a Syrian. Surely he couldn't really believe that Syria under Hafiz al-Assad was less crazy than the CAR?

A *domestique* brought liters of beer, ice cold, and a bottle of Johnny Walker Red. The Syrian poured a significant tumbler of scotch and, with a flourish, mixed in a sweet red liqueur. Not since a high school girlfriend developed a fondness for diet Dr. Pepper and scotch had I witnessed the downing of a more repulsive combination.

After finishing the tumbler, not a lengthy process, and pouring another, the Syrian elaborated at length on the type and condition of every car in Berbérati. Given the sort of community it was, this did not take as long as one might assume—perhaps twenty minutes. Basically three kinds of people had vehicles in Berbérati: missionaries, Muslim smugglers, and non-African businessmen. The latter included an extended family of Lebanese, a German whose ostensible trade was importing big trucks from Europe but who probably was a diamond smuggler, and, oddly, an American of the Bahai faith who ran a store competing with the Syrians'. "All the time his store is full of Africans," the Syrian said with grudging respect, making me wonder who else he thought might be in the store.

Of these groups, the Syrian considered the missionaries preferable. "They are very nice and easy to get a good price. Also, I don't think they lie so much." The worst were the Muslim smugglers. "These Muslims, they are taking over," he said, repeating the refrain I'd heard again and again. "The white man is finished here. My children will have no future in Berbérati!" I would have thought this had more to do with Berbérati and less to do with the Muslims. Besides, the Syrian had no children, he told me. "But we might. We could!" he asserted, as if I had challenged his potency.

The Syrian knew of very few vehicles for sale. One possibility was a Toyota pickup owned by a Swedish missionary. As a better alternative, he recommended commissioning the purchase of a car in Nigeria, where new vehicles could be bought on the black market at a third of their CAR price. Nigeria had a flourishing black market, unlike the CAR, because the Nigerian naira was a soft currency; the CAR franc was tied directly to the French franc and could be traded on open currency exchanges. "So," the Syrian explained, "you give one of my Nigerians the price of a car in hard currency—French francs, dollars—and they go to Nigeria, find what you want and bring it back. It is very simple."

Strangely, I trusted this man; the thought of handing over thousands of dollars in cash to one of his quasi employees did not trouble me as much as logic dictated. What worried me was the time. "It is very fast," the Syrian declared. "Maybe three weeks, maybe a month or two."

Why so long?

The Syrian looked puzzled that I considered a month or two any sort of delay at all. Perhaps, he ventured, I did not understand the process.

"In Nigeria you must bribe everyone! You must bribe the border guards not to search the car and take all your money. You must bribe . . ." He continued with a list that included the person who issued the license plates, the one who issued the export permit, and several other, more arcane officials whose roles I couldn't quite follow.

Wouldn't it save time, I offered, if Ann and I traveled with the car buyer to Nigeria? It was more or less the direction we wanted to travel anyway, and it would eliminate the hassle of bringing the car back into the CAR.

"No, no," the Syrian laughed. "That is too much money it cost you."

Why?

It was, he explained, a matter of race. Any time an official knew a white man was involved with the process, the necessary bribes increased tenfold.

We left as it grew dark. In front of the store, an African wearing a tee shirt that read "Spanish Fly" flailed at a woman with a palm frond. The Syrian chuckled. After a few moments, the woman began hitting the man with a sizable burlap bag. Both yelled simultaneously in Sango but neither tried very hard to block the blows; it looked more like a ritual than a fight. When we walked away down the street to Henri's car, the Syrian stood on his porch with his arm around his wife, both watching the escalating encounter with amused smiles.

"He is a very helpful man," Henri said as we drove away. "I brought him some videotapes from France and he will do much to help us."

On the way back to Henri's, we stopped at the house of an American who ran a general store. "He is the only white man in Berbérati I have never met. I hear his wife is a musician, perhaps we can play together. The Berbérati Symphony," Henri said wistfully. The house was small, surrounded, as was every white residence I'd seen in Africa, by a fence. We entered through a side gate next to the road. Dogs ran everywhere and an African man sat in the courtyard twisting metal rods into an L shape. Judging by the stack of completed twists, he had been doing this for some time.

A white woman in her late twenties hurtled out the door. "There's been an accident," she said, digging in her purse for keys, "on a motorcycle. A Peace Corps volunteer. I think he's wandering around bleeding in a daze. I've got to go help."

We nodded. There didn't seem to be much to say. A naked baby crawled out of the house and began playing in the thick mud of the courtyard. "Jerry!" The woman yelled, moving to her car. "We have to talk when I get back." And then to us: "Who are you?"

Henri, in typically gracious fashion, began his introduction. The woman nodded and backed her car out of the driveway.

"Watch the baby, please." She motioned to the infant now covered in thick red mud. "Oh, there he is." She pointed to a man coming out of the house and then drove off.

"Oo la la," Henri muttered.

This was Jerry, the Bahai store proprietor. Henri repeated the introductions. "We come to talk about a car and about music," he concluded, chuckling.

"What time is it?" Jerry asked.

I told him.

"Good. In ten more minutes the generator will start. I've got it on a timer."

We went inside the cool cement house. After lighting a kerosene lantern, Jerry noticed Ann's St. Louis Cardinals hat and began a lengthy discussion of the ongoing World Series.

Henri moved the conversation to cars. He explained we had heard that Jerry had once owned the Toyota pickup being sold now by the Swedish missionary. Jerry nodded, ducked into an adjoining room and came back with a bundle of metal rods and a piece of wood with three large nails jutting out. "This is an African machine," he announced, and then began twisting the rods into an L shape. He offered no further explanation of the rods but gave a critical analysis of the Toyota, noting it performed poorly in the sand. Since we had to cross the Sahara to reach Europe, this seemed a significant drawback.

The metal rods, Jerry eventually told us, were for the Bahai center he was building on the edge of town.

"Are there many Bahai's in Berbérati?" I asked.

"Not yet," he said, twisting another rod.

Life in Berbérati continued in a pleasant colonial bubble. I woke about six-thirty each morning to the sounds of the coffee workers reporting to work. My room was in a row of guest quarters separate from Henri's house. A Johnny Walker Red bottle filled with purified water sat next to the sink, and at nights bats cruised in through the open shutters.

While Henri worked, I drank coffee on his porch and ate fresh French bread delivered by the local bakery. If the French have done nothing else in Africa, they have substantially improved the quality of baked goods in their former colonies. Breaking a lifelong pattern of sleeping late, Ann would join me, awakened by the hungry nudges of her bedmate, Thompson, the gazelle.

Our social life was dizzying: dinners at the leper colony, a long Sunday brunch at the Catholic mission, drink parties with Henri's co-workers. In between I went running with a host of neighborhood children, read Henri's collection of James Hadley Chase novels and speculated endlessly with Henri on the state of Lucien's Land Rover. He was still optimistic, hoping that one of our envoys would hit upon the right combination of greed, logic and pity to spring the vehicle. As a fallback, I looked at the Swedish missionaries' Toyota pickup, the one that had once belonged to Jerry the Bahai, and conferred at length with various Nigerian car hustlers proposed by the amiable Syrian. The pickup used a quart of oil every 250 miles, and the Nigerians, while confident of ultimate success, were vague in the extreme about everything from price to model of car to delivery date.

Finally Henri received word through the daily radio contact with his Bangui office that there was news of the Land Rover. As the government monitored the radio conversations and as the status of the Land Rover involved certain government officials, Henri had agreed with his office upon an elaborate code. Unfortunately the code was so intricate that neither Henri nor the person in Bangui seemed able to get it straight. Henri shouted into the microphone questions about "package delivery" while the Bangui end talked a lot about "the fruit is ripe."

Ann and I decided to return to Bangui immediately. As Henri's wife, Françoise, was coming from Bangui for a visit, Henri concocted a plan: We would drive with him and meet Françoise halfway. She would then transfer to Henri's car (pickup, actually) and Ann and I would return to Bangui in the coffee company vehicle delivering Françoise. "This way," Henri explained, "we can all four be in the same place to discuss the Land Rover. Françoise will have the latest news for sure."

We rendezvoused in Yaloke. At the hand-pump gas station on the town's one street, we had our Land Rover conference. While we talked, Henri counted about fifteen thousand dollars in CFA francs brought by Françoise. The monthly coffee company payroll—Berbérati had no banks—lay neatly stacked in metal trunks.

Françoise related the news. It didn't take long.

The minister of mines had been in France attending a development conference. That had not helped matters.

"But what about . . . ," and Henri named an African friend in the president's office who had promised to try to find out if there was some hidden reason the vehicle was impounded. Henri had been very excited about this line of inquiry. We'd discussed it at length in Berbérati.

"Oh yes," Françoise said. "I did call but his phone does not work. So yesterday I visited him. He had forgotten but promised to do something right away."

A middle-aged man in Muslim robes stopped in front of us and began to yell in some unintelligible language. I'd seen him before wandering Yaloke streets—or street, as there was only one. He had been yelling then as well. It reminded me of New York.

And what of Chevron, the U.S. embassy employee with a friend in the inspector general's office?

Françoise had visited him as well. He'd heard nothing, but his friend had been busy with one of the World Bank delegations.

That was it. "We must still fight," Henri said, raising his voice over the sounds of the screaming fool. "It is the way in Africa. You must press all these contacts. It is the African way." We agreed on—and wrote down—a code so that we could talk by radio. The payroll and Françoise shifted to Henri's pickup; Ann and I got in the other pickup and, both trucks stirring up a great cloud of dust, we went our separate ways.

On the way to Bangui, the driver, a coffee company employee, stopped a half dozen times to buy goods: a massive amount of manioc, two bamboo beds and an assortment of carved gourds. He intended to sell them in town where the prices were higher. We reached the Bangui checkpoint five hours later.

Chapter Seven

I started getting desperate to leave Bangui when a band of muggers in wheelchairs attacked me. It happened the second night in town, when I was walking back from the telephone exchange after calling Lucien in America. The exchange is a cinder block building not far from the center of town. It's the same office where Bokassa intercepted a telex from a British journalist to his home office; the official on duty at the exchange garbled the telex transmission and Bokassa decided it was a coded message. The police dragged the journalist in front of Bokassa who, after exchanging pleasantries, proceeded personally to beat the man very close to death. A few weeks later, Emperor Bokassa released the journalist from prison, gave him a medal and flew him out of the country.

The telephone exchange is only a short walk from the Novotel Hotel, where Ann and I had taken up residence to escape the high tariff of the Sofitel. Despite the universal warnings from every white person we'd met not to venture out after dark, Ann and I walked alone to one telephone exchange.

The placing of the phone call was a tedious process drawn out over several hours. Once I did reach Lucien, the conversation wavered between surrealism and ludicrousness with a decidedly depressing aftertaste.

"Lucien, look, we've got a real problem here," I shouted into the cracked receiver.

"Oh, yes," he laughed. "Africa."

I groaned.

"You've got to understand, nothing is working!" I enumerated our efforts to free the Land Rover, the frustrations of this person being out of town, that person out of touch, everyone promising everything, and nothing, ultimately, happening.

"Yes, that's how it is," he answered pleasantly. "It just takes time."

This occasioned an outburst on my part as to the limits of my time. Then I moved to present my case. "You've got to come down here yourself. It's a must; or let me throw some money around for a bribe. That might help."

"I don't think my flying there is a very good idea," Lucien said, his voice, for the first time, sounding serious. "How much money?"

We finally agreed upon half a million CFA—about two thousand dollars. It seemed a reasonable sum to offer as a bribe.

"It'll all work out," Lucien concluded. "Really, it will."

This finally depressed me as much as anything. After almost a month in Africa, I didn't have the sense that "it"—the Land Rover, my trip, whatever—would work out well at all. Not one bit.

Sulking back to the Novotel, Ann and I erupted in an argument. It started with her criticism—mild, I must admit—of my lack of patience with the telephone exchange staff's endemic torpor. "Getting upset with those people doesn't do a bit of good," she reasonably asserted.

By "upset" she was referring to some offhand comment I had made to the fellow operating the 1920s switchboard that if I were Emperor Bokassa, I would have eaten him by now just out of spite.

"A little thing," I assured her.

"Telling him you would eat him alive!"

"I never said alive."

The battle escalated from there until Ann stomped off by herself. I warned her—somewhat hopefully, I'm afraid—that she was likely to get mugged.

Bangui, like New York, has a hidden population of homeless

and infirm who emerge after dark dominating the streets. Driving
to and from expensive restaurants in Henri's car, I'd noted with
curiosity the swarming wheelchairs, unlike any I'd seen—ingenious devices powered by hand cranks mounted like handlebars.
Outfitted with wide tires suitable for Bangui's rubbled streets,
the chairs could move with extreme speed and dexterity.

This I discovered while sulking back to the Novotel. On a
side street near the main traffic circle, I suddenly found myself
surrounded by wheelchairs. It seemed, at first, an amiable coincidence. I nodded and kept walking. Two chairs wheeled in to
block my route. *This is ridiculous,* I thought, and turned, trying to
be ever so casual, down a side alley leading to a main street. A
chair manned by a person missing a chin filled the narrow walk-
way. He gave me a horrible, skeletal grin.

The encircling chairs began to move forward, tightening the
noose. I can run, I thought, run right past them, knock them over.
Then a flashing knife made me think otherwise.

As they drew nearer, I reached into my pocket for a handful
of coins. Shaking them alluringly like dice, I scattered the money
in the street.

The wheelchairs instantly broke ranks, scrambling for the
flashes of silver. I bolted for the hotel.

Ann was waiting for me in the lobby. "Did you get
mugged?" I asked her, panting a bit.

"Of course not. Don't be paranoid."

I got the next bit of news on the Land Rover from a scuba diver.
It was unexpected: a tap on my shoulder and I was suddenly
facing a pair of bug eyes behind a glass mask. Darth Vader
wheezes came from the mouth clamped around an air hose leading to a metal cylinder. Floppy webbed feet of rubber brushed my
leg.

"I've been looking for you," the voice rasped.

I felt like laughing. "I've been looking all over Bangui for
you," I said.

A terrorist interrupted to offer us a plate of bean dip.

We were at the American embassy Halloween party. Facing me in the scuba gear was Chevron, the embassy employee from the Ivory Coast with the contacts in the inspector general's office.

"What's the news?" I asked, fully expecting to hear that the inspector general was vacationing in Saint-Tropez.

"My friend, the inspector general, he has investigated and made a report."

"A written report?" I was stunned.

Chevron's mask was starting to fog. "Of course. How else?"

"Do you have the report?"

"Here? In my pocket?" He patted his swim trunks, his only apparel. "Tomorrow." He made swimming motions and turned toward the glass living room doors leading to the floodlit lawn and pool.

"Surf's up!" someone shouted as Chevron wiggled and flopped toward the pool.

The party was at one of the typically comfortable homes owned by the embassy for employees. It came equipped with subtle security measures: a concrete fence decorated with vines and flowers, a winding driveway off the main road, hidden metal shutters and a location backing onto the Ubangi River. Apparently an American evacuation plan existed that involved retrieving embassy personnel in boats. Not that anyone seemed very concerned about coups d'état or native revolts; going to the market was worrisome, but the thousands of French troops "assisting" the CAR government had more serious problems firmly in check.

A few years ago, I'd heard, there had been a halfhearted attempt to stir up rebellion by Libyan-backed rebels. As their first—and last—action, they exploded a bomb at the local cinema. Their choice of films was unfortunate. *Once upon a Revolution* was playing, and when the first small bomb went off—intended, it seemed, to panic the viewers—everyone thought it was part of the film. The second, larger bomb wrecked the screen. This proved to be a very unpopular move as the populace was outraged by the destruction of the town's only cinema. The culprits were caught and duly pummeled by angry moviegoers, ending the revolt.

The luxurious life-styles provided to embassy employees—numerous swimming pools, servants, VCRs and movies flown in from the States—outraged Ann. She'd grown up in a military family and had developed a deep distaste for the perks surrounding government life. But Bangui was such a bleak place, it seemed to me small consolation.

In a corner of the living room, *Conan the Barbarian* played on the VCR for an appreciative audience of children and marine guards. The marines were dressed as terrorists, complete with watergun Uzis.

An attractive woman in her mid-thirties nodded toward the television. "I think it provides a good role model," she said.

"Conan the Barbarian?"

She nodded.

"For the marines?" I asked. The woman wore strips of soft black cloth wrapped all around her body.

"No," she laughed, drinking from a Budweiser can. "For my daughter." She indicated a pretty girl of perhaps six. "She's very feminine but the woman in *Conan* gives her a good model for her aggressions."

A man, also garbed in strips of black but of a different texture, ran up and rubbed his body against her. Everyone laughed. I felt there was something here I was missing. The two pulled apart with a ripping sound.

"Velcro!" The woman shouted. "We're Velcro!"

On the TV, Conan's female accomplice dismembered several people. The young girl watched entranced. "Vegamatic time!" one of the marines cried. *Conan* was a marine favorite; they knew all the lines.

"Slice and dice!" cried another.

Later, I talked for a long while with the ambassador about the professional poachers in the western part of the CAR, where Valéry Giscard d'Estaing liked to hunt when he was president of

France. "They come down from Chad and the Sudan with Kalashnikov machine guns, sometimes on camels, sometimes in Land Rovers. Of course," the ambassador said with a smile, "it is against the law to kill an elephant in the CAR."

"But you see a lot of ivory for sale here," Ann pointed out. She wore a pilot's leather jacket and Ray-Ban sunglasses. One of the marines suggested that she looked like a fighter pilot, which she took, I believe, as a compliment.

"Yes, you do see a lot of ivory," the ambassador agreed. An awkward pause ensued. "It is not against the law to sell it carved."

"Perhaps the CAR government believes the ivory is surgically removed," Ann suggested. "With no harm to the elephants, of course."

"That is probably the case." The ambassador nodded, smiling faintly with the appreciation of a man who had spent the last twenty years dealing with African governments.

Sometime after midnight, a contingent of French pilots in flight gear began jumping into the pool with their Mae West life preservers inflated.

While watching, and wondering how I was to get back to the Novotel—God knows I wasn't walking—a French woman began railing against do-good projects in Africa. She was dressed in a miniskirt and married to a French embassy official. Her cheekbones were high, her mouth a red slash. "Fifteen years ago," she laughed sardonically, "I came to Africa with the Alliance Progrès, like your Peace Corps. We work like hell. I see all the young faces, they come each year now. And you know the truth." She jabbed me in the chest with a long, red fingernail. "It only gets worse! Africa goes downhill so fast!"

She was right. Of the twelve countries in the world with a lower per capita income today than in 1960, nine are in Africa.

"We feel so good about what we do!" Her laughter carried out over the yard, mixing with the splashes from the pool. "We are all so in love with our idea of Africa. Africa!"

Chapter
Eight

I met Chevron the next day in his office at the embassy.
The life revolving around the squat, concrete building had a
certain quirky quality rather endearing in its regularity. There
was always a handful of CAR soldiers lounging in front talking with cabdrivers and flirting with passing women. As a car
bomb preventive, no parking was allowed anywhere near the
embassy, an oddly prim sight in a town where the difference
between parking a vehicle and abandoning it seemed purely
academic.

The entrance to the embassy functioned like an air lock, with
two sets of locking glass-and-steel doors; in this high-tech inspection zone, equipped with a metal detector and, rumor had it,
gas jets to immobilize unwanted visitors, a plastic bottle of drinking water invariably sat sweating on the air conditioner. Behind
bulletproof glass, a marine guard processed papers. His immacu-
late presence was all the more impressive considering the previous evening's debauchery at the Equator disco or the Rock Club.
Somehow it never felt quite right to ask this armed, formal senti-
nel if he'd felt better last night after throwing up, though it was
a question Ann had been known to pose. She came by the embassy a lot to catch up on sports through the U.S. newspapers in
the Martin Luther King reading room. Her frequent forays occasioned a dramatic increase in the reading habits of the off-duty
marines.

Chevron's office featured a large portrait of Ronald Reagan
constructed entirely out of butterflies. It was the finest example

of an art—portraiture by dead butterfly—that is, I believe, unique to Bangui.

As usual, Chevron looked like a CEO whose company was teetering on the brink of total chaos. While most of the embassy staff put in long hours, Chevron looked to be working twice as hard as everyone else. Papers crowned his desk, assistants scurried in and out, he yelled into the telephone with true vigor. The American employees concerned themselves mostly with often vague policy objectives, such as the improvement of trading relations or better military cooperation, while Chevron fought the daily wars needed to keep the routine forces of African anarchy at bay.

"Freon," he explained to me when I asked him what he was working on at the moment. "Freon. Do you have any idea how hard it is to come up with enough freon to chill this embassy and all the residences? And can you imagine what would happen in this building without air-conditioning?"

Sealed against what the marines called "nasties" by bars and slabs of reinforced concrete, the embassy had the makings of a stupendous convection oven. It was, truly, an ugly thought.

"So"—Chevron pushed aside a stack of papers—"we have a problem."

He unfolded a piece of official-looking stationery from the inspector general's office and began to read: "An inquiry into the status of one Land Rover Diesel 110 all-terrain vehicle." The detail of the initial description, at least, was admirable. In terse legal French, the report asserted that the vehicle had been confiscated following the bankruptcy of Lucien's company in the CAR. There was a long quote from the Code Minerale explaining the steps the government was entitled to take in case of bankruptcy, including "confiscation of all remaining assets."

"So there you have it," Chevron concluded.

"But Chevron," I said, trying not to scream, "that's all fine, but Lucien's company never went bankrupt."

Chevron looked at me as if I had disappointed him in some fundamental way. He cocked an eyebrow. "Not bankrupt?"

"Absolutely. This is all new. Before they were claiming to have seized the car because of past-due mining fees."

He squinted at the sheet of paper in front of him suspiciously and said, "It doesn't say anything here about late mining fees."

"I know! That's why it's so crazy."

He peered at the paper intently for a while, as if expecting the answer to jump out and bite him.

"Maybe I should go see the minister," I finally said. Everyone had advised against this seemingly obvious step; the consensus was that once the minister had personally refused to release the car, it would render useless any backdoor channels or the possibility of a bribe.

"That's tough," Chevron mused, his eyes drifting back to the stack of freon orders. "Maybe I can get some from the French army."

"Freon?" I asked.

He nodded.

"Is it hard to see a minister?" I asked.

Chevron shrugged. "It can take a while."

"Like how long?"

"A few weeks. It depends on what delegations are in town. I think the South Koreans might be sending some people right after the World Bank leaves."

I groaned, contemplating long afternoons languishing at the Rock Club waiting for a phone call.

"The Rock Club has air conditioners. Maybe I can trade for some," Chevron mused.

"Trade with what?"

"They always like videos. And we got some videos. The marines love 'em. I wonder how they'd like the new *Rambo.*"

I left him pondering the problem.

There came this moment—a small epiphany, if you will. It happened when I was walking back from the market at dusk with a banana in one hand and a yogurt in the other. An owl swooped down across the road, lighting in a mango tree. A little thing, yes. But suddenly I was thinking about the road to Berbérati and how much more there was *out there* beyond Bangui—West Africa, North Africa, the Sahel and Sahara. It was what I had really come to Africa to see, to feel—the Land Rover was just an excuse. And if I couldn't get the Land Rover, so be it. There were other ways.

That next morning I gave up on the prospect of freeing the Rover and concentrated on surveying the Bangui car market. One of the more promising items was a four-wheel-drive Toyota pickup; it was owned by a Bangui university student. She was visiting Ethiopia with a foreign aid project—it struck me as redundant to leave the CAR to witness poverty—and her uncle was handling the sale. He was an urbane fellow who dropped by the Novotel wearing a Burberry raincoat. He explained that even though advertisements were posted for the truck, the vehicle itself was being repaired; naturally, I could visit it at the mechanic's and, in any event, it was scheduled to be ready in a week or two. By now this sort of business procedure seemed perfectly normal.

As a way of explaining why I was impatient to acquire a vehicle, I related a brief outline of what had brought me to Bangui and my subsequent automotive-related troubles.

"Would you like to speak with the minister?" the Burberry-clad gentleman asked me.

"Of course, but . . .," and I told him how difficult I'd heard it was to see a minister.

He smiled. "Yes, but I have a certain advantage."

"Yes?"

"He's my brother."

The next morning I rose at dawn to stumble out to Henri's coffee company office for the 6:00 A.M. radio broadcast. It was terribly early for any conversation, much less one in code, but I struggled to relay that I had a meeting that afternoon with the minister of mines. Henri's radio-distorted squeal of a voice seemed pleased. He passed on the word that the Swedish missionary had lowered the price on his Toyota pickup and perhaps I should consider it as a fallback.

I felt only vaguely silly stuffing two thousand dollars in CFA bribe francs into my torn canvas briefcase before heading to the meeting. Mostly I felt nervous, recalling with a mixture of fear and guilt the mad hunger I'd unleashed by scattering about a dollar's worth of coins in the street. Now I was a walking lottery ticket of lifetime riches.

At the Ministry of Mines, underlings ushered me through a series of outer offices, finally reaching the inner sanctum.

The minister of mines greeted me in a five-hundred-dollar suit, and grasped my hand with a firmness to please Dale Carnegie. "So, we have a little problem, do we?" he quipped, and then chuckled.

He wasn't alone. Rising from the black leather couch, Capitaine Follope greeted me with a half-embarrassed shrug, as if to apologize for his presence.

Right away, I knew it wasn't going to be as I'd planned. Right away, I realized I was in over my head.

I'd expected the encounter to proceed rather like negotiating with a border guard, a time-consuming ritual in which everyone acted as if the only thing that mattered—price—didn't matter at all. But what I got was more akin to a congressman meeting a concerned constituent; not a particularly important constituent but one for whom he felt vaguely sorry, like a country cousin come to the city and clearly confused.

"Tell me," the minister began, "just what is your relationship with Lucien?" Then he smiled.

Alarms rang inside my head. The minister's voice reminded me of the best sort of prosecutor: low-keyed, friendly, with traps set at the end of each seemingly harmless sentence.

"Relationship?"

"He is a friend?"

I plunged boldly ahead. "Sort of."

A knowing smile. "And you are here doing his business?"

"Oh, no." Then I explained how I had come to be in the Central African Republic.

"Let me understand," the minister queried patiently, "you were having dinner with your friend Lucien and he asked you to go to Africa to transport his vehicle and you said yes. This is what really happened?"

It suddenly sounded like the most preposterous thing I'd ever heard. "Well, yes. That's pretty much what happened."

The minister and the capitaine exchanged bemused looks. "And how long have you been involved in business with your friend Lucien?"

"I'm not. He's just a friend."

The looks came again. "And you come all the way to Africa to pick up a vehicle just for a friend?"

I said in a voice that sounded very tiny, "I thought it would be fun."

"Ahhh. Fun."

Finally we got down to it. "This friend of yours, Lucien," the minister said, still in his oh-so-nice tone, "he is a friend of mine, too. I like Lucien."

I didn't say anything. It seemed the only chance, however remote, to salvage a smidgen of respect.

"But he maybe has done things he should not have."

"What things?" This was a question I had been dying to ask since arriving in Bangui.

"We don't know," the capitaine responded, opening his mouth for the first time. "But we would like to know. We would indeed."

"But if you don't know what he's done wrong, how do you know he's done anything wrong?"

This bit of logic did not seem to faze them in the least.

"We keep the Land Rover, and maybe Lucien, he returns and we can have a chat. That would be nice, don't you think?"

Just great, I thought. *Just great.*

"There is one last thing I would like to ask you," the minister said, turning serious for the first time.

"Yes?" *Oh hell, here it comes.*

"You live in New York, correct?"

"Yes."

"I go to New York for a Third World debt conference next month. Can you recommend the best restaurants?"

We left Bangui for the last time the next day at noon. Joseph, Henri's designated chauffeur, whom I'd yet to see actually drive, was behind the wheel of a coffee company Renault. Riding with Joseph proved very quickly to be an experience utterly unique.

As a driver, Joseph did all the normal things most drivers do: brake, accelerate, turn. He just chose to perform these functions at the oddest of times, ones that bore no relationship with the road.

The morning started with Joseph and me leaving the coffee company office to fill the Renault with gas. He was driving. Backing up, we knocked over a line of metal trash containers, initiating an impressive domino display of physics. Exiting the driveway, the Renault collided with one of the metal uprights supporting the coffee company sign, pinning the car under an inconvenient, if not crushing, load. Once freed, we moved out onto the street; straddling both lanes of traffic, Joseph paused to look both right and left. Heavy trucks rumbled in each direction. I must confess to uttering a choking cry, somewhere between a gasp and a yell. When both lanes of traffic had ground to a stop, Joseph proceeded. Clearly, he was the cautious sort.

Joseph had one redeeming quality: he drove very, very slowly. This provided a margin for error crucial to survival.

It also provided me a chance to savor the Bangui-to-Berbérati drive in a way impossible at the escape-level speeds Lucien drove. For the first time I noticed on the outskirts of Bangui a row of little factories: a hut where three men molded mud bricks, another where a man made chairs and beds with, strangely, a sleek Swedish modern look. At the heart of the little industrial district was a bar, the Passe Temps, crowded with rollicking men and women swaying to reggae.

Passing through Kilometer Five, the shantytown on the edge of Bangui where no whites dared walk alone, laughing French soldiers threw cigarettes from a troop carrier. An African in a hooded University of Oregon sweatshirt, balancing a bundle of wood on his head, toppled to the ground, swarmed by the crowd fighting for the tobacco.

Within fifteen minutes Joseph had crushed his first animal, a small goat trailing a scrambling herd rushing across the road. The crunch resonated through the Renault, a heavy, violent sound. Ann suggested we paint a little goat on the side of the car, keeping a tally of the day's slaughter. "You know, how many goats, dogs, small children."

"People?"

"That's it." She explained that her fighter plane friends wanted to do the same thing "when we fight the big one with the Russkies."

"Paint goats on the side of their planes?" I asked.

Later—not very much later, actually—when the Renault speared a chicken, Joseph, who never said anything, muttered with a half smile, "Appetizer."

Chapter Nine

That night the malaria hit. The chills came and then fever and with it the most extraordinary fever dreams.

The dreams were of confusion. In a slick cocoon of sweat, I pondered visual puzzles I couldn't solve, crowded with people who didn't fit: the minister of mines, the white woman at the Bangui pizzeria whose husband beat her, the Czech bartender, Joseph behind the wheel. Brief bouts of sleep felt like long nights, and I'd wake up fumbling for a light to see what time it was, anxious for the dawn.

I heard the arriving coffee workers with relief. Clear early-morning light brightened the small concrete room. I walked to Henri's house, took a shower that flooded the cement floor with tides of red dirt, and sat on the porch, relieved by the brightness of the day.

After breakfast I went to see the French doctor at the hospital. He asked me what was wrong. I told him I was sweating a lot.

"So am I," he responded with a scowl. "It's ninety-eight degrees."

He examined me in a perfunctory way. "You've got malaria. It happens to everybody."

"But I've taken all the pills. They say it prevents it."

"Yes," he agreed, "that's what they say."

He gave me different pills. "Maybe these will work better," he said, shrugging before heading in to operate on a woman with cervical cancer.

\\\

A mechanic friend of Henri's vetoed buying the Toyota pickup. He was a Belgian of great mechanical renown whose sole diagnostic technique consisted of listening to the engine block with a stethoscope. He wagged his finger, uttered a disdainful "tisk, tisk, tisk," and Henri considered the matter finished. "You must have a vehicle that can cross the Sahara. With Ann." He added the last bit as if to explain that it was perfectly okay if I wandered out in the desert with a dying pickup but having Ann with me made it a different matter.

The last likely prospect was a Land Rover that the Belgian mechanic recommended highly. The inspection of it was a typical African business deal: we left after dark to find the owner, who had a small sawmill somewhere out in the bush; he lived with an African woman whom he considered not his mistress but his wife. Henri and the Belgian referred to him as a "little white." They used the term not in the derisive tone the description might suggest but more as a matter of fact. "Oh, yes, the little white."

We cut a rather pathetic picture bouncing out to the sawmill: Henri and I were both sweating with malaria, while Ann's stomach staged a grumbling revolt. The headlights of the Renault were suggestive rather than effective. They cast a vague light more suited to a cabaret than an African dirt track on a moonless night.

After an hour or so we found what appeared to be a sawmill. There were no lights. As we pulled in, we spotted a disemboweled Land Rover, its engine splayed open and spilling parts. "There must be a different Land Rover," I said confidently. No one else said anything.

The Renault's feeble lights caught an arresting sight: on the top of a little hill near the sawmill's main structure, an African bounced up and down with a spear in each hand. He waved these menacingly and advanced toward us at a trot.

"Oo la la," Henri muttered.

Spears thrust forward, the African greeted us in Sango. Henri responded in French. The African countered in Sango. This went

on for a while until finally some compromise was reached and
Henri threw in a few words of Sango, the African a touch of
French.

The African guard explained that his patron was in town but
would return shortly. Yes, the Land Rover was for sale. No, there
was only one.

We stumbled through heaps of trash to peer into the carcass
of the Land Rover. No one said anything. I couldn't imagine what
ill sounds the Belgan would hear with his stethoscope. We got
back into the Renault and left.

On the long drive back, Henri articulated what I was thinking. "To buy a car you must go to Cameroon. It's much cheaper,
much better selection. You can go to Yaoundé or Douala. They
are wonderful towns, a lot of fun. In Cameroon, you will have
no problems."

Two days later, Henri woke us at dawn. "There is a coffee truck
going to Cameroon. It leaves this morning from Gamboula. Joseph will drive you."

This last bit of information stopped me halfway out of bed.
"Right."

It took a pickup truck to carry all our gear. Spread out in the
dirt in front of Henri's house, the equipment looked sufficient to
outfit a small detachment of paratroopers: one coffin-sized trunk;
a black duffel bag in which, quite easily, two people could sleep
(I discovered this later); a canvas briefcase; and my Himalayas
backpack, out of which jutted a spare radiator hose to a Land
Rover I apparently was never going to drive. Ann had her white,
hard-shelled suitcase that looked a bit like a UFO, a duffel bag
and a leather backpack mainly filled with the single copy of
Italian *Vogue* she lugged around like Sisyphus. We had ac-
cumulated: two metal and two plastic twenty-liter jerricans, a
shovel and a substantial metal toolbox. The latter had been
nipped from a cache of supplies Lucien had left.

Gamboula is a border outpost perched on the CAR-Cameroon line. Blending amiably with the smugglers and the border guards getting rich off the smugglers, Henri's coffee company had a forwarding office to help ease incoming supplies and outgoing coffee over the border.

The idea was for us to transfer our gear from the pickup and leave right away on a coffee company truck destined for Yaoundé, Cameroon. Instead we spent three days.

Chapter Ten

Picture a tropical Santa Claus: a round belly bulging from a half-buttoned Hawaiian print shirt, a white beard on a face darkened by twenty-five years of African sun. The eyes are gleeful, the smile near constant. A mad sort of giggle erupts like champagne.

His name was Gerard, and Gamboula, we quickly discovered, belonged to him. Gerard ran the coffee company's Gamboula outpost and, as sort of a sideline, or a hobby, he ran Gamboula as well. Gerard was a big man with a most intriguing life.

While our assorted gear was transferred from Joseph's pickup to the larger coffee company truck, Gerard suggested we drop by customs and have our passports stamped and visas confirmed. We had known Gerard only a few minutes, and it struck me as odd that the border officials, from the soldiers to the commandant, greeted him with the deference I associated with a presidential visit. *"Patron"* tripped off of everyone's tongue; that there was something they could do to please Gerard seemed to give them the greatest joy. Gerard responded not with the polite yet aloof manner that typified most black-white encounters I'd witnessed, but more like a benevolent father figure. He joked, slapped backs, inquired after children and wives.

It made for the fastest border formalities I encountered in Africa.

"I just need to stop off at the market for a moment," Gerard said as we pulled away from the tin customs shed. "Just a little errand."

On the way we stopped to pick up a lone white figure walking along the road. The sight startled me; white people hardly ever walked in Africa, and that there was someone white in Gamboula besides Gerard was extraordinary.

The tall, bearded figure got in the car, looking equally surprised. He wore cutoff shorts and a ripped tee shirt; his very pale skin was dotted with red bites and abrasions. The total impression was one of a shipwreck victim who'd been barely surviving on a desert isle for quite some time.

We looked at each other and then he spent a while longer staring at Ann. Gerard, launched on a story about hunting baboons, made no introductions. Finally our new companion said, in horrendous French, "Who are you?" just as I asked the same thing in English.

He was American, a Peace Corps volunteer.

"I can't talk in English," he said in English. "It's been so long."

His name was Walter and he'd been in Gamboula for four months.

"How long will you be here?" Ann asked.

"Two years."

"Oh." A long silence ensued.

"What do you do?" Ann asked.

"Teach people to grow fish."

"Grow? Are you planting them?"

We later learned that what Walter mostly did was eat big meals and play tennis at Gerard's.

Gerard stopped at the market. "A little errand," he said. "Just a moment . . ." He hurried off.

The market was a rough square of open stalls selling bolts of bright fabric, most imprinted with President or First Lady Kolingba's picture, tubs of ground manioc, odd bits of cooking ware and various roasted meats, mostly monkey and beef. All around the open area, women squatted in the dirt offering a few meager items for sale: a handful of peanuts, four onions, strange leafy greens I'd never seen. Children closed in on us, hands outstretched; most seemed to know Walter.

I wanted to know more about Walter's fish-growing lessons. "Oh, it's simple," he said. "I just teach them how to build ponds and raise these little fish."

"How little?"

He held up two fingers a few inches apart.

"Aren't they kind of bony?"

"Terribly," he said. "But very nutritious."

"Do people like them?"

"Not so much. But Gerard and I do. We fry them whole and eat them all the time. We'll have to go fishing this afternoon."

"Fishing?" I laughed. It seemed such a loony idea. "For fish three inches long?"

"Some grow to five or six," Walter promised. He had long blond hair he swept off his forehead with quick jerks of his head.

A young African woman rushed past us at full speed. I stared. It was very unusual to see anyone run in Africa.

"Uh-oh," Walter murmured.

The woman reached the far end of the market square and hurled herself on Gerard's back, screaming. She flailed him with her small fists. Gerard, a big man, turned around in surprise, the woman sticking firmly to his back. He began to talk to the woman; his face grew slightly red. He strode out of sight behind a stall, the woman attached.

Ann and I looked at Walter, questioning.

"It's a domestic dispute," he said. "Would you like to go fishing?"

I told him I'd love to but that we were supposed to leave on a coffee company truck to Cameroon that morning.

"Oh, that's no problem. Gerard can fix all that."

Gerard walked out behind the stall holding hands with the woman who had been on his back. A young boy, barefoot and wearing torn white underwear, ran up and leapt into Gerard's arms. "Papa!" he yelled. "Papa!"

Ann and I looked on, saying nothing. Eventually Walter announced in the most matter-of-fact tone, "Gerard has a very complicated life."

After lunch, a long affair with too much wine and gin, Gerard announced, "You leave tomorrow. Now I take you fishing, we do a little hunting." He grinned. "An afternoon in Gamboula."

I was learning that everything Gerard did was oddly convoluted. The seemingly simple act of going fishing required a number of steps. First we had to go back to the market to buy bread for bait. This took about half an hour as Gerard had to finish the flirting that had launched the attack of his mistress. The object of his affection was a pretty young woman who wore her hair in braided spikes and sold stacks of unground manioc root. Naturally Ann and I expected, not without a touch of gleeful anticipation, to see a repeat of the afternoon's encounter. This seemed to be in the making when Gerard's son, still in his dirty white underpants, appeared from nowhere to jump into his papa's arms. But this time his mother did not make an appearance.

She was, we learned a few minutes later, at her new house, one Gerard had just built. It was a four-room cinder block structure complete with the requisite goats, chickens and pigs. We stopped there for armaments: a pair of ancient Spanish shotguns with beautiful scrollwork on the stocks. André, Gerard's son, bustled out of the house with a gun in each hand. He looked like the ultimate Dennis the Menace nightmare: a half-naked seven-year-old armed to the teeth.

André had the disposition of an attack Chihuahua. He rushed everywhere at full speed, babbling in a private language of Sango and French. When he wasn't playing with the guns, he toyed incessantly with his penis. His skin was café au lait, his eyes blue.

The fishing pond lay in a hollow between rolling hills, part of a private preserve Gerard had created for André and his mother. "When I go back to France," Gerard said, "this will provide for them." He swept his hand out over the hills dotted with coffee bushes. André acted like a young lord, ordering the black children who trailed behind us to carry the fishing poles and cooler of beer. He darted between the coffee bushes, fondling the beans lovingly.

We used the fresh bread from the market to bait our hooks, which dangled from cane poles. "If I were a fish, I'd eat this," Ann said, ripping off a handful of the delicious loaf. I agreed.

The fish bit urgently but I couldn't get away from the feeling that it was all some sort of elaborate sight gag: four people, apparently sane, earnestly working their poles to pull in the tiniest of fish. "Wow, this is a big one," Walter said excitedly. "Look at this!" He dangled a five-incher proudly.

When a flock of white egrets settled in a tree across the pond, André jumped up and down and babbled in tones even more animated than his norm.

"You," Gerard addressed me, "must go shoot one of the birds."

I demurred.

"No, no, it would please my son. You must do it as a favor to me."

It seemed to me that shooting André would be more to the point.

André bounced up and down some more. Gerard looked at me imploringly, his bright eyes pleading.

I picked up one of the twelve-gauge shotguns and grabbed a handful of shells. André clapped his hands and squeezed his penis enthusiastically. Together we tromped off toward the birds.

Halfway around the pond, I looked back at the band of anglers. From this distance they appeared to have large cockroaches on their lines. But then, I wasn't seeing anything too clearly. Sweat poured down over my eyes. The hints of malaria chills jolted me like electric shocks. The jungle greenness blurred and refocused into a pointillist painting.

André squealed and pulled frantically on my arm. The egrets took flight, their long white wings flopping lazily. I raised the

shotgun, half-wondering whether it was going to blow up in my
face, and waved it generally in the direction of the white forms.
André jumped up and down on my foot and I pulled the trigger.
The report rolled around in the hills, launching new flights of
parrots. A hummingbird hovered in front of my eyes, as if inves-
tigating. André, I was glad to see, look crushed that I hadn't hit
anything.

All afternoon I wandered around the hills, hypnotized by the
green heat. André, frustrated by my refusal to fire at every living
target, abandoned me. For a while I heard him yelling, "Papa!
Papa!" but then I was covered in the lushness, my ears ringing
with the shotgun blast and the throb of the crickets.

Later, in that special late-afternoon light that seemed soft
enough to touch, I slaughtered ducks. They were fenced in Gerard's private mud pen, forty or fifty wild ducks raised to
brighten Gerard's table. We had one twelve-gauge shell remaining. Gerard handed it to me with a solemn command: "We need
three ducks. Our dinner's fate is in your hands."

Tromping around in the mud, I scrambled to line up three
ducks, as it were, in a row. This was not particularly easy to do.
Ducks have little sense of symmetry and are not noted for their
cooperation. Duck herding is an art I am yet to master.

That André ran amok, giggling maniacally and throwing
mud everywhere, did not speed the process.

Finally I isolated three and let fire with our precious remaining cartridge. Two ducks fell mortally wounded (one decapitated), but the third scurried off, all feathers and appendages
intact.

Gerard looked at me with grave disappointment. He counted
up the number of dinner guests on his fingers. "No," he said,
shaking his head, "we must have three." Gerard asked André to
get another cartridge from the car parked about a mile away.
Without a moment's pause, André turned to one of the black
children hanging about and repeated the order.

The shell was fetched, the duck slayed.

On our way back to the car, we stopped at Gerard's vast

garden, terraced into the hillside: rows and rows of vegetables to delight any European. "Why does all this stuff grow so easily," I asked, indicating the carrots, lettuce, broccoli, cabbage, "but you can never find it in African markets?"

"Africans don't eat it," Gerard answered, looking at me as he would at an idiot child. "Why should they grow it?"

That night I lay alternately sweating and shivering under the mosquito net, listening for sounds of thunder. "It's no good if it rains," Gerard explained. "The roads turn to mush. It will take forever to get to Cameroon."

At dawn I woke up to sounds of rain on the metal roof and the ardent cooing of Gerard's pigeons. Over breakfast, Gerard announced happily, "It's impossible to leave today. You stay another day. We go fishing and maybe shoot some monkeys."

We stayed.

Chapter Eleven

I didn't worry about the soldiers until I realized they were drunk. It was 2:00 A.M. and my body felt as if somebody had beat on it with a baseball bat. For twenty hours we'd bounced around inside the cab of a forty-foot semitrailer, the last eight hours in darkness over mountain streambeds.

Gerard had promised that "the roads in Cameroon, when you get close to Yaoundé, they are very good." As did everyone, he talked about Cameroon as a wonderfully developed place, where beer was half the price it was in the Central African Republic and cars, thanks to the port in Douala, were a bargain.

He was right about the beer. But if he turned out to be as wrong about the price of cars as he was about the road conditions, I was headed for big trouble.

He'd also neglected to mention a few dominant characteristics of Cameroon life—like the police roadblocks every few miles.

In our twenty-hour journey from the Cameroon border to Yaoundé, the capital, army and police patrols stopped us twelve times. The driver, who made the run frequently, thought this was rather good. "Sometimes the police are a problem," he told us. This was not a joke.

We had left Gamboula at dawn. Except for our considerable luggage covered by a tarp, the open flatbed trailer was empty. Pierre drove. An imposing figure of perhaps fifty, he walked with an upright carriage that suggested a military background. He had a graying mustache and wore a neat short-sleeved safari suit not unlike the sort sold by Hunting World.

We stopped first at Pierre's house, a tidy concrete block building like the one Gerard had built for his mistress. This was Gerard's work as well, a bonus for Pierre, whose services Gerard valued highly. "My best man," he explained. "A superb driver."

As Pierre maneuvered the huge truck in front of his house, blocking most of the dirt road, eight or nine children rushed out. They clambered up to hug their father, who sat regally behind the wheel in the elevated cab. He let them play rough tunes on the screeching air horn and demonstrated the multiple gearshifts. Pierre's wife held up the baby of the family to give him equal opportunity on the horn. Pierre laughed. Ann and I laughed. I felt as if I had stumbled into an African Norman Rockwell scene.

After a few moments of play, Pierre shook off his family, went into the house for a black leather purse of the sort French men carry, and climbed back into the cab. Two teenagers, apparently not family members, scrambled onto the flat bed of the truck. Pierre gravely started the coughing diesel and, with one last wave to his family, eased the big rig down the road.

The Cameroon border consisted of three separate posts. This struck me as odd. Pierre explained what should have been obvious: "It gives them three chances to make money from bribes."

For each station, Gerard had written a letter addressed to the commandant. At the first, Pierre led us to the only visible authority, a soldier clad in green fatigue pants, a Bugs Bunny tee shirt and sandals. He appeared to be asleep, lying against the mud wall of the customs hut, cradling an AK-47 assault rifle; his precise level of somnolence was difficult to determine as he wore sunglasses. Pierre murmured greetings; the soldier turned his head slightly to stare at me; banana trees reflected off his mirrored glasses.

The soldier held out his hand. Thinking he wanted our documents, I nodded and handed him Gerard's letter. He shook his head and held out his hand further. I stared at him, confused. Finally I realized he wanted to shake hands. Feeling like an uncouth cad, I mumbled apologies.

Using his assault rifle as a cane, the soldier slowly rose and ambled inside the hut. A metal helmet hung on a peg over the wooden counter, where two old bikes were propped next to the frame of a small motorcycle. A sign proclaimed "Unity, Dignity, Work." The soldier carried the letter into a side door labeled "Commandant du Corps Urbain."

He reemerged followed by a man in a rumpled warm-up suit who was yawning and rubbing his eyes. This, apparently, was the commandant. We shook hands, and he opened Gerard's letter, deftly removing the five-thousand-franc note folded inside. He shook my hand again and requested we fill in a longish customs form. We did. Our passports were stamped.

That Gerard had not mentioned the enclosed money, nor requested that we provide it, was typical of the sort of generosity I'd encountered in Africa. Like the letters of introduction I was carrying from Henri to various friends in Cameroon and Chad, the hospitality was a charming throwback to a different era.

I'd been warned by Gerard that the first stretch of the journey, a winding 150 kilometers, was on a "very bad road." That he considered it bad even by Central African standards made it a warning not to be discounted. "After Bertoua, though," Gerard had added, naming the first major town in Cameroon, "the road is very good."

Had Pierre not been every bit the driver Gerard had claimed, the truck would never have made it to Bertoua. Less than five miles over the border, on a steep downhill grade with a sharp turn at the bottom, four trucks lay overturned. One semi had just toppled, its wheels still spinning. The driver, evidently unhurt, sat on top of the door, waving a frantic warning to Pierre. The road was muddy, littered with sharp boulders.

Pierre shrugged but did not hesitate. Sliding like a log in a chute, the truck shot down the hill. At the critical turn, passing just inches from the earlier victims, we swayed precariously, a ship tossing in heavy seas. Then with a rapid downshift, never touching the brakes, Pierre regained control.

It took just under five hours to travel the 150 kilometers to Bertoua. We stopped for lunch at a market on the edge of town.

On this Sunday afternoon, a raucous crowd spilled out of the bar, dancing to the music blaring from a stand selling cassettes and records.

We ate strips of beef pared off a haunch roasting on an oil drum stove. Three pickup trucks filled with young men waving Cameroon flags roared up from the direction of town. They shouted slogans, and when the bar throng responded tepidly, they yelled louder. Several jumped off the truck and ran about the market brandishing flags; the scene reminded me of male cheerleaders taking the field before a football game.

The crowd liked this more, raising bottles in tribute. One flag bearer caught sight of Ann and stopped suddenly, kicking up a flurry of dust. Ann smiled and saluted with her beer. She wore shorts and a tee shirt featuring a picture of oversized sunglasses at a rakish angle. The young Cameroonian patriot looked confused, uncertain whether to smile or scowl. Finally he thrust his flag toward Ann and shouted, *"Liberté!"*

"Égalité!" Ann yelled.

This pleased him. He bounded back to his truck.

Pierre, when I asked, explained that this was a Cameroonian national holiday, Independence Day, he believed. He indicated that it was not a good day to travel.

"Why?"

He paused, seeming to search for the right word. Eventually he said, simply, "Politics."

By African standards, Cameroonian politics are stable, at least for the moment. President Paul Biya assumed his title with the aid of his predecessor—an African rarity—and since assuming the presidency in 1982, he has faced only one serious coup attempt, also an African rarity. That the threat came from the man who had granted him power in the first place, the former president, Ahmadou Ahidjo, is very much *not* an African rarity.

Cameroon is one of those African countries with no real reason to exist as a national unit. Within its arbitrary boundaries, carved by European politicians, live over two hundred ethnic groups, each with a separate language and none able, in size or strength, to dominate the country. Geographically it is equally confused, with swamps and tropical rain forests in the south transforming into arid savanna and desert in the north.

Officially the country is bilingual, split between French and English. Had World War One ended differently, German would have prevailed.

Cameroon's colonial history is appropriately muddled. The Portuguese explored the coast in the late fifteenth century, but the British evidenced the first serious Western interest, signing a commercial treaty with the chiefs of Douala in 1856. Like most African ports, Douala developed as a slave market and the local chiefs acquired international trading skills. Looking to expand their influence, the Douala chiefs asked Britain to declare a protectorate over the area, and when Britain failed to respond, they turned to Germany.

The Germans brought the full complement of mixed blessings that characterize European influence in Africa. Roads and schools followed troops. The northern Muslim reaches of the country were "pacified," beginning a pattern of domination by the south that continues today. As a spoil of World War One, the French and English divided the territory, hence the two official languages.

Had I visited Cameroon before spending time in the Central African Republic, I doubtless would have been struck by the poverty, the primitiveness—all the clichés of sub-Saharan African life. But after the CAR, I marveled at the signs of sophistication in Cameroonian life. Like soccer.

It may seem a silly thing, but the sudden appearance of schoolchildren playing soccer in the roadside villages came as a shock. For the first time I realized that in almost a month in the CAR, I had not seen one organized or spontaneous athletic event outside the walls of the Rock Club. Young children and teenagers either worked or hung around looking bored, with a preponderance of the former.

But in almost every village in Cameroon, a fierce soccer battle was under way. And truthfully, the games did indicate Cameroon's more developed status. Though only eight hundred dollars, the annual per capita income of Cameroon was almost three times that of the CAR and ten times higher than neighboring Chad. Sport is a function of schools and leisure time, of a society organized enough to field different teams, of an economy rich enough to support at least a little nonproductive endeavor.

The other thing, besides soccer, Cameroonians apparently cared for was dancing. I had never seen so many people dancing in my life.

Perhaps that it was Sunday had something to do with it. Surely the people in the little town of Minta undulating down the road in what looked exactly like a conga line were going to or from church. They wore bright dresses with fringed hats and crisp white shirts and narrow ties. A man who appeared to be flirting with rapture led the group, laughter and song spilling from his lips. He waved an umbrella like a baton.

In other villages, lone dancers moved to a private rhythm. They stood by the side of the road, looking at us and dancing. I liked it.

By the end of the day, I felt as if I'd spent most of my life in the cab of Pierre's truck. Several times during stops, I'd tried to shift from the cab to the flatbed so that I could stretch out or stand, but each time Pierre stopped me. He said it was a Cameroonian law that three people must ride in the front, though I suspect he was mostly worried that I might bounce out at a vicious bump or tumble down the open rear during one of his frequent power-slide turns. But it may have been a law. God knows there were enough police around to enforce the most perverse regulations.

The roadblocks started as soon as we reached the main highway in Bertoua. Within the next hour we hit five more; before we arrived in Yaoundé, police or army patrols had stopped us twelve times.

Most of the roadblocks—except for the last one, the one with drunks and guns—fell into a pattern. An improvised barrier, such as a log, a chain, maybe an old car, slowed traffic. Pierre

would sigh, curse and reach for his leather purse. He always tried
to get out of the truck before the guard reached him so that the
official would be less likely to spot something in the cab—a pair
of sunglasses, cigarettes, a cassette tape—that he wanted.

Some of the men were local police, some belonged to state
units patrolling the road; various army units joined the proceed-
ings, including paratroopers in red berets. Each group wore a
different uniform, but all shared a crisp neatness that was extraordinary in the heat and dust. Some wore sandals; the paratroopers had intimidating high boots of shiny black leather. The
boots of the motorcycle patrols resembled riding garb, knee high
with chunky heels. Everyone carried guns.

"That's all they give them," Pierre said, "clothes and a gun.
All their money they make like this, stopping people."

The exchange of money occurred in a surprisingly discreet
fashion, more like tipping a maître d' than paying off a bribe
encouraged by weapons and the hint of jail. Invariably the exam-
ining officer noted some irregularity in our papers. This problem
could only be solved by a commanding officer not present at the
time; in fact, this commanding officer might not return for hours.
A small fine, however, would suffice.

Three thousand CFA, about eleven dollars, was the standard
amount Pierre turned over. Once a motorcycle patrol demanded
more. The two men, very large and dressed all in black, did not
appear to be in the best of moods. For some reason they had
picked a very sunny stretch of road to run their little scam and
both sweated profusely under layers of black cloth and leather.
The two men took turns harassing the unlucky occupants of a
white taxi van. On the front and back, the van proclaimed its
name in large letters, *La Bonne Volonté*.

Known as "bread loaf" vans because the poor souls inside are
stacked like bread, these decrepit, often windowless metal canisters on wheels are the most common form of transportation in
Africa. The motorcycle police made everyone get out of *La Bonne
Volonté*. I counted. Seventeen people disembarked.

About half the passengers were Muslims in white bou-bous;

most of the others wore the normal ragtag assortment of second-hand Western clothes. One man had on a neat dark suit and carried a briefcase. Others clasped plastic bags and two men held straw baskets stuffed with squawking chickens. Everyone was coated in a layer of red dust and looked exhausted. I wondered how long they had been trapped in the van. The heat was choking.

One policeman demanded to see everyone's papers. The mood was one of quiet resignation, except for the driver. He jumped up and down and pleaded with the officer. "But we have this all worked out," he cried. "We agreed! We agreed!"

The other cop looked on disgustedly and then walked over to us. He was a big man with the build of a fullback. Typically, Pierre steered the man away from the truck. They talked for a moment and then Pierre, with a sigh, reached into his purse for three thousand CFA. (One's attitude turning over the bribe was important. It was no good seeming untroubled by the bribe, as then they would ask for more; too surly, and the recipient took offense.)

Unexpectedly, the motorcycle policeman shook his head violently. Pierre said something, gesturing with his hands outspread. The cop strode over to the truck; Pierre trailed, rolling his eyes.

"What's in here?" the cop asked, gesturing toward the small mountain of baggage in the back of the truck.

We explained it was just personal items.

"Open them," he said. "All of them."

Ann and I looked at each other and then over at the white van. The other policeman had ordered all bags unstrapped from the roof of the van and was searching each one. Clothes were thrown everywhere in the road, as if a small bomb had exploded.

I took Pierre aside and slipped him a few thousand CFA. He renegotiated with the cop. When we left, the driver of the van had collapsed in the middle of the road, head buried in his hands.

A couple of hours after dark, we stopped in a little village comprised of three bars and a restaurant jammed together. It was a popular place. Other trucks were parked, and a rowdy crowd rumbled from bar to bar downing Coastal beers. (The low price of beer in Cameroon seemed to have a decided effect on drinking habits.)

On the exterior wall of a bar, an ancient film projector illuminated a French version of *Halls of Montezuma.*

I stayed by the side of the truck to watch the baggage, while Ann went in search of food and drink. Pierre and his two teenage assistants disappeared. The crowd, friendly but curious, swirled around me; some people asked for money or gifts in a halfhearted way. Reggae music mixed with the soundtrack of *Halls of Montezuma.* It reminded me of nighttime at a country fair, shadowy forms searching for elusive sex and happy to settle for beer and music.

Ann returned with a young African man whose face was marked with tribal scars. Both carried handfuls of banana leaves wrapped around hot chunks of roasted beef. Ann introduced me to her friend. "He saw me walking through the crowd and asked if everything was okay, if I needed any help," she explained.

"She was walking so fast, I thought maybe a bad person was chasing her," he smiled.

"Are there bad people here?" I asked.

He laughed. "There are bad people everywhere in Africa." He paused, chewing on the tough meat. "Are there no bad people in America?"

It wasn't until we stopped at the next roadblock, about five miles further, that we realized Pierre's two teenage helpers were missing. The five miles had taken a half hour to drive. Pierre fumed as we turned around.

We found one of the young men planted on the front row of *Halls of Montezuma.* Pierre berated him and he sheepishly climbed into the back of the truck, eyes still turned toward the screen. Ann promised she'd tell him how the movie ended when we got to Yaoundé.

Pierre cranked the truck to leave, and when I asked about the other teenager, he explained that he lived nearby and had left for home.

About four hours later I thought about this when we were rumbling down what was essentially a riverbed. The horrendous condition baffled me because I'd heard so much about the good roads in Cameroon, and I was certain they would only improve the closer we got to Yaoundé, the capital. My Michelin map of West Africa, number 153, indicated a veritable highway extending several hundred kilometers from Yaoundé.

Were we on the main highway? I finally asked Pierre.

No, he responded.

Why not?

The main highway, he said, was worse than this road. Everyone took this road.

This troubled me. I found it hard to believe that the other road, touted as one of the best highways in West Africa, could be worse than this boulder-strewn horror that held our speed to ten miles an hour. And if this road was in fact better, why wasn't there more traffic? Why were we almost the only truck on the road?

At a shack where we stopped to stretch and drink a Coke, I unfolded my Michelin and asked Pierre where we were. He pointed to a thin black line that snaked above the main highway, arching into the hills before descending into Yaoundé. I stared at this, confused and tired. If this wasn't the best route—and I was convinced it wasn't—why did Pierre take it? Perhaps, I thought, he might have taken a wrong turn and was reluctant to admit it.

And then I remembered the teenager we had left at *Halls of Montezuma*. He was some kind of relative of Pierre's, and that made for the only logical explanation: Pierre had taken the longer road into the hills so he could deliver his cousin to his house.

I brooded over this while the truck bounced toward Yaoundé. I told myself that I should have watched our route more closely and complained when we left the main road hours ago. I had been friendly and open with Pierre and his helpers in a way

I knew Henri or Gerard would never have been. Clearly, I thought, I'd played the fool and been taken advantage of. "They can smell weakness miles away," Henri once said in passing, "they" being Africans. I'd been weak.

But as soon as these thoughts rolled through my head, I felt ashamed. I sounded like a caricature of every budding racist I'd ever known. It was a nasty, dirty feeling.

And that's how I felt, nasty and dirty, when we finally reached Yaoundé at 2:00 A.M.

Chapter
Twelve

"Yaoundé: this is the capital of Cameroon—a clean, modern city which is hilly and picturesque and has a refreshingly cool climate."

This passage from the guidebook *Africa on a Shoestring* reverberated inside my head that first morning in Yaoundé like a mantra. In my frazzled state, still shaken from the truck ride and three hours' sleep, I felt as if I must be hallucinating. There had to be some horrible mistake. Clean? Modern? Picturesque? This was Yaoundé?

It's tempting to say my introduction to the city unfairly flavored my attitude, but what happened to us the first five minutes in town was, I'm convinced, a quintessential Yaoundé experience.

The soldiers stood at the edge of the first main intersection in town. It seemed, at first, like every other shakedown, but soon it took a sullen turn. "Get down!" the soldier barked. "Now!"

I climbed down. "Your bag!" He pointed to a canvas briefcase on the floor of the truck.

The soldier talking wore sunglasses and a rain poncho tossed over his shoulder like a cape. He had a mustache and a jutting jaw. When he jerked the bag from my hands and spat, "Open!," tottering back on his heels, I realized he was drunk. I looked around into the glazed eyes of his comrades. They were all drunk.

From my early experiences on weekend deer-hunting trips in Mississippi, I've had a marked aversion to drunk people with guns. These drunk soldiers had automatic weapons.

Curiously, I felt calm. The irritation of twenty hours in the truck, my seething annoyance with Pierre, the frustration of not knowing why our supposed eight-hour trip had taken twice as long: all of those petty concerns disappeared staring at this man with the jutting jaw, the poncho that I suddenly realized he wore like Clint Eastwood, the sunglasses, the weapons.

As they lifted each item in the briefcase—tape recorder, binoculars, books, flashlight—the soldier in the poncho cape barked, "You give to me."

Each time I shook my head. Twelve hours ago I would have parted with a small item, say the three-dollar penlight, but now I was steeled to see it through.

I found myself enjoying the moment. Everyone had said I was crazy to go to Africa, that there were dangerous sorts of people and situations worth avoiding. Now, at least, I'd found a bit of both.

"You give to me!"

His voice rose. As he moved my tape recorder toward his pocket, I reached out to stop his hand. Jerking his head upward, he stared at me through his dark glasses, chin jutting forward. Around us, the soldiers shifted, waiting.

Pierre stepped between us, a flash of money in his hand. Speaking softly to the soldier, he steered him away from the briefcase. A few thousand CFA changed hands. The soldiers waved us on.

But in truth I don't think it was the tête à tête with the soldiers those first few minutes in town that made me question Yaoundé's star billing. It wasn't the people that troubled me, because except for the overzealous soldiers, Cameroonians were the kindest people I'd ever encountered, with a natural gentleness that was extraordinary. It was the place itself that rose up in one lusty assault.

Most of all, Yaoundé was confusing. If Los Angeles ever experiences an extended period of siege warfare, when all the fighting is over and the city labors to return to normal, in those first trying days I suspect it will have much in common with

Yaoundé. Both cities give the sense of having exploded from within, flinging roads and houses at frivolous angles over unmanageable quantities of land. Neither possesses a center, and navigating either requires a car (preferably, in Yaoundé's case, a large, well-armored vehicle as local driving habits resemble a lethal version of bumper cars).

None of this, of course, I understood that first night in Yaoundé. Though our arrival had been a bit rough, I still expected, at least by Bangui standards, a très chic metropolis. The first problem was finding a place to sleep.

The Hotel Deputy, everyone insisted, was the only hotel worth considering. Creeping around, as much as one can in a forty-foot flatbed truck, trying to avoid any major intersections where there might be more police, we finally located the hotel on a slight hill overlooking what seemed to be the center of town. It was big and modern and completely full, with a fair number of African men in business suits sleeping in the lobby. This was not encouraging. The problem, we learned, was that the Cameroon Congress was in session. We drove on.

On our fourth try, just as dawn was lighting up the sky, we located a hotel of sorts over a restaurant, with one vacant room. Its unoccupied status was understandable. Large sections of the rug and one wall were charred from a very recent fire. It had an air conditioner, however, that vaguely worked and a large carved log rather like an American Indian totem pole rising to the ceiling between the beds.

To inquire about the room, we woke the unfortunate clerk, who slept on the counter in the lobby. As soon as he indicated there was a vacancy, Pierre backed the flatbed truck to the front door and we began to unload our gear. The clerk, perhaps wondering if he was in the midst of some unpleasant dream, watched as out came the footlocker, jerricans, shovel, toolbox, body bag duffel: all our stuff.

"All of this is yours?" he asked, rubbing his eyes. "You want this in your room?"

The room was on the fourth floor. There was no elevator.

"If we have to take all this crap up to the fourth floor, I'm sleeping right here," Ann said, indicating a plastic couch. She was serious.

"The couch is good for sleeping," the clerk agreed quickly.

We did a sensible thing; we locked all the luggage and equipment into the hotel office. This, not surprisingly, filled the office but the clerk assured us that was okay. "It's only the office," he explained. No one argued.

Two hours later, I stumbled out of the torched room downstairs to the restaurant. A middle-aged African wearing an orange fez stood behind the bar. "It's Monday," he responded when I urgently requested coffee.

"Yes," I mumbled, "it's Monday."

He nodded and started to walk off.

"Wait!" I cried. My voice froze him in midstep. The clerk, stretched out on the lobby counter, woke up with a start. "What," I asked, lowering my voice with effort, "does Monday have to do with coffee?"

"There is no water on Mondays."

I groaned. The lack of water in the bathroom upstairs I'd noted, but I hadn't speculated that it was an endemic condition.

"Some Mondays we have water," the desk clerk rose up to brag.

"Only in the afternoon," the man in the fez corrected.

"That is true," the clerk conceded, lying back down and closing his eyes.

I sat forlorn at the bar, staring at the line of bottles under the cracked mirror, thinking hard about turning to gin as a coffee alternative. Then I spotted a plastic bottle labeled Elephant Water.

"Can't you just heat some of that water," I asked, pointing to the liter bottle, "and I'll have instant coffee?"

"The stove is electric," the man answered, "and . . ."

"Let me guess. There is no electricity on Mondays."

The desk clerk spoke up. "Sometimes on Monday but . . ."

"Only in the afternoon," I finished.

He nodded, pleased. Somewhere in my massive duffel there was a gas stove and a battered pot. In my mind I went through the motions it would take to find it, starting with digging the duffel out from the mountain of jerricans, shovel, and toolbox in the office. I settled for a South Dallas martini: a glass of warm gin, straight.

"Are you an alcoholic?" the desk clerk asked me pleasantly. I looked up from my glass to find him standing next to me at the bar.

I explained to him about being on the truck for twenty hours.

"How long did it take you from Bertoua?" he asked.

"Twelve hours."

He frowned. "Why? It should take five. The road is very good. We have good roads in Cameroon."

I had another drink.

He asked why we were in Yaoundé and I told him I needed to buy a car. Then I asked him if he knew where the local branch of Henri's coffee company was located. Henri had given me the name of the manager along with a letter of introduction and suggested I start the car search by getting in touch with him. In my brief time in Africa I'd seen how much knowing someone could help.

"This is a coffee company," the clerk said, reading over the name and address Henri had given me.

"Yes."

He paused. "They do not sell cars." For an instant he glanced at my gin glass sitting on the bar, doubtless thinking of the havoc alcohol wreaked on the logical functions of the brain.

I tried to tell him why I wanted to find the coffee company. With the gin and the lack of sleep, I doubt I did it very well.

"Do you know where this is?" I asked.

He went into a lengthy explanation. His directions were the sort one reads in wilderness guidebooks: go north for a few hundred meters, turn right at this landmark, then north again.

"Can't you just draw me a map with street names?" I finally interrupted.

He shook his head. "I don't know the names. But I will show you."

That the clerk—whose name I repeatedly asked but could not, in my besotted state, retain—did not know the names of the streets of his native city struck me as ludicrous until we got in a taxi and I discovered that there were no street signs in Yaoundé. Apparently signage was an affectation of Western life the city fathers had rejected.

"How far is it to the coffee company?" I asked.

"It is close."

We drove for forty-five minutes up and down Yaoundé's hills. I had no idea where we were, nor, I realized with a sigh, did I remember the name of the hotel where we were staying. I didn't have my passport or my wallet, just a pocket stuffed with a few thousand CFA. Thanks to the therapeutic qualities of a gin breakfast, this bothered me not at all.

Even in my alcoholic haze, I could see that Yaoundé thrived commercially in a way unimaginable in the CAR. There were actually stores filled with more than the routine canned food and rudimentary hardware items that were all Bangui or Berbérati offered. I spotted one window advertising freon and thought of Chevron. We traveled through a district of tin-roofed shanties selling auto parts and tires; I gazed longingly, wondering if I might ever have a car that could use such goodies.

On almost every corner there were little stands advertising duplicating machines and typing. This puzzled me but I concluded that it was a sign of the great commerce under way in Yaoundé. Later, I understood that copying services were essential as the Cameroon bureaucracy, which I came to think of as a giant spider webbing up the entire country, required all forms to be submitted in multiples of ten. And there were forms for everything.

Just as I was beginning to fall asleep, the taxi stopped and the driver patted me gently on the knee. We were in front of a grocery store jammed in between two five-story brick buildings that looked to be new but had an unfinished, crumbling quality reminiscent of China.

I stumbled inside behind my friend. The large room was dark and pungent with the aroma of coffee. I felt as if I had crawled inside a coffee can.

"Coffee!" I exclaimed.

"Coffee!" the taxi driver, who'd followed us, echoed.

We were in some kind of coffee warehouse. But it had nothing to do with Henri's company. A teenage boy behind the counter thought he knew how to get to the right address. He started to explain but then said, "I'll show you."

He climbed into the taxi. Twenty minutes later we reached a small grocery store whose only connection with coffee, as far as I could tell, was that it sold little jars of instant coffee. A man standing in front wearing a pin-striped suit asked what we were looking for and, when he saw the address Henri had written down, assured us he knew where it was.

He got in the taxi as well, which was now getting somewhat crowded. I fell asleep.

When I woke up, we were in front of what appeared to be a French villa. There seemed little chance it could be the right place.

A bearded Frenchman came out the front door. He paused, hands on his hips.

"Do you know Monsieur Blanchard," I asked weakly from the back seat of the taxi.

"I am Monsieur Blanchard!"

A small round of applause broke out in the cab. I got out, explaining who I was and what I was doing, or trying to do. He nodded distractedly then motioned me aside and asked in a low voice, "Who are all these people?"

What happened about buying a car was this: we looked everywhere in Yaoundé. We found nothing remotely capable of making it across the Sahara and all had price tags, to my horror, just as crazed as in the CAR.

"You should go to Douala," Monsieur Blanchard told us, using the same tone of voice as Henri when he'd advised traveling to Yaoundé. "There are many, many cars there." Henri, I believe, had said that as well.

But short of constructing a car from spare parts, there was nothing else to be done. We took the "shuttle"—that is, I promise, Cameroon Airlines' own description—to Douala. Within twenty-four hours we were sitting in front of a Mr. Richards, an Englishman who ran the largest Nissan agency in town, and spilling our story. He was amused. We had, it turned out in one of those odd twists of fate I thought only occurred in Evelyn Waugh stories, attended the same college at Oxford. This was by far the most tangible benefit I'd ever accrued from any educational institution.

Mr. Richards sat behind a half-acre oak desk littered with phones. For over an hour he shouted alternately into each, managing, by my count, to complete two calls. But he found us a car. Two cars, actually.

"They're Toyota Land Cruisers, big diesel things, so they won't go *bang* when you carry fuel on top."

That it was dangerous to carry gasoline on top of a vehicle was something, I thought, I'd read before in one of my guidebooks. This talk of motion pleased me. It made things sound as if one day we might drive somewhere.

"Both are '85s. You'll just have to take a peek at each and take your pick, won't you?" He named a price not too outrageous by West African standards.

"Great," I said. "Can we see them this afternoon?"

He looked at his watch. "Probably not. I reckon you've just missed the last flight."

"Flight?" Ann and I looked at each other. There was something here we didn't grasp.

"Don't want to walk back to Yaoundé, do you?" Mr. Richards grinned and selected a pipe from a rack.

"Yaoundé?

"That's where the Land Cruisers are. We've got a branch there. King Motors. Now what you want to do is see Mr. Robertson. He'll fix you right up. Handle any problems you have. First-rate man, Mr. Robertson."

Chapter Thirteen

"You are very lucky," Mr. Robertson told us. "Two perfect cars to choose from. Very lucky."

Mr. Robertson was a tall, angular man in an expensive gray suit and shiny black shoes with sharp toes. He wore his hair like the rock-and-roll singer Little Richard's: swept up on his forehead at an unlikely angle and glistening with something slick.

I was very excited. Sitting in Mr. Robertson's small office just off the showroom floor (even though there were no automobiles on the floor), I felt like a teenager about to get the keys to the family car for the first time.

"Let's go take a look!" Mr. Robertson cried.

I echoed his sentiments and jumped to my feet.

"This is unbelievable," Ann said.

It was an apt comment in its most literal sense. What had us both thrilled was the prospect of being allowed to remit an exorbitant sum for a used vehicle we knew nothing about and to which we intended to entrust our lives. That it seemed a great privilege probably says something about what five weeks in West Africa can do to one's way of looking at the world.

In a bit of sales bravado, the two Land Cruisers lumbered from the King Motors garage and executed, in tandem, a series of maneuvers across the sprawling back lot. They reminded me of a pair of elephants having a go at synchronized swimming.

Finally, in a swirl of diesel fumes, they shuddered to a stop in front of our small reviewing committee.

I stared, not wanting to believe.

"Nice, huh?" Mr. Robertson bragged.

They looked awful. Both appeared to sag in place like exhausted runners after a marathon. One was emblazoned with the initials of the Cameroon armed forces in foot-high letters. The other was a shade of light blue I'd never seen, lacquered with a rough, pebblelike texture. Later, I learned it had been painted with a vacuum cleaner.

"These are 1985 models?" I asked in disbelief.

Mr. Robertson frowned. "I don't think so. I think they're 1982."

"How many miles?" I asked, feeling a need to make this resemble a normal car-buying experience, with emphasis on mileage, warranty and service records, as if I had a choice other than the Land Cruisers. It was an effort no less absurd than requesting an aisle seat on a lifeboat.

"Oh, not many," Mr. Robertson responded automatically. We examined the odometers. Both were close to ninety thousand kilometers.

"That's not so bad," Ann murmured hopefully.

"Yes," Mr. Robertson hastened to agree. "And I think the numbers"—he indicated the odometer—"have only gone around once or twice."

"Oh."

"Take your pick!" Mr. Robertson declared. Ann and I examined the two Cruisers for a few minutes, then walked over to a nearby bar to discuss the situation.

King Motors sat at the bottom of a steep, rubble-strewn hill. Halfway up the slope, a bar with a metal roof was dug into the hillside, rather like a gun emplacement. Just inside the bar's open front, a black kettle bubbled over a fire. This gave the interior of the bar an enveloping saunalike quality. Ann asked the old woman hunkered by the fire what she was cooking. She dipped a rusty spoon into the opaque liquid and came up with a mess of meaty bones.

"Looks great," Ann said, and started chewing on a bone without hesitation. I was appalled.

Sitting on the porch of the bar, we drank Cokes and pondered our situation. This was more an exercise in therapy than decision making. We both knew there were only two choices: either buy one of the two Land Cruisers or give up the trip and fly home.

Even though we moaned about the moment-to-moment travail of African travel, we both knew we were securely seduced by the lure of *out there:* that stretch of country from the bottom of Cameroon to the Mediterranean. It was irresistible. We had to make the trip.

An army sergeant came into the bar, laughing with a friend.

"You should try the food," he suggested, pointing to the kettle.

"She did," I answered, indicating Ann.

"She did?" He rolled his eyes.

We finished our Cokes and walked back down the muddy hill to buy a Land Cruiser from Mr. Robertson.

Eight days later, in sheer desperation, I hit upon the idea.

"Mr. Robertson," I announced, after trapping him in the bathroom (he had begun to avoid me), "I can't buy the car."

"What's wrong now?" he moaned.

"My visa expires in three days. I must leave Cameroon."

"Umm," he said, looking concerned for the first time since he'd counted my money a week ago. "Your visa. We must prepare the car quickly."

"Three days," I repeated. "Seventy-two hours."

"Visa problems," he muttered.

I followed Mr. Robertson out of the bathroom to the back lot where the Land Cruiser sat. At the moment, it had no doors. In fact, after a week of work, it looked significantly worse than ever.

"Visa problems," Mr. Robertson said.

Quietly I gloated over his concern. My "visa problems" were a complete lie. This bothered me not at all. I considered my falsification of the problem a sign that I was learning to cope with Cameroonian life. Like picking up a few words of West African pidgin or learning to carry an umbrella for the afternoon deluge, it was a sure indication of local adaptation.

"We must fix the car," Mr. Robertson declared, sounding for the first time as if he meant it.

The visa gambit had punch because backing it was the most feared element of Cameroonian life: the bureaucracy. It had the same impact as, in a more primitive culture, informing a tribal chieftain that the Volcano God intended to erupt in anger. The bureaucracy was a fact of life: cruel, capricious, ultimately devastating.

Mr. Robertson summoned the workers and, in English, pronounced: "This man's visa expires in three days. We must work hard!" Then, in pidgin, the true language of Cameroon and one I don't speak, he told them what he really wanted to say.

I had made an effort to learn pidgin but had not progressed much further than *pickaninny child* for "children." In his book *The Africans,* David Lamb quotes a sermon in pidgin by the Reverend M. G. M. Cole, an English-educated Cameroonian: "Teday the country happ. Made dis thing fo as ee de go, en den de go. Nor cause any trouble. Nor gee the president headache. . . . Oona nor amborgin am . . . nor forget two party. We nor want one party."

What he said translates as: "Today the country is happy. Let's continue things as it is, as they are. Don't cause any trouble. Don't give the president a headache. . . . Don't you humbug him. . . . Don't forget the two-party system. We don't want a one-party state."

In the last week I'd developed a sort of affection for the crew at King Motors, further proof, I suppose, of the bonding ability of really horrible experiences. My favorite was Richard, a tall, slender fellow who always wore a bicycler's racing cap canted over one eye. He walked with an odd gait, a slouching, sliding motion that gave him a rhythmic dip, not unlike the effect of posting on horseback.

Richard always carried a small sledgehammer. At first I

thought this to be an affectation, like a young executive's fondness for Montblanc pens. But then I realized Richard employed
the sledgehammer to attack any and all mechanical problems. He
was the Michelangelo of sledgehammers. I once saw him align the
bent threads of a headlight with this tool of choice, and on another occasion he used it to straighten a twisted fuse.

After contracting to buy the car, Ann and I had made a long
list of things to be done before we took possession. The main
function of this itemization, it turned out, was to afford the
hard-pressed Mr. Robertson a little comic relief. Whenever I
presented it to him—always, of course, complaining how nothing
had been done—Mr. Robertson would take it from me and
chuckle over its points. This was the only time I ever saw him
smile. Because it annoyed me so much to see him happy, I finally
tore the list up.

Ann and I had settled into a routine in Yaoundé. Each morning we took a cab to King Motors. This was never uneventful. We
learned that the price varied from about twenty-five cents to
forty-seven dollars, the latter the amount one driver insisted was
the normal fare. What was truly normal, of course, was for foreigners—a category Ann and I could not escape—to pay exorbitant sums for all services. The idea of paying two or three times
the normal price, I had accepted as something of a tax. But when
this soared to multiples of ten, I felt obligated to object.

Employing exceedingly clever tactics, cabdrivers frequently
agreed to transport us for a reasonable price then renegotiated
once we were in the car. This gave them significant leverage in
the negotiating process. They could, for instance, refuse to stop
the car while the matter was under discussion. Worse yet—this
happened twice to me—a driver might *insist* on stopping in a
locale in which tarrying was not an advisable course of action.
Then, while the local residents stared at us with the obvious
delight of those sensing their net worth about to skyrocket, the
driver would say, "Well, you can just get out . . ."

Right.

Once deposited at the top of the sheer hill leading down to King Motors, we picked our way through boulders and mud craters, past the Artisans Relais bar, to the car dealership, where two salesmen in ties and jackets always sat waiting on the empty showroom floor. (The positioning of King Motors at the foot of such a treacherous slope was a brilliant marketing strategy; once someone was crazy enough to drive a vehicle down the hill, repairs were sure to be necessary. The odds were also considerable that new repairs would be required once the vehicle made it back up the hill.)

Each morning I felt obligated to locate Mr. Robertson for our ritual questioning. This was more along the lines of a catechism than effective information gathering. I asked the same questions and he gave the same answers. Typically this occurred in a dark corner of the garage or in the half-lit bathroom, adding to the religious atmosphere.

After I had rid myself of the need to confront Mr. Robertson, I could go about doing something productive. This meant coaxing, pleading, bribing and occasionally threatening Richard and the crew working on the Cruiser. Of these modes, bribery was by far the most effective.

In the final analysis, the bureaucratic problems rivaled the technical. What it came down to was this: either the car would be fixed and all papers prepared, all documents executed by Friday, or it would remain in the clutches of Mr. Robertson for another week.

That was a horrible thought. And an expensive one. The price of living in Yaoundé was forcing me to desperation. I remembered with a bitter wistfulness the assurances everyone had offered about the cheapness of Cameroonian life compared to life in the CAR. What I now understood was that such comparisons were standard fare for Europeans in Africa. Everyone talked about how much cheaper it was in some other country. In Cameroon the favorite greener pasture was Togo. I heard some of the exact phrases used to describe it as had previously been employed

to laud Cameroon. The main difference seemed to be that everybody bragged about the lobsters in Togo and no one had made
such claims about Cameroon.

The reason I had to get the Cruiser by Friday or wait another
week—at a minimum—was the onset of a mysterious
Cameroonian holiday. Some people thought it was Independence
Day—or Week—and others insisted the break was in celebration
of the president's birthday. A smaller, though adamant, group
maintained the holiday related to an ongoing census. The logic of
why this would necessitate a holiday was, to me at least, totally
obscure.

I learned of the impending holiday on Wednesday morning.
It was then that I launched the visa gambit, setting off what was,
by King Motors standards, a veritable orgy of labor.

The major mechanical problem was the doors. For some reason the crew had removed all four doors of the Land Cruiser. The
problem now was getting them back on.

To be fair, I contributed significantly to the difficulty of the
situation. By chance I had stumbled onto Richard banging at one
of the doors with his ever-present sledgehammer and strenuously
objected. Richard protested, claiming that it was the only way to
refit the doors. I said there must be a better way, though, of
course, I had no idea what it would be.

My concerns slowed matters considerably. At one point,
Richard removed the door of the companion Land Cruiser, the
one we had elected not to buy, and discovered that it would fit
on our car in its unsledgehammered state. Why this substitution
worked better than the original door made no sense but it seemed
a good solution—except that the Cruisers were not the same
color. I didn't really care if the big diesel beast was converted to
a two-tone color scheme, but I feared it might trouble a prospective buyer when I attempted to resell the car, which I had to do
at the end of the trip if I was to avoid total bankruptcy. Already
the car had plenty of oddities that might trouble a non–West
African buyer: it had been painted with a vacuum cleaner, the

interior appeared to have been feasted on by rats, and there was no heater. In Cameroon no one even thought about the latter, but it stood to reason that in Switzerland, my ultimate destination, this might be considered an inconvenience.

By Friday morning, the door problem—along with a host of nagging details such as two missing shock absorbers—had not been solved. But the big problem loomed on the document front. Of the vast array of papers we needed to drive legally in Cameroon—a title, insurance, a tax sticker called a *vignette,* an inspection sticker—none had been obtained. Mr. Robertson, naturally, had promised all of them a week earlier.

I was not pleased. As all government offices were closing down in a matter of hours, the only hope was to appear in person in front of the various officials responsible for the documents and bombard them with cash.

"We must go quickly, quickly," Mr. Robertson insisted, as if I were reluctant. "We go now!"

But of all the cars at King Motors, none actually worked. Except for our Land Cruiser, which did not have doors.

"We must take your car!" Mr. Robertson cried. "It is the only way!"

So we did. It is difficult to describe the restraint it took not to give Mr. Robertson a firm nudge out the doorless doors.

Before we stopped in front of the motor vehicles office, a mob of peddlers had descended upon the car. Many were selling license plates (in Cameroon, as in England, a driver must buy his own plate); others offered their services as bribe masters, a form of bureaucratic guide supposedly knowledgeable in the local lore.

"Without me you pay too much in bribes!" an old man, who looked to have seen his share of successful bribes, shouted.

"I have an uncle!" a teenager boasted. "A very important uncle!"

It is not unusual in Africa to be besieged by imploring throngs. If in a car, the usual defense is to roll up the windows and wait it out. However, inasmuch as the Land Cruiser did not have doors, much less windows, it made for an awkward situation. Four or five of the more agile peddlers immediately jumped into the car.

"Please wait," Mr. Robertson said to us. "This will not take long."

This was a line with a familiar ring. As soon as Mr. Robertson had gotten out of the car, I started the engine and explained to him that we would be waiting for him at King Motors—an explanation underscored with various vile threats as to what would happen if he returned without the necessary papers.

He pleaded with us not to abandon him in such a dangerous location.

"But it's a government office!" I yelled, trying to push away a teenager who was crawling into my lap.

"I know!" he answered desperately.

I drove back to King Motors. Richard greeted us, sledgehammer in hand. I sighed and nodded and then Richard did what he had been wanting to do for days—pounded on the Cruiser doors until they fit.

We walked up to the Artisans Relais bar to drink Coastal beer, the sound of sledgehammer against metal wafting up the hill.

Chapter
Fourteen

Our last night in Yaoundé, Ann and I sat in the dining room of the Hotel Terminus. We stared at each other while picking over plates of petrified meat rumored to be beef. It was a celebratory occasion but we were too dazed from the last week to give any of the normal signs associated with celebration.

The Terminus dining room was a large, airy room hung with white curtains that fluttered charmingly during the regular late-afternoon thunder shower. Though Congress was in session and most hotels brimming, the Terminus remained curiously empty. I wondered if perhaps the owner had committed some grievous political sin resulting in his ostracism. Each evening the proprietor, a balding man of significant dignity, ate alone in the nearly vacant dining room. A pair of French engineers, who gave every sign of being lovers, were the only other regular diners. The food was bad and frighteningly expensive, but the view over the sprawl of Yaoundé was pleasant. I considered it, all and all, a choice spot.

Every evening the hotel staff gathered in the foyer to watch a videotape of a movie called *The Harder They Come* featuring the Jamaican reggae star Jimmy Cliff. I can't really say how many times this ritual had been repeated, but the staff's familiarity with the work did not diminish their appreciation. They knew each line and repeated them enthusiastically like a Greek chorus. For some of the staff it was the only English they knew and, when greeted in English, they would respond with random phrases from the film, always delivered in the correct Jamaican accent.

To "Good morning," they were likely to answer:

"Dat man, he no good. Bad man, what to do. We talk to him with dis gun."

"Of course."

While Ann and I sat staring at each other, we were surprised by the appearance of Mr. Ngi, one of the staff of King Motors. He had a front-office job of indeterminate description and had often intervened on our behalf with Mr. Robertson. Each time we thanked him for his efforts, he responded, "Call me Mr. Dependability and Responsibility. I will always help."

Mr. Ngi asked what time we were leaving the next day and promised to come by the hotel so that he could lead us out of the maze of Yaoundé streets to the proper road heading north. "Call me Mr. Dependability and Responsibility. I will be here to help."

By noon the next morning we were still waiting on Mr. Ngi. With fading hope, we puttered around, packing and repacking the Land Cruiser. Neither of us wanted to admit how intimidated we were by the thought of leaving Yaoundé and finally being on our own.

What I felt was a sense of dread. I had no confidence the Land Cruiser wouldn't break down in the first two hundred miles. And even if the car made it, there was the question of paperwork.

It was impossible, I'd learned in Africa, to have too many documents. There was a piece of paper for everything. Late at night at the Hotel Terminus, I lay sweating in bed wondering what quirky little official stamp or permit would be demanded that we'd never heard of. I imagined the scene with chilling detail: "You don't have a vignette?" The border guard wore shades and shorts and waggled an AK-47. He chuckled. "This is quite impossible. You'll have to go back."

There were other problems. We had insurance (liability only—the Cruiser was on its own) for Cameroon but none for other countries.

"Just buy it in each country," the insurance salesman had

assured me. "It's very easy." This last line disturbed me as I'd concluded that there was a direct correlation between the actual difficulty of a situation and the degree of confidence with which people insisted there would be no problem.

Then there was the question of a carnet.

"This is one of the most valuable documents you will have with you and must be carefully guarded for its loss or theft could prove very expensive," asserted *Africa Overland.*

"A carnet *(carnet de passage)* is required for the majority of countries in Africa with the exception of Morocco, Algeria and Tunisia," explained the ever-helpful *Africa on a Shoestring.* "The purpose of the carnet is to allow an individual to take a vehicle into a country where duties would normally be payable without the necessity of having to pay those duties. To get a carnet you first need to make an application to one of the motoring organizations."

Actually, I had a carnet. Warned that travel by car in Africa was impossible without one, I'd gone to considerable trouble and expense to acquire one from the Automobile Association in England. Unfortunately, my visit to England coincided with the worst hurricane to hit the country in a century, silencing all telephones, littering the streets with uprooted trees and knocking out the rail line from London to the Dover ferry. My life had not been made easier by the fact that I was hauling around enough Land Rover parts to launch a dealership, plus assorted camping gear—though my stove and lantern did come in handy in my hotel when the electricity died for two days.

But the carnet I had so diligently acquired was applicable strictly to Lucien's Land Rover—or, to be more precise, the minister of mines' Land Rover. Each of its pages bore the serial number of the ill-fated vehicle. Though I brooded on ways it might be fraudulently altered, it was hopeless.

I had asked the English car dealer in Douala if I really needed a carnet to cross borders with a car.

"I suppose so," he answered, puffing on his pipe. "That's what everyone says, don't they?"

"But where can I get one?"

"The Auto Association in London, I should think."

"But there must be someplace in Africa!"

He thought for a while then finally looked at me and shrugged.

"Look," I said, "this doesn't make sense. Africans cross borders every day in private cars. They don't have carnets issued by the Automobile Association."

"No, but then again you're not African, are you?"

We left it at that. Everyone else I asked had differing opinions on what documents were needed to get from one country to another with a car. And though we met other Westerners who were driving through Africa, all had started their journeys in Europe and were equipped with the full range of paperwork outlined in books like *Africa Overland.* I began to get the sense we were the first non-Africans who had ever attempted to drive a car purchased in Africa back to Europe. Even Mr. Robertson had asked, "Why you want to do this thing? Cars are much cheaper in Europe," and then he'd tried to talk me into going into the car transport business with him, ferrying vehicles down through the Sahara from Europe.

"But we can make so much money! I can come visit you in America!" He proposed this quite often. In truth, I warmed up to the idea. I thought how wonderful it would be to have him call me from JFK Airport.

"Mr. Robertson," I'd tell him, "just take a bus to Times Square. Got that? Times Square. And wait for me. Just wait right there on the street for me. And you brought your daughters? Wonderful."

While waiting for Mr. Ngi, Ann and I walked to a grocery store below the Hotel Terminus. Everything, as usual, was appallingly expensive. For some reason, cans of ravioli were on sale and we bought a dozen. It seemed an awful lot at the time, but if I'd known then what a treat the gooey pasta squares would be in comparison to the rest of our diet, I would have purchased every can in the store. We rounded out our supplies with a few tins of evaporated milk, a pile of the tasteless sort of cow cheese that never seemed to spoil, a couple of boxes of Ritz crackers (quite a splurge), a pound of rice and more packets of Knorr lentil soup than I could ever imagine eating.

Though the Land Cruiser looked enormous when empty, it proved difficult to get all our gear inside. (Unlike many African vehicles, ours lacked a roof rack.) Making matters worse, we'd moved the spare tire from underneath the vehicle, where it was designed to go, and placed it inside. Though it was comforting to know the thing wouldn't fall off or be punctured, the tire was enormous and occupied an amazing amount of space in the rear.

Trying to find the perfect configuration for our equipment developed into a recurrent theme of the weeks ahead. The process had much in common with a contact sport: a profusion of sweat accompanied by loud moans and groans, numerous curses, at least a bit of blood and, invariably, threats of blows between all parties concerned. After an hour of this, we collapsed exhausted and stared at our handiwork.

What I had hoped would be a model of planning and symmetry looked much like a hurriedly packed getaway car at the robbery of a war surplus store. On the back seat sat my duffel bag and Ann's suitcase, the toolbox we'd liberated from Lucien in Bangui and my Himalayan pack jammed with odd-sized auto parts, including a radiator hose that jutted from the pack, grotesquely suggesting the neck and head of a sci-fi monster. Underneath this, chained to the seat struts, was a metal lockbox about the size of a baby's coffin. The box gave me inordinate pleasure as it was precisely the sort of security precaution recommended in my guidebooks. Feeling quite smug, we placed money and valuable papers into the box. Unfortunately, getting things in and out was such a pain and the need to produce car papers and passports so frequent (some days ten to fifteen times) that we quickly took to leaving these items in plain view on the front seat.

In some perverse way, I was disappointed that no one ever seemed interested in stealing them.

In the rear, my footlocker rested on top of the spare tire; seven jerricans of twenty-five liters each filled the remainder of the space. Five held diesel fuel and the other two water. Wedged in between the canisters were the extra tire tubes I'd bought from King Motors.

We stuffed as many cans of ravioli as we could under the seats and tossed the rest helter-skelter into the rear. There they bounced around like grapeshot whenever we hit a bump.

By one o'clock we had to face what had been apparent for hours: Mr. Reliability and Dependability was not going to make it. With a melodramatic sense of occasion, we climbed into the Land Cruiser and headed off into the maelstrom that was normal Yaoundé traffic.

The thought of having a wreck in Africa had been a recurrent horror. One of the U.S. embassy personnel in Bangui had nonchalantly warned me, "Look, if you're driving out in the bush and you hit something like a person or vehicle—animals are fair game—*Don't stop.* Just keep going until you get to a police station. A police station you can trust."

I wondered how you could discern the trustworthy stations from the other kind, but asked a more basic question. "Why don't you stop?"

"It's simple. If you stop, the local people will rip you out of your car and kill you."

This little bit of advice ran through my head when, about two hours outside of Yaoundé in the village of Obala, I had the unpleasant realization that the Land Cruiser was rolling downhill into a parked van. At the time I was standing outside the Cruiser holding the keys in my hand. The door was locked. Ann was off buying something to eat.

I leapt forward and tried desperately to unlock the door. But the key wouldn't fit into the moving lock. Sweating furiously, I latched onto the door handle and tried to pull the car backward. On the boardwalk that ran over a sewage ditch parallel to the road, a policeman gnawed a piece of beef and chuckled.

Ann ran across the road with a stalk of bananas. She dropped them and grabbed onto a door handle. The Cruiser continued its steady roll. With a soft thud, it came to rest against the bumper of the van. The policeman finished the last of his beef snack and walked over, wiping his fingers on a banana leaf.

He inspected the two vehicles. Both bumpers were well dented and, no doubt, had been for years. I braced myself for a fierce argument over the relative age of each pockmark.

I began to explain.

The policeman held up his hand to stop me. He looked again at the point where the two vehicles had kissed, chuckled, then waved us back into the Cruiser. "Leave," he said.

We did.

To drive toward the Mediterranean from Cameroon, one has the choice of heading northwest into Nigeria or Northeast into Chad. Entering Chad near the capital, N'Djamena, one could theoretically drive across Lake Chad (largely dry for the last ten years) and into Niger. There were problems with this approach. For starters, Chad was fighting a war with Libya and though most of the fighting occurred in the northern desert near the border, the Libyans had bombed N'Djamena just a few months earlier. Another consideration was the lack of a road across Lake Chad. On Michelin map number 173 (the African bible) it appeared as a splotch of bright blue against a dark brown background. But in truth it was possible to drive across the dry lakebed, though the sand would float up to the doors.

By all accounts, however, the prospect of getting bombed by the Libyans or lost in the sands of Lake Chad was preferable to driving even an inch into Nigeria. Everyone from Cameroon police to Europeans had described the experience as deeply painful. The Nigerian police were touted as ravenous predators who roamed the roads like pirates.

"Not worse than Cameroon," I'd insisted to one German

who washed up at the Hotel Terminus in an old Mercedes. He hoped to sell the car in Douala; the trafficking of cars was a popular enterprise with a certain globe-rat set of Europeans. "My friend," he rasped, grabbing my arm. "A white man in Nigeria driving a car is nothing but a raw, bloody," he pronounced each word carefully and slowly, letting the graphic image set in to full effect, "piece of meat floating in a fishbowl of piranhas." He shuddered and downed most of a Coastal beer in one pull. His eye caught the TV screen and the gathered crowd for the evening showing. "Is that *The Harder They Come*?" he asked.

Road maps of Cameroon show one red line bisecting the upper two-thirds of the country in a north-south direction. Repeatedly this had been touted as an excellent road, a claim that, of course, made me suspicious. But if we were to drive through Chad to avoid Nigeria, this was the only road. The difficulty was reaching it from Yaoundé. The choice was either to backtrack east toward the Central African Republic on the same charming road we'd ridden with Pierre, or to bushwhack on a series of tiny roads from Yaoundé through the central section of the country, finally intersecting with the fabled main road in a town called Tibati.

"I wouldn't try that," Mr. Reliability and Dependability had warned. "Those roads are terrible, with many bad mudslides, and you may not be able to get any fuel. It would be a mistake."

This clinched it. I was rapidly becoming a contrarian on all matters relating to advice in Africa. Using our Michelin 173 map, we charted a course northeast from Yaoundé linking a series of tiny roads through Obala, Batchenga, Mankim and Yoko, eventually reaching Tibati.

This was the course that brought us in contact with the back half of a parked van.

I drove rapidly from Obala, waiting for the gunshot and the cry, "You hit this man's van, you must pay. Look, it is ruined!"

But none came. A giddy happiness seized me. After over a month of speculating on the fate of Lucien's Land Rover, and after the assorted difficulties of acquiring the Cruiser, we were at last driving through Africa. Our car papers might be hopelessly inadequate, the drive shaft could plummet from the undercarriage at the next bump, and other, more debilitating wrecks might be in store down the road, but at least for one afternoon we were actually driving through Africa toward Europe. This was wonderful.

Cameroon is a country that spans much of the geographic variety of Africa. The tropical rain forest of the south is gradually transformed into the near-desert of the north along the Chadian border. That first day out of Yaoundé, we drove on a rutted red dirt track that wound through thick growths of leafy banana plants and coconut trees shooting toward the sky. It was a lush forest broken by unexpected clearings. One minute we'd be wrapped in a green tunnel of foliage like some tropical hallucination, and the next we'd break through into a vista of undulating hills. The heat closed in on us and we drove in a quiet daze, happy to forget the noise and confused frenzy that is the essence of African cities.

At Batchenga we stopped to hunt for something cold to drink. Along the wide, dusty street, mud brick houses caked with a peeling white plaster slumped against one another. In the blue double doors of the store, kids sat on Coke cases listening to a soccer game on a battered transistor. Somewhere in northern Africa a tournament was under way and Cameroon was playing. The store's shelves held only a few tins of canned meat and some sweltering bottles of Fanta. A Slavia beer poster featured a frosty glass with a rich head of foam; "Le Savoir-Faire," it bragged, and I longed in the worst way for a single sip. Several photos of Cameroon's president framed the teasing picture of cold beer.

Ann asked if they had cold Fantas. The Muslim shopkeeper shook his head and pointed across the street to a house. "There?" Ann questioned.

He nodded.

"That is a store?"

He nodded. A pretty woman in a bright yellow dress and matching turban giggled and motioned for us to follow her. We walked across the street, kicking up little clouds of dust, and knocked on the door. A teenage girl holding a baby answered and let us in. At the center of the one room sat a square white refrigerator. Somewhere a generator hummed. The girl opened the refrigerator; a rush of cool air escaped. Inside the refrigerator sat four Fantas. We bought them all and drove away.

An hour later, we realized something was wrong. We were in a town that was too large, a town with an Afribank and a traffic circle. We consulted our map. No town existed along the road we thought we were on.

We drove around the circle searching for a sign giving the name of the town but there was nothing. Finally we stopped the Land Cruiser in the middle of the road and waited. Within a few seconds we were surrounded by a curious crowd. Two friendly young men inquired if they might be of assistance. On the hood of the car, I unfolded our Michelin map and asked, quite simply, where we were.

The map created great amusement and confusion. It took a very long time to establish the basics: this is Cameroon, this is Chad, that is Nigeria.

What is this? one of the young men asked.

The Mediterranean.

Who lives there?

No one, it is an ocean.

A what?

A lake. A very big lake.

The other young man teased his inquisitive friend. You don't know what an ocean is, he laughed. Don't you go to school? Together they joked for a moment before returning their attention to the Michelin.

Staring at the map with our new friends, I felt as if I were seeing the colorful display of countries and water for the first time. It suddenly seemed like such a beautiful thing, this map, resplendent with promise and hidden mysteries.

Eventually we established that we had missed a turn in Batchenga. I groaned, contemplating the last hour spent bouncing over the rough track. Since leaving Yaoundé hours before the

Cruiser had not left second gear, except for a few brief bouts of thrilling thirty-five-mile-per-hour speed.

We probed. Wasn't there some connecting road? A shortcut? The answer was negative. Everyone seemed puzzled that we wished to travel north at all. Didn't we realize that the north of Cameroon was a barbaric place full of backward people? Had we seen the beauties of Douala and Yaoundé?

Bouncing back to Batchenga Ann and I fumed, each quietly blaming the other for the missed turn. You're the driver, she thinks. You have the maps, I charge, playing out the argument in my head.

In front of the store with the blue double doors, we asked directions. Engrossed in the soccer game on the radio, their answers were brief, confusing. We drove in and out of town several times, looking for a sign or an intersection. Though the map indicated a small road leading north, we couldn't find it. This all took a long time. It was very hot. We had been driving for five hours and were still only forty-two miles from Yaoundé.

Ann leapt out of the Land Cruiser to confront a truck driver climbing down from his cab. He appeared startled, almost frightened. He explained that the road we wanted was five miles away in the direction of Yaoundé. It was near a church, on the right. But why, he asked, did we want to go north? Didn't we understand that it was a backward place? "Not like here," he insisted.

Less than a mile later we passed a crumbling church next to what looked like a mud driveway. I stopped, puzzling. A white Peugeot 504 pickup exploded from the bush on the narrow track. Frantically I jammed the Cruiser into reverse; the Peugeot braked, mud flying everywhere. Several people bounced out of the open rear of the truck.

Ann asked directions from the people lying in the mud. I was impressed. In the long discussion that followed, we were told that yes, this is the road to Yoko, the next major town heading north, but a bridge was out along the way. The only thing to do, the Peugeot driver insisted, was return to Yaoundé and take another, more circuitous road.

There must be another way, I insisted. We have four-wheel drive, I boasted with more hope than experience; we can go over even the worst roads.

Yes, the driver responded calmly, but four-wheel drive does not make the car swim.

Ann giggled.

It might be possible, the driver mused in the skeptical tone one might use to discuss the likelihood of UFOs, to avoid the fallen bridge by going this way. In the mud, he drew an elaborate map routing us through a village called Saa. None of the roads existed on either my Michelin or Baedeker. Ann sketched the map in a little pink student's notebook she'd bought in Yaoundé. The cover read "Le Afrique Magnifique" and had a drawing of the African continent; a skull and crossbones covered the location of South Africa.

The sun was fading as we left the Peugeot and drove down the narrow track. The brush was ferociously thick on both sides and I worried about a campsite. While we discussed trying to clear out a place along the road, realizing that we had no axes or machetes, we came to a collection of a half dozen huts in a clearing. "Home for the night," Ann said.

She was right.

Chapter Fifteen

At the center of the small clearing sat a hut built on a concrete slab. There was another slab in front of the hut, like the rudiments of a basketball court. Some sort of dark beans covered the concrete, where women crouched picking through them. Everyone else in the village sat around a radio listening to the last moments of Cameroon's soccer match against Guyana. "We are losing two to two," a teenager in a tee shirt that read "Spanish Fly" told us. Like the others, he looked very sad. Under the rules of the tournament, he explained in a low voice, Cameroon must win or be eliminated.

Perhaps because of the focus on the soccer match, our arrival made little impact in the village, almost as if we were expected. This was a welcome change from the usual instant melee. We asked the young man in the Spanish Fly tee shirt if we could camp in his village. He told us we were welcome, of course, but that it would be necessary to ask permission of the chief. This he said rolling his eyes, as if to stress the silliness of such formalities.

Our Spanish Fly envoy summoned the chief from the large hut. A slight man, perhaps in his mid-fifties, emerged sleepily in a pair of nearly transparent powder-blue pajamas. His hair was white, his manner dignified, friendly but aloof. He directed chairs to be brought from inside the hut. When I asked about the beans piled on the concrete, he responded with a long, sophisticated treatise on cocoa beans, laced with numerous statistics on price, yield per hectare and harvesting methods. He did not seem to accept my avowal of ignorance when he asked what beans sold for in my village. I suspect he believed I was withholding information for some shrewd bargaining to come.

We set up my small mountain tent next to the Cruiser.

"I've never done this before," Ann said.

"Me either," I answered, puzzled. It was the first time we'd used the tent since arriving in Africa. "It's a great little tent," I assured her. "Maybe a little hot. It was made for the mountains. See how it slopes downward in the middle between the poles? That's so it won't fall down in big storms; aerodynamically designed."

"What I meant," Ann said patiently, "is I've never camped out before."

I stopped unfolding a sleeping bag and looked at her. "Never?"

She nodded.

"Not even in the backyard?"

"Do you know what backyards look like in Oklahoma?"

It rained off and on all night; the inside of the tent felt like a sauna with mosquitoes. I slept quite wonderfully.

I had forgotten it was Sunday. The girl's voice, high and lyrical, reminded me. It came from a church with a thatched roof and no walls; it was a pleasant, open space, inviting and cool. Rhythmic clapping joined her voice.

The church was in a village of only a few huts; some of the large crowd must have come a great distance as there was no major village for miles.

At least, I thought there was no major village. In truth I didn't know. We were lost.

Ann disagreed. She maintained it to be a gross exaggeration to consider ourselves formally lost.

"We know we're on this road and this road goes to Saa and from Saa we can reach Ntui and Ntui is on the main road to Yoko."

This struck me as factually inaccurate in the specific and insanely overconfident in the general. "First," I pointed out, "we don't know this road goes to Saa. Second, once we get to Saa—if we do—we have no idea if we can cross the river. And about this main road to Yoko. What main road? Do you see a main road?" I waved the Michelin map at her. It was sprinkled with drops of sweat; we had just finished a session of unfolding it on the hood of the Cruiser and staring at it earnestly, as if by power of concentration we could will our location to appear on the map, perhaps with a flashing red light and a sign: "You are here."

A Peugeot 504 pickup appeared in the distance heading our way. Ann jumped out immediately to flag it down. This had become a habit. We never allowed Peugeot 504s to pass without asking directions. In two days there had been three. Each seemed able to tell us where *they* were going but unable to explain how to get where we wanted to be.

"You seem like intelligent young people, you should have no trouble." This is what the driver of the Peugeot told us after detailing instructions on how to reach the only working bridge to Saa. His urbanity startled us. The man had gray hair and wore a clean, freshly pressed blue shirt. Everyone else in the truck was dressed with equal flair. By comparison, Ann and I looked like derelicts.

"You must take my son with you," the elegant driver insisted. "He will show you where to go."

We protested. He insisted. Standing in the back of the pickup, the son nodded enthusiastically.

After climbing into the Cruiser, the son explained that his father was going to a funeral in Batchenga. He seemed very glad to escape from such drudgery. He wanted to know if we were soccer players and was amazed when I said I wasn't and Ann said she was. "She plays but you don't?" he marveled. The rest of the way he chuckled without prompting and I felt certain he was thinking of what a horrible wimp I was.

Thanks to our guide, we found the bridge. We found Saa.

We even made it to Ntui, where we left our friend. "When there is another funeral," he said, "you must come back." We promised to try.

After Ntui we spent the rest of the day in one long green tunnel of thick growth bordered by huge baobab trees with bases as wide as the Land Cruiser was long. This was the African jungle of my dreams.

Sections of the narrow dirt road were smooth, tempting me to try third-gear speed. It felt wonderful the first time I nudged the lumbering Cruiser up to thirty-five, jolting around the frequent turns with, I imagined, inordinate grace.

Until I rounded one turn and faced a road full of cattle. The Muslim herdsmen walked languidly along, carrying open umbrellas in one hand and swagger sticks in the other. They both waved at us in some mad semaphore. The lead steer bolted sullenly out of the way. We ground to a shuddering stop.

From then on I kept the car in second gear.

We hoped to reach Yoko by nightfall, but while we waited for another herd of the floppy humped cattle to pass, a kindly Muslim pointed to our left rear tire, dangerously low. With great pride, I pulled out the small, portable air compressor I'd brought from America. It plugged into the cigarette lighter and produced a steady, if meek, stream of air. The effect it had on the tire was imperceptible. I felt betrayed. It had looked like such a wonderful gadget.

We drove for a few miles and then, as if a change of scenery would improve the efficiency of the compressor, I tried it again. By now the tire had lost all air. There was nothing to do but change it. This mandated taking everything out of the rear of the Cruiser—the jerricans, the trunk, the odd spare parts, the ravioli—to get to the tire, which weighed some sixty pounds.

All this took a long time. In the dimming light, we rested in a clearing of tall grass pressed downward by a passing herd of cattle. In the wonderful peace of African twilight, we ate a supper of lentil soup. By the sputtering flame of a small gas lantern, Ann read Gerald Durrell's Cameroon story, *A Zoo in My Luggage;* one passage in particular impressed her, a description of the eating habits of a Cameroonian lizard.

> Their prey was the immense population of tiny creatures that inhabited the forest floor, the small black beetles hurrying along like undertakers late for a funeral, the slow, smooth-sliding slugs, weaving a silver filigree of slime over the leaves, and the small, nut-brown crickets who squatted in the shadows waving their immensely long antennae to and fro, like amateur fishermen on the banks of a stream.

"Let's sleep on the roof of the Cruiser," Ann suggested.

"Right," I agreed.

At first I thought it was rain. Little pinpricks of sensation danced across my chest. As I nudged upward into consciousness, I realized it was mosquitoes. My hand waved them away.

At once the pinpricks turned very nasty. Bolting up in my half-opened sleeping bag, I stared at my chest convinced someone was burning me with a lighted cigarette.

It was completely dark, the moon not yet risen. Struggling awake, I tried to piece together the bits and pieces of stimuli: something was biting me. Wasps, I thought, a nest of wasps had fallen on me. But there was no humming or buzzing; I didn't feel anything flying. Something crawled all over my face, into my ears, biting.

"Ants!" I cried.

"What?" Ann asked sleepily.

"Ants!" I jumped up and broke into a wild Saint Vitus' dance. "Ants!"

"Oh," she said, completely calm. I had the sense she might fall back asleep. Frantically, I hit at my arms and legs. "Ants! Ants!"

Insanely, I wondered if the biting creatures had selected only me for assault.

"Oh, shit," Ann mumbled, finally staggering up. "Oh, shit." We bounced up and down on the car. Between hops, I grabbed the flashlight I'd left between the two sleeping bags.

The flickering light (flickering because I was jumping up and down) exposed a horrible scene. We were in the midst of an ant blitzkrieg. The tiny things were everywhere.

Ann and I slipped down the windshield onto the hood. It was less ant infested and gave us a moment of calm.

"How?" Ann asked. I'd been wondering the same thing.

Searching for a clue, I played the flashlight over the roof.

"Don't bounce up and down," Ann admonished. "Give me that thing." She took the light and held it steady.

We both saw it at the same time: several palm branches brushed the roof to form a natural bridge. What appeared to be an endless stream of ants cascaded down the branches onto our sleeping bags.

The day before, we'd encountered it several times: a column of ants crossing the road. From afar it appeared to be a black board laid across the road, say a two-by-six. Then slowly, as you crept closer, the board came alive, transformed into thousands of crawling creatures. I liked driving the car slowly over the column and watching with morbid fascination the disruption it created. I'd read about these ants in one of my African texts: "If an obstacle is encountered in the line of march the ants instantly swarm all over it, biting viciously. . . . Anything that cannot escape by flying or crawling is killed and carried away if small enough, or eaten alive if too large."

Obviously the thing to do now was to move. I jumped off the hood but before I could get the door open, ants seized control of my bare lower appendages. Like a high jumper spurred by dreams of Olympic glory, I leapt back on the hood.

Ann looked unimpressed. "So much for heroics," she chuckled.

"Why don't we crawl in the windows?" she suggested.

"They're rolled up," I said.

"Why don't we roll them down?"

This seemed like a constructive suggestion. Leaning over, I opened a side door and jackknifed over the frame to lower the window. Ann did the same. We each grabbed a sleeping bag and, flailing at the ants, flew in feetfirst through the open windows. To start a diesel engine, one must first allow a little thing called a glow plug to warm up. This always seemed to take a long time.

When the engine finally kicked over, I threw the car in reverse and, jerricans bouncing crazily, drove furiously away.

Chapter Sixteen

I woke up to the sounds of roosters and the stares of children. A lot of children, all carrying books. I smiled at them, they smiled at me and then I fell back asleep.

When I came to again, I could hear singing floating in the dawn; rolling over on the Cruiser's roof, I saw a line of schoolchildren tromping off to a small building across the road.

A young man standing by the Cruiser offered his hand. Though wearing a torn tee shirt and cutoff shorts, he held himself with a tangible formality, as if waiting to be introduced. I told him my name; Ann, her feet fluttering in my face, woke up and did the same. He nodded. I sat up, embarrassed, as if I'd overslept an appointment.

Everyone in the village who wasn't at school stood around the car and stared. I asked the young man his name. He said, in French, that it was Robert. Did he have a another name? One from his village? Yes, he answered: Yakubu Ngi.

It is a rare person, certainly, who relishes the thought of waking up to a crowd. That vulnerable transition between the strangeness of dreams and the inevitability of day is best negotiated alone or in groups no larger than two. This is particularly true when one is waking in an unknown place, without the slightest hint where the morning requisites—coffee, a bathroom or semblance thereof—might be found.

Ann asked Yakubu if we should speak to the chief. He replied, a bit sheepishly, that we should have asked permission from him before spending the night. We apologized.

"Do you have insect lotion?" he inquired.

Ann and I both were covered in red bites from the previous night's combat. I assumed Yakubu was advising medical treatment.

"The chief likes insect lotion," Yakubu continued.

"Has he been attacked by ants?" I asked.

He looked puzzled. "Ants?"

Quite dramatically I told the story of the evening's trauma. Yakubu was unmoved; he seemed puzzled that I should even mention it.

"Yes," he finally said, "there are ants. It is best to avoid them."

He repeated his request for insect lotion. I pulled out a tube of first-aid ointment. While excited at first, on examination he seemed disappointed. This was not, he said, insect lotion.

I thought he was being a bit picky. While it was true that the ointment was not *specifically* for insects, it would do just fine and, anyway, there wasn't exactly a drugstore down the road. With some annoyance I demonstrated on my ant bites that the salve would function. "This is not insect lotion," Yakubu insisted.

We went around like this for some time until it finally struck Ann that what he was talking about was insect *repellent.* That was what the chief liked.

We dug up a small bottle for his future comfort.

I needed to go to the bathroom. In a nonchalant way, I tried to slip away down the road with the aim in mind of darting into the bush. About fifteen people followed me. I accelerated, trying to ignore them. This made it appear a game and they chased merrily. Grumpy and unrelieved, I tromped back to the Cruiser.

Yakubu had our flat tire out of the Cruiser and was beating on it with a log. It was a novel, not unimpressive sight: he held a five-foot log in both hands and crashed it repeatedly at the point where the tire met the metal rim. He employed a sweeping overhead motion reminiscent of a woman grinding grain.

It was a technique of tire repair I'd read about in one of my African books. At the time—I think I was eating scones somewhere in Knightsbridge—I'd been amused by the description and impressed by its ingeniousness, in the remote way one might react to an account of Eskimos crafting boats from seal skins. It had not, I must confess, seemed very important.

But now it was suddenly more relevant. What he was doing was trying to break the "bead" formed by the seal of the tire and rim. This was an essential step before removing the tube and repairing the leak. The bond between tire and rim is maternal in its clinging strength; powerful machines separate the two in garages all over the world. None, however, were available in this village along the back road to Yoko, Cameroon. Nor was there likely to be one between here and Chad.

Yakubu's exertions captivated the audience. I snuck away unnoticed into the underbrush.

Returning in a more serene state, I found Ann backing the car over the tire. While it seemed logical that this would inevitably ruin the tire by crushing the tire wall to Jell-O, I'd seen the same thing done in Bangui. (Of course, that hardly served as an endorsement.) Loosened by the log beating, the tire broke free of the rim under the weight of the Cruiser. Cheers rang out.

The rest was relatively easy. With a pair of improvised tire tools, Yakubu pried the tire away from the rim and snaked out the tube. A huge hole gave it the appearance of a mortally wounded eel. But this was no problem: from the good Mr. Robertson, I'd purchased extra tubes.

The new tube was passed around for inspection and met with hums of admiration. I was feeling very smug, the epitome of the well-prepared African voyager.

This warm sensation lasted about two minutes. "This is the wrong tube," Yakubu said, frowning.

"Wrong?"

"It is not the right size." He pointed to the numbers on the tube and the numbers on the tire. The two did not match.

I cursed Mr. Robertson in a thunderous voice I'm certain they heard in the school. What made it worse, of course, was the knowledge that I should have personally checked the numbers before leaving Yaoundé.

Yakubu explained gently that if the tube were *larger* than the tire, it would probably be okay. But it was smaller. He pantomimed an exploding tire to illuminate what would happen if we tried to use it.

We had breakfast with Yakubu before leaving. He took us to a hut on the edge of the village with piles of charred and rotting goat meat out front that reeked of death. But inside a young boy pulled fresh loaves of bread from under a rough counter. It tasted light and delicious, with a fresh smell that fought the stench of the goat meat. I buried my nose inside the soft dough.

We drove on toward Yoko wondering what we'd do if we had another flat. Stupidly, I hadn't bought a patch kit for tubes. I put it on a list of things we needed. At the top was "metric wrenches"—the tools stolen from Lucien's stash were English, perfect for the Land Rover but useless for the Japanese-made, metric Cruiser. The second item was "toilet paper," followed by "engine oil" and "sand ladders." The list was arranged vaguely by precedence of urgency. The sand ladders—devices to free a vehicle trapped in deep sand—we would not need until Chad. The other items, particularly the second, had more acute applications.

About thirty miles outside of Yakubu's village, we were surprised by big mountains of gray rock rising out of the plain. As we wound upward, the air grew cooler and less damp until the road leveled off on a high plateau with vistas of rolling hills.

On the outskirts of Yoko, an ancient Land Rover heading out of town swerved in front of us. Four Africans, visibly angry, bounded out. In the half moment I had to think before they reached the car, I wished for the can of mace—a last-minute gift from a friend in New York—stored somewhere in my duffel bag.

"Did you see a white van?" they yelled.

"A van?"

They were looking for a van that had been stolen from a

friend. Where had we come from? they wanted to know. How long had we been driving?

No vans had passed us, we assured them. We were certain.

"We'll find them," the largest of the group, a six-foot-plus man, promised. He waved a piece of pipe for emphasis. It occurred to me that this was one of the few times I'd seen Africans threatening violence, an occurrence so frequent in New York one hardly noticed. "Oh, you're going to kill him, are you," I once found myself saying to a cab driver as I half-listened to the details of a dispute with his brother-in-law. "How nice."

Before this posse remounted into their Land Rover (which they started with a hand crank) we asked about the best place to get a tire fixed. They seemed puzzled by our specification of the "best" choice. "There is *one* place in Yoko. You must go to the Catholic mission."

"The mission fixes tires?"

"Of course. They fix everything."

"Even souls?" Ann asked.

They laughed loudly and inquired in a flirtatious way how broken the madame's soul was.

"The mademoiselle's soul has numerous cracks," Ann told them, smiling.

This was taken as highly suggestive. A couple of the men looked embarrassed, but others, including the big fellow with the pipe, suddenly appeared more interested in talking to Ann than chasing van thieves.

I drove on.

The Catholic mission of Yoko sat on a big hill overlooking the town. Shaded by trees, it was a cool retreat with inviting whitewashed buildings. A black man in a flowered dashiki and jeans met us; he was friendly but puzzled that we had come to the mission with a flat tire.

"Why did you not go to a garage?"

We relayed what we had been told by the men in the van. He laughed.

"It is because you are white. They think white people like to go to white people with problems."

"But you aren't white," Ann pointed out.

He laughed louder. "You noticed?"

When we asked about a garage, he shook his head, insisting that he would fix the tire. "You see?" he smiled. "The men in the van were right!"

Sitting on the steps in front of the wide wooden doors to the church, he worked on the tube with a Tip-Top repair kit. When he observed my keen interest, he explained the necessary steps, stressing the need to roughen the rubber so that the patch bound to the tube. "Did someone shoot you?" he asked, sticking three fingers into the hole. "It is good you have come to a mission; this tube requires a miracle. You must buy a new one as soon as possible."

Later, when a precarious patch had been secured, we retired to his apartment in one of the stone buildings. A stretched bull-hide and a bow and arrow hung on the wall. "African crafts," he said, and it was hard to tell if this too was intended ironically. I took it as such, from a man who bridged the two worlds of black Yoko and the white mission fathers. He had worked for the mission since he was a young boy. Twice he had been to France for theological study.

"Are you a priest?" I asked.

He gave us a knowing look that I was beginning to like. "There are very few black priests in Cameroon. None in Yoko."

Before we left, he insisted we fill one of our jerricans with the clear, good water he had poured through the mission's large ceramic filter. Using my hand-held filter, it would have taken us an hour to "make" that much water. That was how I referred to the filtering process. "Let's make some water," I'd say to Ann, as the device required two people for effective operation. She invariably objected to this description on scatological grounds.

On the edge of town, we stopped in a little grocery store. We

never passed an opportunity to acquire food, and this was something of an event: an actual store with shelves and counters.
Unfortunately, most of the stock consisted of canned meats
donated by the leading relief organizations of Europe. I bought
a can of chocolate syrup; Ann a load of bubble gum. We also
acquired some tuna fish that looked museum quality and several
bundles of pasta. It was quite a haul.

Our friend at the mission had warned us about the road
heading north from Yoko. There had been, apparently, a recent
wreck of spectacular proportions.

The abundant likelihood of disaster quickly manifested itself
as we left Yoko. Entering a forest of tall grass, the Cruiser tun-
neled through a world of brown stalks topped with lingering
green from the passing rainy season.

The road—path would be more accurate—twisted and
turned, as if unsure of its northern path. The packed-dirt surface
made speed irresistibly seductive. I leaned on the horn, trying to
edge the Cruiser to the right as we whipped around curves; but
this was a road without left and right, too narrow for the wide
Cruiser. The high grass flailed the windshield as I dared to slip
into third and sometimes even fourth gear. Ann and I giggled like
schoolchildren.

In the early afternoon we broke from the grass onto a plateau
and we could see behind us the sea of grass we'd crossed. Furtive
baboons darted across the road and into thickets of low trees.
Dust hung in the air, coating the inside of the Cruiser with a
patina of gray. Muslim cattle herders and their charges crowded
the road; I thought about what would have happened if we had
met them a half hour earlier in the tunnels of grass. The Muslims
carried walking sticks and bright prayer rugs.

Tibati was the next large town. ("Large" had taken on a
relative meaning; Tibati was billed as about the same size as
Yoko: one long street.) Still charmed by the cool retreat in Yoko,
we asked at a gas station along the way if there was a mission in
Tibati. A Muslim in white skullcap assured us there was. The
conversation took place while he and I tipped a round ten-liter

flask full of diesel fuel into the Cruiser. The station was a crumbling shack with a few fifty-gallon drums out front; using a hose as a siphon, the man measured out the fuel into the bottle which, wrapped in straw, resembled a large wine flask.

Henri and others had warned me of the dangers of water in diesel fuel. On their recommendation, I'd acquired a length of clear tubing that I'd tied to a broken radio aerial. The idea was to gather a sample in the tube from the bottom of a fuel container where any water present would gather. This sounded easy enough that even I could master it.

When put to the test, though, I found myself wondering how to tell the difference between water and diesel. Weren't they both clear? While the Muslim watched in amazement, I held my fingers under the tube and let a little of the fluid spill out. Then, like some mad petrochemical connoisseur, I rubbed the liquid between my fingers and raised it to my lips. Not surprisingly, it tasted like diesel. Sagely, I nodded my approval while Ann attempted, without notable success, not to laugh.

With visions of mission comforts, we decided to try to reach Tibati that night. It was the magical time of day in Africa; the late-afternoon haze enveloped the landscape in soft light, welcome as a caress after the beating of the sun. Neither of us said anything.

It was near dark when we reached Tibati. Ann had brought with her two baseball caps—one from Notre Dame University (a gift from her boyfriend) and the other her red St. Louis Cardinals hat. We debated which might have the strongest appeal to a Catholic clergyman, finally deciding on Notre Dame: the Cardinals hat featured a bird swinging a baseball bat, not the variety of cardinal most associated with clerical life.

The mission was behind a large soccer field where children kicked a ball almost invisible in the fading light. I thought of long games of kick the can and capture the flag in Mississippi, when I'd hide in the darkness and dream of the time when I could leave and go to the places I read about every afternoon in the coolness of the air-conditioned Jackson Public Library.

The mission father was on his way to a night school catechism class. He was a short, efficient Frenchman who'd driven his Peugeot down through Spain and Morocco to Cameroon the year before. He had a small room for visitors in a separate building, a one-story concrete bunkhouse. To our disappointment he made no mention of Ann's hat.

"I'm sorry," he said, opening the door to the dirty room, "some Germans stayed here last."

Dirty or not, the accommodations seemed like pure luxury: electric lights (he had a generator) and a shower. Under a mango tree in front of the bunkhouse, we heated a can of ravioli and read scenes from *The Long Goodbye.* Before the lights went out at ten o'clock, I unfolded my Michelin map and traced our route. We had gone only a few inches across Africa. The route we'd charted to the Mediterranean ran through Chad, Niger, Mali and Algeria. Before us lay little complications like Lake Chad and the Sahara Desert. It was already the second week of November; my wife planned to arrive in Algeria for Christmas. At the pace we were traveling, we would make Algiers long after the new year.

But I was developing a certain African mind-set. It seemed silly to worry about anything as far away as a month. More acute concerns screamed for attention: like getting a new tire tube and unclogging the Cruiser's air filter. I fell asleep outside on the roof of the car—the German-dirtied room had little appeal—to images of wondrous new Michelin tubes and gleaming air filters. Ahh, the stuff of African dreams.

It seemed an unlikely bit of good fortune the next morning when we spotted what appeared to be a tire repair shop on the edge of town. There was even a sign in front of the blue, pockmarked building that read, with unaccountable wit, *"Pneu Clinique."*

The proprietor assured us he had a tube to fit. "Of course, of course," he said, then turned to a youth on a bicycle and whispered urgently, "Go find a tube! Hurry." As the boy pedaled away, he asked, "Do you have sunglasses you could give me?"

As it was apparent that this might take a while, I thought it wise to move the Cruiser from the street where I had stopped. While we appeared to be the only vehicle moving in that part of Cameroon, one never knew when a massive lorry might turn the corner at fifty miles per hour.

The Cruiser, alas, would not start. I was shocked. In our brief time together, I'd developed great faith in the machine and took this failure quite personally.

While Ann and I looked under the raised hood, a man appeared whom at first I took to be a fool. He wore a big floppy hat in the style of a sixties hippie, and smiled with a manic frequency. Shifting back and forth from one leg to the other, he appeared to be dancing a continual jig to music only he heard.

The man asked questions about the car. We answered curtly. He said he could fix the car. I muttered my doubts. "There," he said, pointing to a wire coming out of the starter. Though I hadn't noticed it before, it hung at an odd angle, frayed at the contact point. The man told me to try to start the car while he worked with the wire. Less skeptical now, I obeyed.

Within a few moments, the engine fired. The mechanic danced a few steps and doffed his hat just as the boy on the bicycle returned holding up a tube triumphantly. Never had so many fortuitous omens graced us at once.

The tire tube was the wrong size. I compared it to the one I'd purchased from Mr. Robertson. Our happy mechanic frowned in confusion when he saw Mr. Robertson's tube. "But why don't you use this one?" he asked.

I pointed out that it was the wrong size.

He scoffed, assuring us that the size was close enough to make no difference.

"Why not try it?" he asked. "What could go wrong?"

"Well," Ann answered, "it could blow out and cause us to run off the road, crash and burn."

He chuckled. "Yes, that could happen." He seemed sorry that he wouldn't be around to witness such a bang-up good time.

By now I had great faith in the man. By my interpretation, he had appeared on the scene like a character in a fable with the clear mission of assuaging our troubles, sort of a mechanical saint of the bush.

We changed the tube and afterwards the three of us sat around eating the can of chocolate syrup I'd bought in Yoko. It tasted not remotely like chocolate syrup but had a pleasing, sweetly smoky flavor.

The rest of the day we drove through high plains filled with rollicking baboons and herds of Muslim cattle. In the late afternoon, we camped on a knoll under a eucalyptus tree. Brush fires burned across the horizon. A cool breeze repelled the worst of the flies. I fell asleep while the sky was still lit by the afterglow of the fading sun.

Chapter
Seventeen

I grew up in a part of the world that thought little about Catholics. Mostly the subject came up when Notre Dame came down every fall and beat one of our good Southern football teams. Mississippi, my home state, was so dominated by Baptists, Presbyterians and Methodists that a lot of my pals figured my family had become Catholic when we left Galloway Methodist for Saint Andrew's Episcopalian. "That's, like, run by the pope, huh?" my best friend asked.

While Catholics were considered unusual, I never sensed any real animosity toward the church. When my grandmother took up Catholicism after her fifth marriage, everybody figured it was far preferable to another husband.

But Africa washed away any ambivalence I might have had about Catholics. Even now when I see a nun walking down Lexington Avenue, I feel compelled to run up and ask if she needs a place to stay for the night. What the Catholic church has done to and for Africa is eminently questionable, but what it did for Ann and me isn't.

Like in N'Gaoundéré. If you were transported to N'Gaoundéré from just about any place in the First World, there's little doubt that your initial thought would be, "What a sad little place," and your second would concern when you could leave.

One of the appealing aspects of slow driving, however— *motor touring* in the old-fashioned way—is that perceptions are granted ample time to adjust to the changing circumstances of a journey. Instead of being depressed by the dusty streets, the little shacks and soldiers everywhere, when Ann and I reached N'Gaoundéré we talked excitedly about how many streets there were, the several auto-parts stores and, of course, the omelet shack.

We didn't notice the omelet place at first. It was an insider's tip from Danny Beck at the mission. Not a priest or religious student, Danny was a volunteer from a church group in Wisconsin who taught at the high school in N'Gaoundéré. "I didn't want to join the Peace Corps," he explained when we asked why he had stepped on a plane one winter afternoon and emerged, sundry changes later, in N'Gaoundéré. Danny made it sound as if the only logical thing to do if you didn't join the Peace Corps was to teach English and math in N'Gaoundéré.

Danny Beck was one of the few nonclergy members at the mission and, except for a nun from New Orleans, the only American. She was a small, cheerful woman in her late thirties who belonged to the Ursuline order. I liked her right off when we fell into a detailed discussion of New Orleans's better bars and she offered a superb comparative analysis of the Maple Leaf Bar versus Tipitinas, a famed dance club. She seemed touched when I told her I'd met my wife at Tipitinas. "How romantic," she said, and then asked if Dr. John had played that night. "Or was it the Wild Tchoupitoulas Indians?"

We stayed at the mission in N'Gaoundéré for two days. Though our accommodations were in cement cubicles surrounded by a barbed-wire fence, it felt like a resort. Built on a high plateau, N'Gaoundéré is graced with a cool and dry climate. The first morning, I sat at the shaky desk in my square mission room wearing wool socks and a sweater, reading a pamphlet I'd found called *Why God Made Me Black.* Across a dirt courtyard from my barred window, the Ursuline nuns held mass in a tiny chapel. When they finished, the nuns talked for a while in front of the stained glass doors then hugged each other before heading to class. I thought it must be a good way to live and felt a pang of jealousy for the peace they seemed to have found.

At night, led by Danny, we walked deep into what everyone

at the mission called "the African quarter." This struck me as an odd distinction to make in the middle of Africa, especially in a town with precious little non-African influence. (There wasn't even an equivalent of Bangui's Rock Club.) We sat on benches in front of a charcoal fire and ate grilled meat. When finished, one paid by the number of skewers. From the house next door, we bought a plate of black beans and beignets. The beer came from a Lebanese grocery. It was a feast. Ann and I devoured twenty-six skewers.

Accompanying Danny was a young Frenchman serving in the Alliance Progrès. He wore penny loafers, khaki pants and a Lacoste shirt. With his short dark hair and intense manner, he reminded me of the civil rights workers who came to Mississippi in the mid-sixties from colleges like Bowdoin and Swarthmore. I expected him to hum Peter, Paul and Mary songs at any moment.

Jean-Marc was his name. He had traveled across America by bus, evolving an elaborate rating system for bus stations along the way. "I have been to your Jackson, Mississippi," he told me, after asking where I was from. "The station there has a very serious problem—the video games are horribly loud. It makes sleeping very difficult."

I expressed my sympathy, though I would have placed video game loudness far down on my list of reasons not to spend the night in the Jackson, Mississippi, Trailways station.

"Amarillo—that is a station with wonderful food. The tacos!"

After Jean-Marc finished his bus station critique, he explained why his country continued to "be involved" with former West African colonies like the CAR, Cameroon and Chad.

"I tell you, my friend," he said, twirling a coat hanger meat skewer, "they may talk about the prestige, the sentimental attachment, but it is money! Yes, money! Okay, my government pours a lot of francs into these countries but they get more out. The trade agreements, the minerals, the timber. How you say? Money talks, bullshit walks?"

\\\

What I liked most about N'Gaoundéré were the auto-parts stores.

As a kid, I never had the car fever in the serious way my friends did. Though I owned a '55 Chevy, inherited from my grandmother, I didn't put in the hours taking apart engines and memorizing each issue of *Car and Driver;* I knew what Hooker headers were and what they did and why Hurst was the name in four on the floor, but I couldn't have done a valve job if my life depended on it.

It seems predestined that when you're sixteen, everybody— adults, that is—urges you not to waste your time on motorhead pursuits, to concentrate on useful endeavors like algebra and Latin. Driving around Africa was gratifying if for no other reason than it proved all those people wrong. I constantly found myself trying to remember the offhand mechanical comments of my friends and cursed myself for dedicating even a moment to algebra and Latin when I could have been doing something productive, like taking apart transmissions.

Whenever Ann and I encountered other travelers driving down from Europe, we gawked enviously at their superbly outfitted vehicles, equipped for maximum comfort and all contingencies. In our beat-up Land Cruiser, a jack was a luxury and a window that worked for two days straight a miracle. Walking into the auto stores of N'Gaoundéré—there were three, for some reason—we were thrilled.

The pleasant Lebanese shopkeepers understood our giddy joy at finding a Tip-Top repair kit for tubes, with a full assortment of patches, and motor oil that was actually new, not recycled, plus a headlight and 30-amp fuses. These kindly, wise merchants realized they offered automotive delights not readily available. "Between Yaoundé and Chad, this is it!" one bragged, adding, "And in Chad, it is sometimes easier to buy a machine gun than a new tire tube."

\\\

It is curious how quickly the appeal of luxury—and the mission qualified as such by our standards—can fade. It was like the good stretch of paved road north of N'Gaoundéré leading to Garoua, the next sizable town. When we first lumbered onto the smooth tarmac, I was so astounded that I stopped the Cruiser, got out and took a photo. The gleaming road stretched into the distance like a black mirage.

Riding on the slick asphalt carpet, we noticed for the first time the tremendous noise generated by the Cruiser's diesel engine. This acoustical fact had been lost midst the routine deafening rattles of the jerricans smashing against each other and the cannonading of ravioli tins as the Cruiser's tanklike suspension negotiated the canyons of Cameroon's road system. Ann and I rarely attempted normal conversation as we were too busy bouncing against the roof. (There were, alas, no seatbelts.)

But within an hour on the trouble-free Garoua highway, I felt bored, a novel experience on an African road. It was a relief when, after a couple of hours, the route returned to its familiar, outrageously bumpy condition.

The same went for Garoua, reached in the late afternoon. By force of habit we steered toward the Catholic mission, and it wasn't solely because it seemed to lack the friendly charm of N'Gaoundéré's that I was pleased there were no rooms. A night at the mission would have been comfortable—any insect-free environment had appeal—but I longed for the feel, the texture, of an African evening.

And that night I found it: under a baobab tree near a Muslim village a few miles north of Garoua. Across the stretch of fields, a red band of fire swept down a hillside. In the soft light of the day's last moments, the wailing call to prayers floated from the village mosque. Waves of heat shimmered from the dry ground, the earth giving up some of the burning it had received that day.

This, I thought before nodding away, was why I had come to Africa.

\\\

Two days later we burned all our letters. We did this in a large field where children gathered grasshoppers in burlap sacks. There were about ten children, and they scurried across the recently burned field in an efficient pack, scooping up the grasshoppers and pulling off their wings before depositing them in an old grain sack bearing the name of a Dutch relief agency on the side. Charcoal smudged their faces and clothes—torn bits of shirts and shorts—making them look like a band of apprentice chimney sweeps.

We'd spent the night in this field, somewhere near the Chadian border. The paper burning before me was the stuff of journalistic accreditation: press passes, letters from my publisher, copies of a few articles I'd written. A brief story in a *Herald Tribune* I'd found at the N'Gaoundéré mission prompted the little bonfire: the government of Chad had recently expelled the *New York Times* correspondent and banned all journalists from the country.

Other travelers had billed the search by Chad's border guards as fanatical. As I really wasn't a journalist, and certainly not traveling on a journalist's mission, it struck me as a shame to be expelled for carrying papers whose sole purpose was to *solve* problems, not create them.

This was a part of the world called the Sahel, the dry band that stretches across Africa, dividing the tropics from the Sahara. Here there was still a semblance of a rainy season, enough to support stubby wheat fields and the acacia trees whose thorns I'd dodged for days.

Not far away in the field was a collection of abandoned machines: tractors and what appeared to be a road grader. They had been stripped of all removable parts. It might have been a year since they were left here, or a decade. Not long ago, these tractors could have harvested a serious crop, but the Sahara was expanding by 250,000 acres a year, drying the earth. Africa was a place that defeated the large machines of the West with careless ease.

It will be like this, I thought, after the apocalypse: dirty children playing in scorched fields with the hulks of ruined technology hovering in the background. Perhaps Africa was better prepared for the future than we were in the West.

The strong wind that had been blowing since sunset the day before whipped the flames of my little fire. "We're going to be blown off the roof," Ann had calmly declared during the night while the Cruiser rocked beneath us.

At least this dry hurricane kept the gnats and mosquitoes at bay. Caught without a mosquito net, I'd begun sleeping with a canvas shirt draped over my head. It limited the insect assaults enough that I could fall asleep, but invariably I awoke in a panic, covered in sweat and half-asphyxiated from sucking on the smelly cloth. It made for interesting dreams, like the one I'd had about border guards refusing us entry when we failed to produce the right papers. This was another visit from the bureaucratic demons that had plagued my sleep in Yaoundé. The word "vignette" rumbled throughout the dream.

Vignette was the document a police patrol had asked for the day before. The soldier, a tall and skinny youth not long out of his teens, was polite but insistent. A vignette was required. It did not matter that no one else had requested it. With sound logic he said, "You have been lucky. But that you have not had problems before does not mean that you do not have a problem now."

What we had to do, he explained, was to return to the nearest regional capital and acquire a vignette from the authorities.

Which authorities?

He wasn't sure and, as we asked more questions, it became apparent that he wasn't entirely positive that a vignette could be obtained anywhere outside of Yaoundé.

What made this all the more maddening was the memory of the first time we'd heard of the vignette. It was back in Yaoundé and several people, including Henri's colleagues in the coffee company, had mentioned that it was something we needed to take care of before leaving town. The vignette was a round sticker placed on the upper left corner of the windshield certifying that the yearly vehicle taxes had been paid. Several times I had insisted that Mr. Robertson acquire a current vignette (he asserted all taxes had been paid). Naturally he agreed in the most forceful terms. And naturally it had not been done. When I pointed this out on that last, fateful Friday afternoon in Yaoundé, he'd shrugged and said, "I guess you can stay and we try to get it next week, or leave without it. I promise you, it will be okay. No one asks for the vignette. Never. I swear."

Without Ann's persuasion and the easy disposition of the soldier, we would never have been allowed to pass the checkpoint. As it was, he relented after we promised to take care of it "as soon as possible."

The next morning, while I disposed of journalistic traces and watched the band of kids depleting the grasshopper population, Ann and I debated what to do. Returning to Yaoundé was preposterous. Short of being dragged at gunpoint, there was no way we would consider it. But I argued for driving back to Maroua, the nearest regional capital, about three hours south, to try to obtain a vignette. "If we can't get it, we'll just turn around and keep going toward Chad. At least we'll have tried."

Ann made a good point. "What happens if we don't get the thing? Driving back, we'll have to go through the same checkpoint. You think they'll let us through again? And what about the cops in Maroua when they find out we don't have a vignette?

"What we ought to do," she said, "is just keep driving toward Chad until they stop us."

"And what happens if they ask at the border for the vignette?"

She shrugged. "We wing it."

And that's what we did.

"What can my American friends give me?" the customs officer asked. We were on the Cameroon side of the bridge leading to Chad.

I was so delighted he hadn't mentioned the vignette or any other arcane credentials that my instinct was to offer just about anything he wanted. A warm, tingling spirit of International

Brotherhood washed over me. You want a camera? Of course. A radio? Why not.

Fortunately, the officer's request was more modest. "A photo?" he asked. "A photo with my American friends!"

I had lugged from America a cheap Polaroid instant camera for this very purpose. With great care, I arranged him and Ann in a pleasing two-shot in front of the Cruiser. The results so delighted him that he called out the other five people in the customs shed and they all posed with Ann. It was a toss-up which they appreciated more, Ann or the photos. I started to wonder if my strategy was inherently flawed. By detaining us on the Cameroon side of the border, the officials would gain access to a large (though finite) number of photos and, in theory at least, an unlimited opportunity to enjoy Ann's company.

But when the ten-shot pack of film ran out, the friendly officials waved us through. "If you don't like Chad, come back," one invited.

"Our visas are expired," I pointed out.

He laughed. "You think that matters to your friends?"

We drove over the bridge into Chad. Beneath us, the riverbed was wide, with only a narrow strip of clear water bounded by sand beaches.

A long line of trucks stretched in both directions waiting to clear Chadian customs. This was not a promising sign.

There were five cement huts with tin roofs lined up in a row. This comprised the most impressive border installation I'd seen in Africa. At first I took the presence of the multiple buildings as an indication of efficiency. This is great, I thought, five different offices to speed things along. But then I realized that to enter Chad you had to have your passport stamped at each hut by contrary officials, each with his own agenda, questions and, of course, long, detailed forms to complete.

No one wore uniforms of any kind, making it difficult to tell who was an official representative and who was merely a nosy hanger-on. It was generally a good guess that the fellows carrying guns were customs executives, but in Chad this could hardly be taken for granted. Swirling wind and passing trucks kicked up a toxic cloud of diesel dust, covering the sheep and goats that wandered between parked trucks. Many of the men wore white robes and strode from hut to hut with their arms held in front of their faces blocking the dust.

I did what seemed the most reasonable thing at the time: I suggested to Ann that she go into the first customs shack while I stayed in the car.

"Why me?" she asked.

"They'll be nicer to you."

"I bet."

"Look," I said, "I'll stay out here and make friends with the guys who come to search our car. If you have any trouble just yell."

"That's very reassuring." She gathered our papers and walked toward the first shed, dodging a herd of goats.

Feeling guilty, I upheld my end of the arrangement a bit too enthusiastically. When two young men came out and asked me to take everything out of the car, I assailed them with good humor and charm. Like a college freshman at a fraternity rush party, I was determined to be liked. By the time Ann returned some half an hour later, the car remained unsearched but my friends were discussing when they were coming to visit in America.

"How nice," Ann said, looking at me.

More immediately, they promised to drop in on us at the Catholic mission in N'Djamena.

"Wonderful," Ann told them. "We will look forward to it ever so much."

It wasn't until we were driving into N'Djamena that Ann mentioned that all the car papers—registration, insurance, everything—had been confiscated at the border.

Chapter
Eighteen

We spent over a week in N'Djamena.

Our home was the Catholic mission next to the new prosthesis clinic. Each morning the mutilated lined up to be fitted with shiny new limbs. The prosthesis clinic was but one of many new buildings in N'Djamena. This was not due to a sudden surge in tourism or a gold strike but a more basic reason: much of the town was destroyed during the civil wars that raged sporadically in Chad in the years following independence from France in 1960. At its climax the American ambassador swam the border river into Cameroon to escape the fighting.

Westerners have often fared poorly in Chad. Before independence, N'Djamena was called by the French Fort-Lamy, named for the legionnaire major killed while attacking the Chadian fortress in 1901. One of his fellow officers recounted the battle in a letter Douglas Porch quotes in *Conquest of the Sahara*:

> It was a terrible atrocity which I will never forget. This mass which swarmed and jostled, the men stepping over the bodies, climbed over each other to grasp the top of the rampart, where a bullet would bring them tumbling back down. Faces upon which was painted the anguish of death turned toward us, a few in desperation firing their last shot at us which would hit someone. The horse of a chief reared up and added to the disorder. This is the vision of the horror which I still have before my eyes.

But a stability of sorts currently reigns in N'Djamena. Now there is a huge new American embassy compound with fortifications to ensure it will be a long while before another U.S. ambassador takes another midnight dip.

N'Djamena has a charm that defies the customary guidelines of taste and logic. Visiting in 1962, Martha Gellhorn thought it was a "horrible country. The squalor is even greater than in Garoua, and here there are mosquitoes to boot . . . It is appalling."

Cloaked in a perpetual layer of dust, the town still resembles what it was for years: a battlefield. Only the newest buildings are not bullet riddled. There is almost as much garbage crowding the street as in New York City. Young men roam these streets in Land Cruiser pickup trucks mounted with machine guns. Almost everyone is armed with some combination of knives and automatic weapons.

But war-zone capitals of a winning side are usually graced with an infectious optimism difficult to resist. And Chad definitely feels it is winning. After years of watching Libya annex its northern territory, Chad finally put aside internal feuds and struck back. In a series of blitzkrieg assaults, Chadian forces overran Libyian desert bases previously thought impenetrable. Their attack methods quickly qualified as the stuff of legends.

"The Libyans had planted these huge minefields around their positions," a U.S. embassy aide told me one night in a rooftop bar, "and figured only an air strike could touch 'em. But the Chadians snuck a bunch of Toyota pickups mounted with machine guns up north. They drove at night and hid out during the day.

"They attacked at dawn with the rising sun behind them. It must have been some sight. They drove so fast over the sand that the mines—most of them, anyway—blew up behind them. They came in firing machine guns and waving swords, scared the hell out of the Libyans." He chuckled. "For good reason, too. Taking prisoners is not very high on their priorities list."

The American government aids Chad in its war with Libya and this helps create a benevolent attitude toward Americans in

N'Djamena. America has influenced not only the battlefield but the fashion front as well. It is a common but disconcerting sight to see men wearing the white headdress of the desert and a U.S. Army shirt with "Stubberfield" or "Smith" stenciled over the pocket. Several times I was asked by these warriors if I had an extra Stinger missile to spare. The high-tech U.S.-supplied surface-to-air missiles are very popular in Chad, and it's a common opinion that most Americans must have a few extras lying around. In an armament-obsessed place like N'Djamena, the small, portable projectiles are the ultimate status symbol. I was offered some outstanding handmade swords in exchange for my Stingers; when I tried to explain that I actually didn't have any, my denial was taken as either unnecessary modesty or selfishness.

It is fortunate that Ann and I enjoyed N'Djamena because it appeared for a while that we might never leave. The problem was a simple one: our car papers. As long as they were held by customs, we were effectively under arrest. Without car documents, passing the checkpoints that surrounded N'Djamena was impossible.

We discussed the problem with a group of Belgians staying at the Catholic mission. (N'Djamena has no hotels at the moment, only a few bombed-out shells from its posher colonial days.) The Belgians arrived in a pair of diesel Land Cruisers modified with a staggering display of camping gimmicks. With their built-in kitchens, sleeping platforms and generators, they were every bit the well-equipped African voyagers Ann and I were not.

All four Belgians—three men and one woman—were nurses. Somehow, despite six weeks en route from Europe, their clothes were remarkably clean. This may seem a little thing, but it amazed Ann and me; everything we owned had taken on a dusty brown tint that defied the most vigorous scrubbing (though, of course, we hadn't seen hot water in weeks and had only hand soap of a dubious Lebanese origin). Ann suspected the Belgians had a washing machine hidden somewhere in their Land Cruisers.

The Belgians appeared in N'Djamena our first night. They

had spent a week crossing Lake Chad, using the same route, in reverse, we intended to travel.

"We had many difficulties," André said. He was about thirty, with the spiked hair, aviator sunglasses and stubby beard of a rock star. Ann thought he was very good looking. Michelle, his blond girlfriend, seemed to agree. "The sand was so deep it came into the car through the bottom of the doors. One of our vehicles overheated and we finally had to stop and cleanse the radiator. There is no road and the way is hard to find. We would have been lost without our guide."

"We were lost *with* our guide," Michelle said, laughing.

"Is your guide good?" André asked.

Ann explained that we didn't actually have one.

André whistled. "You are very brave."

We characterized this as a gross exaggeration.

"It's not bravery when you just don't know any better," Ann said simply.

But a more pressing problem than the lack of a guide emerged when André took a look at our Land Cruiser.

"This is very bad," he said, pointing to the rear springs. "The springs will never make it through the desert."

For the first time since Yaoundé, I examined the rear end of the Cruiser. The leaf springs, designed in a U shape to support the car, were totally flat. In fact, on the left side the metal had passed the horizontal level, forming an inverted U pointing the wrong way.

"Très fatigué," André pronounced gravely. "This," he said, "you must replace while you are still here in civilization."

That he considered N'Djamena civilization said not a little about where he had spent the last month.

"Très fatigué," André repeated.

The next morning we embarked on a search for rear springs. After several futile inquiries at roadside garages, I took a more direct approach and flagged down a Land Cruiser on the street. It belonged to a UN development group (like Bangui, N'Djamena is awash in international aid), and the startled American passenger seemed to know less about N'Djamena than we did. But the Chadian driver had a suggestion.

"We go to Control Data," he said. "They have springs."

Just hearing a name like Control Data startled me, evoking memories of a world I'd almost forgotten. It was akin to a telephone ringing in the middle of the desert.

"Yes," I agreed immediately. "Let's go to Control Data." I liked the crisp sound of the words.

Control Data was one of those strange hybrid stores you find in out-of-the-way places, the sort of establishment that sells everything from gas stoves and shortwave radios to odd car parts like thermostats and headlights. One of the few items not sold was rear springs for a Land Cruiser. But the blond female proprietor, who was inexplicably Finnish, suggested we go to the garage run by CARE, the charity organization.

"They have everything," she promised. "Everything."

The mere sight of the CARE garage set my heart racing. In a walled compound stretching a city block, forty or fifty Land Cruisers labeled with the olive branch seal of CARE waited for service in an aircraft hangar of a structure outfitted with hydraulic lifts and brimming tool chests.

A bearded, barrel-chested African ran the show. While Ann and I gawked at the array of vehicles and equipment, he consulted a microfiche viewer and announced that he didn't have any rear springs that would fit our Cruiser. (This was not surprising as most of his Toyotas were pickups built on a different suspension.) He advised us to look in the market.

"In the spring section," he specified. Ann and I laughed, assuming he was joking. We had seen the market, a sprawling area near the mosque in the center of town, and though the various stalls sold the typically eclectic mix that ran from razor blades to jerricans, we had seen no auto parts.

The CARE manager looked puzzled by our laughter, as if there were a riddle he didn't get. "Iman will show you," he said, gesturing to one of his employees.

With Iman wedged into the front seat, we drove through town to the dirt streets of the market. He directed us through back alleys until we emerged in front of a line of stalls. I was amazed. In front of every corrugated tin shack sat a stack of auto springs.

A great cry went out when Iman announced what we were looking for. Springs of all sizes and shapes were dragged forth, each presented with the guarantee that it was the perfect factory-original part.

Most were clearly homemade, welded from bits and pieces of bed parts or flattened steel bars. One looked promising. It had a Toyota parts sticker and seemed, at a rough measurement, to be the right size.

Iman negotiated the price for us. In a matter of minutes it plummeted some 1,000 percent from the horrifying to the merely painful. Clearly a shrewd sort, he insisted on a prepurchase inspection by his pals at the CARE garage.

The owner of the spring followed us back to CARE on a tiny moped that moved so languidly the tassel of his red fez hardly budged in the hot air.

At CARE, the head mechanic had departed but in his place, yelling at everyone, was a Hawaiian. At least I assumed he was Hawaiian. The man had dark, almost olive skin contrasting with a brilliant Hawaiian shirt. White love beads and sandals completed the outfit. His name was David and, we learned, he owned Control Data. The blond Finn we'd met was his wife.

"These black bastards," David hooted good-naturedly when he saw our spring with the Toyota sticker, "they'd sell you the Bible and call it the Koran." He marched into the CARE office and consulted the microfiche. The part number on the Toyota sticker corresponded to a light switch.

"Does this look like a light switch?" David yelled at the man in the fez who had followed on his moped. The man smiled.

Though David was shrieking, neither he nor the would-be spring salesman seemed in the least angry. Apparently it was all very routine.

David picked up the weighty spring, opened the door to the Cruiser and started ramming the heavy steel toward the dash. "Is this where the light switch goes?" he yelled. "Will it fit?"

Other CARE workers gathered around for the show. The man in the fez shouted, *"Oui! Oui!* It is for a big light!"

When everyone stopped laughing, David took Ann and me aside, his arms around our shoulders. "Who the hell are you?" he asked pleasantly.

We told him our story and what we were looking for.

"I don't understand," he said, laughing. "Some fool at the border has your car papers and you're driving around trying to buy a spring that might be a light switch? Are you crazy?" he shrieked. "Crazy!"

He directed us inside his new Mercedes jeep. "You want air-conditioning?" he asked. We nodded frantically, like a pair of country rubes come to the city.

David proceeded to explain the facts of life in N'Djamena. We must, he stressed, retrieve our documents from customs as soon as possible. "This may seem crazy to you," he ventured, "but here in Africa, these officials, they take cars for their own use. Have you ever heard of such a thing?"

We acknowledged that it was a phenomenon we'd previously experienced.

"Good. Then you know what these black bastards can do. Anything. They can do anything."

David instructed us to see the head customs official immediately to inquire why our documents had been confiscated. "No, that is no good," he corrected himself. "I'll take you. The bastard owes me. That's what you say in America, right? Owes me?"

On the way over to the customs office, David told us his history. He was Malian—"a black bastard like these other black bastards," he insisted. David struck a perpetually upbeat note that seemed unrelated to what he was saying. He was a trader by profession, a descendant, he crowed, of the great Malian traders who built Timbuktu. "It's in my blood!"

The customs office was part of a compound of government bureaus that included the police headquarters and tax offices. The buildings were off the main road in a walled compound dotted with trees. It would have been a pleasant, shady spot were it not jammed with a milling crowd one notch below a mob.

"What's wrong?" I asked David.

"Wrong? What do you mean, guy?" He finished a lot of sentences like that. "So what you think, guy?"

I gestured to the angry mass.

David shrugged. "It is like this every day. There are many minnows trying to swim upstream."

David worked through the crowd like a fullback shedding tacklers. He passed a pair of armed guards at the door to the customs office with a pat on the back. With Ann and me following in a bewildered daze, he knocked on a door marked "Director" and, without waiting for an answer, strode inside.

"Come on," David urged us with a smile. "He won't bite."

The director greeted David warmly. He listened to David outline the situation and then yelled for an aide in the outer office to bring a file. He returned with an overflowing shoe box of papers.

"Good," the director said. "Now we analyze the situation properly." He began stirring through the papers.

"Did they keep your carnet too?" David asked.

We explained that we didn't actually have a carnet.

At this admission, David and the director exchanged troubled glances. The director put down the shoe box and, after the appropriate drawing-room-comedy pause, said in a grave voice, "You don't have a carnet?"

This occasioned a lecture by David on the impossibility of traveling through Africa without a carnet. When he was finished, the director leaped in. "This!" he exclaimed, "is why my people kept your documents!" He appeared delighted that there was some logical explanation. "Without a carnet, we have no guarantee that a visitor will not sell his car in our country on the black market." He stopped for a moment and cocked his head. "You would not do that, would you?"

He seemed disappointed at my ardent reassurances. Later, I realized he was interested in buying the car.

"It is very difficult," the director finished, throwing up his hands.

David thanked him and steered us out of the office. He walked between Ann and me with his arms on our shoulders and talked in a low, confidential voice, like a football coach on the sidelines just before a big game.

"That son-of-a-bitch, he wants your car! Bad springs and all. Your only hope is to get a letter from the U.S. embassy."

"What should it say?"

"That doesn't matter so much as having a letter on the embassy's stationery. And lots of stamps, it *must* have lots of stamps. These black bastards love stamps.

"Then you might have a chance at saving your car."

We rode in depressed silence back to CARE. "Good luck!" he yelled with a wave as he dropped us off.

The spring salesman in the fez was lying against his merchandise, sound asleep. We woke him up and drove the spring back to the market.

Tim Whitset understood the problem right away. "What you need," he said, smiling, "is a perfectly meaningless letter that impresses people. Official people."

We nodded enthusiastically.

"That," he said, "is something of a specialty of mine." He called in his assistant, a young African with an ironic smile.

"Silas, we need a letter. The usual sort of thing. Let's see . . ." Tim Whitset paused, running his finger back and forth over his upper lip. "Let's make this good. They like professors, so we'll make you a professor on a research project. Say from Yale?"

I nodded.

"Right. And Ann can be your research assistant. That should do it nicely."

Silas smiled shyly and retreated to the typewriter in his outer office.

"Now, what other problems can we solve?"

Tim Whitset worked for the U.S. embassy. A big man in his early thirties, he'd lived in Africa for over a decade and relished matching wits with the local bureaucracy. His office in the newly fortified embassy compound was, in essence, a large vault with a heavy combination lock on the door. From this windowless crypt, he launched his rescue missions in the complicated bureaucratic wars that raged through the Chadian government. On his desk, he had a souvenir of a more traditional war.

"It's a piece of a Libyan plane, actually," he responded to my question about the charred piece of twisted metal. "It was shot down a few months ago over town. Poor suckers flew all the way from Libya to drop a few bombs in a mud flat outside of town and then got blown to hell and back. A U.S. missile operated by the French. A true United Nations effort."

Silas returned brandishing a letter. *"Oui, patron,"* he announced with exaggerated formality, bowing deeply. Everyone laughed. "This should stick it to them," Silas said.

Whitset read the letter aloud, translating from the French:

To Whom It May Concern:

Dearest sirs, before you is Stuart P. Stevens, a famous and world-renowned scholar of the Greatness of African Culture, and his assistant, the highly respected Ann Bradley. Mr. Stevens is researching a book which is titled *Why Africa Is Better than Europe.* It is, of course, a very long book.

Please offer any assistance possible. He is traveling in a Toyota Land Cruiser, Cameroon registration BKC-289, in which he will return to Europe upon completion of his research.

When he finished, there were smiles all over the room. Silas bowed elaborately.

"Tell me," Tim Whitset asked, "do you like milk shakes?"

There are two great appeals to the Étoile du Chad restaurant: the milk shakes and the view from the rooftop bar. The combination propelled the Étoile to great popularity during the last bout of fighting in N'Djamena. Snipers could enjoy a fresh papaya shake while spotting targets across town. Elaborate patterns of automatic weapons fire decorated the walls.

While Ann, Tim and I sipped the delicious cool drinks, the N'Djamena vehicles of choice, Toyota pickups with machine-gun accessories, cruised the streets below like sharks. I mentioned to Tim, in an offhand way, that a similar truck had narrowly missed ramming me that afternoon. The comment drew a heavy frown.

"But they missed?" he asked.

I nodded. He relaxed.

"Was the driver wearing a red beret?"

I thought for a moment. "Yes, I think so."

"You're a lucky man," he said flatly. "The fellows in the red berets are Gourara. They belong to a tribe from the north. They live in caves, love to fight, speak a language nobody can understand and are *ab-so-lutely* wild. The Libyans are scared to death of 'em. They're right, too."

Tim explained that the Gouraras served as bodyguards to the president, who was also from the north. "They're quite a stabilizing force, in their own peculiar way. As long as they remain loyal to the president, the odds of a coup go way down. And despite their fierce reputation, I've always found them perfectly friendly. But you don't want to have an accident with any of them. Which is sometimes hard to avoid since they can't drive worth a damn."

"Yes."

"Any—I mean *any*—accident with a Gourara is an automatic four-million-franc fine. Automatic."

This was terrifying. The Land Cruiser cost only three million.

"The way I figure it," Tim explained, laughing but serious, "the best thing you can do after an accident is just throw the keys at 'em and run. It has to be cheaper."

Later that evening, David of Control Data dropped by the Étoile and insisted we join him at home for a drink. He lived in a brick house behind a high wall and locked gate that reminded me of a miniature U.S. embassy. Inside, the dim rooms were strewn with thick pillows and dark rugs. Expensive electronic gear glowed in each corner of the living room, and hidden speakers serenaded us with disco, an effect heightened by a lighted circular ball spinning from the ceiling in the best disco style. I felt as if I had walked into a Middle East bachelor pad.

We drank Johnny Walker scotch (sixty dollars a bottle at the market down the street) and talked about Hollywood films. At some point I noticed my mouth was full of blood. Going into the bathroom, I made faces and glared at my bared teeth; a steady flow of blood seeped from the gums. Somewhere I'd read this was a sign of a vitamin deficiency, which seemed highly likely considering my diet of canned ravioli and flat bread. I washed my mouth out with scotch and went back into the living room, where David and his wife tried to talk to each other in English. It was their only mutual language. His English was excellent, hers atrocious. The two appeared quite in love, which argues, I suppose, for the benefits of nonverbal communication.

We left at dawn and drove back to the Catholic mission. I realized it was Sunday when we passed the nuns walking across the mission courtyard to mass. I fell asleep to the pleasant sound of organ music.

That afternoon I drove the Cruiser around the corner from the mission to a vacant lot the size of a city block. From the piles of rubble and shattered bricks, I suspected that artillery or mortar shells had played a role in emptying the lot of buildings.

I had chosen the spot as a place I could change the engine oil without worrying about disposing of the old oil draining from the engine. As I stopped the car, raised the hood and started to work, a crowd quickly assembled. I took no notice of this at first; it seemed impossible in Africa not to draw an audience for even the most mundane of activities. One didn't think about it after a while.

But as I emerged from under the car where I'd been loosening the drain plug, I stared at the bodies and faces surrounding me. It was a nightmare vision. Everyone was deformed or mutilated. A teenager with a ghastly swollen face stood next to a young girl with teeth jutting through her upper lip. A one-legged boy with no fingers leaned on a large youth, perhaps twenty-five, with high, handsome cheekbones and no nose, just two holes punched in his face.

The hot oil dripped out of the car, spreading over the packed dirt like blood from a wound. I felt it burning against my leg.

I rushed through the final steps of the oil change. The crowd grew larger. Children fought over the empty oil cans.

When I drove away, hurrying to the sanctuary of the mission, the children were playing in the lake of dirty oil.

Chapter
Nineteen

The problem was the sand ladders. They kept digging into the deep drifts, causing the Land Cruiser to buck and snort. There was a certain irony to this as the sole reason one carried sand ladders was to *extricate* not impale.

The theory is that when you travel through the desert you should carry these huge, awkward things called sand ladders designed to go under a vehicle's wheels when stuck in the sand. "Drive up onto the sand ladders and use them as a short piece of artificial road to give the vehicle a run and sufficient momentum to get through more sand," advises the *Sahara Handbook,* warning, "To get out of a large stretch of soft sand it may be necessary to use the sand ladders several times."

The theory, I'll grant, is impressive. But as far as I was concerned, simply carrying the devices—or trying to carry them—created an instant crisis.

The *Handbook* features pictures of neatly rigged vehicles with sand ladders attached in ingenious manners. Bolting the long metal strips to the roof rack is the most common method. The ladders in the photos are handsome devices made of aluminum that, as one picture demonstrates, a woman can easily carry.

While I am willing, if begrudgingly, to admit that the photos are genuine, I promise that nothing of the sort can be had in N'Djamena. In fact, it took a massive search to locate the frustrating substitute we finally acquired. It was a big long steel plank intended for use with the semitrailers that ply, perilously, the desert routes. We acquired it from a truck driver who lived on the edge of town in a small mud brick hut with a courtyard. He had been using it quite effectively as a perch for roosting chickens ever since he acquired it from a Japanese relief organization that had abandoned N'Djamena during the last fighting.

It was a single, fifteen-foot-long piece of metal perforated with holes. We needed two smaller lengths.

"No problem," the truck driver exulted, "my brother will cut in half."

His brother was a junk dealer who worked out of a walled compound stacked with dead cars and various military vehicles punctured with violent holes. He examined the merchandise and announced that it would take an hour to cut. He also wanted a small fortune for the job.

"An hour?" I gasped. I was very hot and covered in chicken shit from wrestling with the plank. For days I had wandered N'Djamena trying to locate the essential items to cross Lake Chad: additional jerricans for water and fuel, tire tubes, a rear spring, food and, alas, a pair of sand ladders. I had begun to feel like an automotively obsessed Don Quixote.

Once he had payment in hand, the junk dealer sliced through the metal in less than five minutes. "Not so hard," he said, trying to muster his most convincing tone of surprise. I groaned, rolling over in my mind a phrase popular with the American embassy crowd: WAWA—West Africa Wins Again.

Figuring out how to transport the sand ladders was the next urgent problem. We decided to hang both sections from a single hook that juts from the front bumper of the Land Cruiser as a towing aid. The end result resembled a lethal battering ram, an effect I rather enjoyed. Unfortunately, as we learned that first morning out of N'Djamena, in practice it worked more like a scoop than a ram.

Contemplating Lake Chad, I'd always envisioned a flat expanse of deep sand, like the bottom of a dry pond. But the reality was a constantly shifting terrain of rolling sand hills. As the Cruiser crested one rise and started up the next, the sand ladder jammed into the ground. In essence we were digging up a large portion of Lake Chad. I thought of what our tracks must look like from the air, the trail of some wounded beast rolling through the sand.

After a morning of this, something had to be done. At the top of a rise, Ann, Bertrand and I dismounted. Bertrand took a look at the front of the Cruiser, shook his head and walked off to squat in the sand, his long white bou-bou draping on the ground. He smiled pleasantly but with an air that indicated fixing sand ladders was not in his job description. He was a guide.

Bertrand lived in a village on the far side of Lake Chad. He'd guided the Belgians across the lake to N'Djamena and now was returning home with us.

The economics of our arrangement baffled me. For the privilege of chauffeuring the amiable teenager back to his village, he wanted to charge us a staggering fee. The Belgians had encountered a similar situation when they employed Bertrand for the trip to N'Djamena.

It was a function of supply and demand. All travelers across Lake Chad passed through N'Guigmi, Bertrand's village. The guiding business was a local monopoly controlled by a union of sorts; the locals knew their services were essential for the inexperienced and that no guides were available other than those in N'Guigmi. All they had to do was stick together to demand a high price.

The Belgians were not loose with money. For two days they had sat in N'Guigmi refusing to pay the going rate (about three hundred dollars), threatening either to go it *sans* guide or to retreat the way they had come. And then they found Bertrand.

Actually, he found them. One morning he turned up at their camp on the edge of town to volunteer his services for only a "small" fee. Bertrand needed to go to N'Djamena to pick up a new identity card, having lost his old one. After hours of discussion over many cups of coffee, a deal was struck for Bertrand to guide them for a mere third of the normal fee. (Bertrand neglected to mention that his lack of an identity card meant that he would be harassed at each of the numerous checkpoints along the way, delaying the crossing several days.)

Having acquired his new papers in N'Djamena, Bertrand appeared at the mission and asked the Belgians if they would like to take him back home. They demurred but suggested he talk to Ann and me. We needed a guide and Bertrand wanted a ride home—it seemed a fair enough swap. But when I suggested to Bertrand that he should consider making the trip without a fee, he erupted into a pout that lasted two days. It was all a bit strange. Instead of making a simple arrangement with a teenager, I felt as if I were trying to coax Greta Garbo out of retirement.

Finally we came to terms and Bertrand became our guide—but not, apparently, a sand ladder repairman. He squatted and watched while Ann and I worked on the problem.

In N'Djamena, I had secured the metal planks to the bumper hook with a cable and padlock. The locking cable was one of the gadgets I'd brought from America and, as was the case with all my toys, I was inordinately proud of it. But what had seemed so clever in N'Djamena had been transformed by the desert into a mistake; sand clogged the lock, making it inoperable.

While struggling with the lock, the sand whipping into my eyes and mouth, a figure appeared on horseback. He—or she—was dressed in a flowing white robe, a brimmed straw hat and a scarf wrapped around the face, hiding all features. In other circumstances, the garb would have seemed fantastical but here I merely thought about how practical it was and envied the person for his or her superior protection from the elements. The figure waved and continued over a rise. A moment later I wondered if I'd imagined the scene.

By pouring water into the keyhole of the frozen lock, we eventually freed the cable and secured the sand ladders next to the Cruiser's grille. Bertrand rose, nodding his approval. We followed him back into the Cruiser.

When I turned the key, nothing happened. We got back out and raised the hood, trying to figure out whether it was a bad connection or faulty battery. We poked and pulled to no avail. Positioned at the crest of a small hill, I assumed it would be a simple matter to push the Cruiser down the slope, jump-starting the engine. But I failed to consider the weight of the fully loaded vehicle and the adhesive qualities of sand. With our hands, we dug the hot sand away from the wheels; we pushed, sweated, dug and pushed some more. Twice the Cruiser started to roll and twice, as we jumped in, it ground to a halt.

I began to think about how long we might have to wait until another vehicle chanced our way. Now I envied our visitor on horseback, not only for his clothes but for his more dependable transportation as well.

We dug and pushed again; this time when the car began to move, Ann leaped in while Bertrand and I pushed. Just as the hill began to bottom out, the engine fired.

"What did he say?" I asked Ann, who could vaguely understand Bertrand's twisted French. We were back in the Cruiser now, jolting over the sand.

"I think he said not to turn off the engine."

That night when we camped, we left the Cruiser idling contentedly. We were in a little grove of trees, scrub thorns that had grown up in the ten years or so since this section of the lake had lost its water. Above the low grumble of the Cruiser's diesel, voices floated across the sand. It would have been difficult to imagine a spot that appeared more isolated, but I had grown accustomed in Africa to the inevitable presence of others, however unlikely and surprising. It was a hard place to be alone.

The sky presented its usual spectacular display of stars. I had the aching exhaustion I'd come to expect on the road. Africa was turning me from an insomniac into a narcoleptic. Under me, the sand radiated a soothing heat. For a moment I ran through a list of nagging difficulties: the faltering battery and the electrical gremlins, the grinding sounds of the transmission in low gear, the scores of acacia thorns sticking from the tires that made them look like black porcupines with crew cuts, the questionable amount of fuel left in the tank and jerricans.

But I was happy, deeply happy, falling asleep in this strange place with a contentment I'd rarely known.

If one were looking to shoot a film at a location that epitomized a bedraggled, fly-ridden, godforsaken desert border station, Bol would do nicely. It was the last official town in Chad, though the actual border lay somewhere beyond at a point that once was the middle of Lake Chad.

The look of the crowd hanging around the customs house made it seem an evil place. A sullen bunch, they stared at us with bored disgust.

The customs office was a mud building surrounded by acacia trees that cast a thin shade over the tin roof. Ann went inside with our papers while I opened the hood of the Cruiser and fiddled with the battery and starter, still puzzled by its intermittent response. A tall man with tribal scars inquired as to the problem and volunteered his services. Perhaps, I thought, I was wrong about this place. Maybe it was not so bad.

The volunteer mechanic requested tools, and I brought out the odd-fitting nonmetric set I'd stolen from Lucien. He grunted and went to work with a set of pliers. After a few minutes of messing about, he rose and said, simply, "Fifty thousand."

"I'm sorry?" I asked, not understanding.

"Fifty thousand CFA to fix the car."

That was almost two hundred dollars. I wanted to laugh but felt somehow that wasn't the prudent response. My suggestion of an alternative, say ten dollars, was met with a sudden burst of anger. He threw the pliers into the dirt and stormed away to pace in front of the customs office. Low-voiced invectives flew back and forth between him and his friends.

The outburst caught me by surprise. Almost without exception, the Africans I'd met had a gentle manner that usually left me feeling loud and insistent. Often preposterous sums of money were demanded but only a few times had anyone responded with true anger when I'd pushed a more reasonable price.

This did not seem like the best place to incur hostility. I'd heard stories of travelers stranded at borders for days, even weeks. It was a fear Ann accelerated when she emerged fuming from the customs office.

"We have to wait. The commandant"—she rolled the title around with relish—"has left for the day. He might be back tomorrow. He might not."

The commandant, Ann explained, and *only* the commandant could stamp our passports. I looked over at the would-be mechanic and his friends. It was a smug bunch.

"Look," I said, with some heat, "what you have to do is go back inside and tell them that we must send a message to the U.S. embassy explaining that we will be late for our meeting in N'Guigmi because the commandant will not stamp our passports. Show him Tim Whitset's letter."

This, of course, was a lie. It was the sort of vague threat I often bandied about with officials. "I'll need to contact the embassy . . ." To date, no one had seemed to care in the least.

Ann groaned. "Look around," I suggested, "and think about spending the next week here."

Glumly she tramped back inside the office.

When I turned to work more on the car, I had this sudden paranoid rush that the thwarted mechanic had sabotaged the machine. I stared at the hot, sand-encrusted engine, wondering if those loose wires had dangled as uselessly this morning.

Ann returned from the customs hut with a smiling official in a long white robe. He wore tennis shoes and carried a plastic briefcase.

"We go to the commandant," the man said blithely.

"It worked," Ann whispered as she walked around to get into the car.

"We should help our American friends," the official pronounced. "You are working for the embassy. You are my friends."

The magic letter had worked again. I knew Tim Whitset,

sitting in his vault-office plotting against the African bureaucracy, would be chuckling.

"I'm not sure I'd get in the car just yet," I warned, as Ann and the official began to squeeze into the front seat.

"Why?"

I turned the key and pushed the starter. Silence.

"Those guys didn't fix it?" Ann asked, gesturing toward the gloating mechanic.

"We have to talk about that," I answered dryly.

Fortunately the customs office sat on a slight hill. We got out and pushed. Ann stood by the open driver's door while the official and I worked from the rear, our feet digging into the hot sand. The engine fired suddenly, lurching forward, leaving the officer and me sprawled in the sand.

"We are friends," the official repeated with only a slight waver. We looked at each other and nodded while picking acacia thorns out of our palms. "We are friends."

Bol has few streets; all are deep sand, affording a natural advantage to the small donkeys that move people and goods at a pace suited to the rhythms of Bol life. We passed the skeleton of a Land Rover, its aluminum frame, stripped by the sand and wind of all paint, gleaming in the sun. The houses were mud brick, jammed one against the other.

We found the commandant in a dark room strewn with rugs sitting cross-legged like a pasha. A veiled woman moved through the rear of the two-room house.

The commandant was a shrewd man. As our escort from customs explained our story, stressing that we were traveling on official United States embassy business and had an important meeting to attend in N'Guigmi, the commandant nodded with the hint of a smile. It was not, I believe, my imagination that his eyes lingered over my attire before he asked in a quiet voice, "You travel on official business?"

Ann and I both were filthy. I wore torn red shorts and an Ole Miss tee shirt encrusted with sweat and sand. My knees, jutting noticeably in the squatting position I'd assumed, bled from scores of sand scrapes. Swirls of grease decorated my face like war paint; my hands were mostly black.

"This meeting in N'Guigmi. Tell me more about this meeting. Your letter does not mention a meeting."

We were a bit of amusement for the commandant. Two oddball Americans washed up to relieve the tedium of a fiery afternoon. He wanted us to understand that he was no backwater fool to be awed by a thin piece of paper no matter how many seals or signatures shouted for attention.

In the end, reluctantly, he let us go, sorry to see the finish of such sport. From a little wooden box, he produced a metal seal and stamped our passports, adding under his name an admirably ironic note: "Important visitors."

Driving back to the customs post, where, not surprisingly, there was more stamping and signing to be done, the official asked if we needed fuel. In the middle of Lake Chad, the answer to such a question is invariably yes.

"You sell fuel as well as do customs duty," Ann teased. With the commandant's signature in hand, we were in a good mood.

He looked confused. "I have no customs duties," he answered.

Why, I asked, was he at the customs office when we arrived?

"It is very cool with the shade of the trees. And I meet friends there. Like my American friends!"

We bought the fuel from fifty-gallon drums on the back of an ancient Land Cruiser pickup. It was bootlegged fuel from Nigeria, dyed a wine red and speckled with clumps of dirt and thorns. I strained it through a metal strainer and an old baseball hat. The price, at least, was reasonable.

"Do you stay with the Italians tonight?" the customs official/fuel salesman asked us.

Ann and I looked at each other. Italians? There were Italians in Bol?

"There are many Italians," he answered. "I will show you.

I am also a guide," he added, casting a jealous eye at Bertrand, who seemed unfazed by the potential competition.

There were moments traveling with Ann when I expended great energy contemplating exotic ways to do away with her. (There were more times—and for infinitely better reasons I'm sure—when she pursued similar lines of thought about me.) But often she proved invaluable, and I wouldn't have traded her for a carload of trilingual mechanics.

Meeting the Italians was one such moment.

Our new guide, bouncing happily on the seat between Ann and me, directed us to a large compound on the edge of Bol. It looked like a military base: a collection of buildings behind a high hurricane fence topped with barbed wire. Some of the buildings rose two and three stories, while others were like Quonset huts, lined barracks-style in a row. A swamp of sorts lay to the side of the installation, a remnant of the disappearing waters of Lake Chad. A sign read, "Calabrase Construction."

Enhancing the military effect, two Africans stood watch over the locked gates. Our guide, having delivered us here, did not seem to know what to do next. I stopped the Cruiser and Ann approached the guards.

Their surprise was understandable: a white woman appearing from the desert? A discussion ensued. I wondered what language they were using: French? Italian? English? Eventually one guard left, leaving Ann standing at the gate: a small figure in dirty khaki pants and a Ralph Lauren shirt torn at the sleeves.

The guard returned with a white man who looked to be about fifty. He radiated cleanliness—clean in a way I had forgotten was possible. He wore pressed shorts and a white shirt, a neat, smiling man, deeply tanned, with a trim goatee. He reminded me of the sort of fellow one saw having lunch in Saint-Tropez with a bottle of cool white wine, a fresh salade Niçoise and several pretty women; always the pretty women.

When Ann began talking the man stopped dead in his path and then rushed forward, hugging her. Inside the steaming Cruiser, Bertrand and our new guide looked at me, as if I were expected to explain. After more hugs, Ann started to walk inside the compound, led by the neat figure in pressed shorts. They had gone several yards when Ann, as if suddenly remembering us, jogged back to the Cruiser.

"You can come in now," she said, making it sound as if we were being invited into her house.

"You're sure?" I asked, trying to muster all my sarcasm.

"Sure. Fernando says it's fine."

"Fernando," I said flatly.

Fernando ran the Calabrase Construction complex. The Italians were in Bol building roads on a United Nations grant. Why someone thought it was a good idea to build roads in the middle of Lake Chad escaped my logical powers. There seemed to me two problematic questions. One: what happens if water returns? (I suppose the answer was fairly simple: the roads would be underwater.) And two: once constructed, who would use the roads? There were less than a dozen vehicles for two hundred miles in either direction.

But as far as I was concerned, it was a stroke of good fortune that someone at the UN was troubled by the state of local roads in the middle of Lake Chad. And that Calabrase Construction had been selected to improve the situation.

They loved Ann. That an attractive woman (albeit a bit dirty) speaking Italian had appeared in their midst must have seemed like a miracle, and the men—there were only men—responded like pilgrims blessed with a personal appearance by the Virgin Mary: reverential, thankful, gracious to the extreme. I mostly trailed around in Ann's wake enjoying the benefits.

When we explained our troubles starting the Cruiser, Fernando Diamond grew upset. "Oh, this is terrible," he said. "My best electrical mechanic is out in the field and this sounds like an electrical problem."

Ann and I exchanged glances. The luxury of choosing among

mechanics with various specialties was like a dream from another life. It had, after all, been less than an hour since I was staring down at my engine with an old pair of pliers, praying for inspiration. "Electrical mechanic?" I asked. "You have other mechanics?"

He nodded vigorously. "We have many mechanics. Come, I will show you."

We followed him to one of the large metal structures. Inside was a replica of the CARE garages in N'Djamena: elaborate work stations with hydraulic hoists, tools galore, spare tires. We gawked.

For the rest of the afternoon, mechanics swarmed over the Land Cruiser. I watched, hoping to learn as much as I could. Ann wandered off, returning later with Perrier and cheese. At the time I was cleaning out the air filter caked with four or five inches of fine-grained sand.

"Would you like some lemon with this?" she asked, holding up a glass of Perrier.

An African mechanic who radiated competence removed the starter and disassembled it, cleaning each part in an oil bath. He made clucking sounds through his teeth as he worked.

"These springs are very poor." Fernando pointed to the Cruiser's rear springs.

"Yes."

"I wish we had some for you. But this model of Land Cruiser we don't use. You go across Lake Chad now, yes?"

We explained our route.

He shrugged. "Let us pray. But come now, first you take a hot shower and then a little espresso and a beer, then we have a real Italian meal. A big meal."

All of those things happened. Each was exquisite, but perhaps the shower emerged triumphant in the competition of the senses. The purifying event took place in Fernando's house, a metal three-room structure placed, as befitted his position, at the head of the row of sleeping accommodations. Most of the workers had roommates, but Fernando had the house to himself. The walls were covered with posters of Italy and Vargas drawings of pinup girls. Two black women, servants, I presumed, sat quietly in their veils, eyeing us with amusement. (It is an appealing side effect of wearing veils that it draws attention to a woman's eyes, which, in turn, appear uniformly more animated, as if in compensation for the masked features.)

One by one, including Bertrand, we took showers. By the time we finished, the bathroom resembled the site of a hotly contested mud pie war; crumpled towels once white, now a deep sienna, littered the floor. Fernando's servant took one look and giggled. Ann and I tried as best we could to clean up. It helped—a little.

Before dinner, we stopped for an espresso in the prefab building next to the prefab dining room. Though constructed like a house trailer, inside it had the feel of a working-class suburb of Milano. Freshly showered from their day in the desert, the sunburned men sat drinking beer or espresso from one of the two machines.

They were large men who talked about sports and debated fiercely the choice of movies for the night. (The videocassette player has permanently altered the Bol social scene.)

A friend of Fernando's named Marcus escorted us to the bar. Marcus's nickname was Little Valentino, a tribute to his good looks and elegant clothes. Marcus was an accountant, with the smooth hands of an office worker. There were others like him, the front office executives of Calabrase Construction. Though they looked and talked like Florentine intelligentsia, Marcus and his friends mixed easily with the other workers. The conditions of employment in Bol blurred management and labor lines; everyone worked fourteen hours a day, ate the same food at the same time, had equal say in the vociferous arguments over the evening's film selections. (Marcus and friends wanted Bertolucci's *The Spider's Stratagem;* others lobbied for *Rambo III.*)

No one I met at Calabrase complained. Their salaries were triple what they would have been in Italy and, like the Frenchmen I'd met in the CAR, the Italians welcomed their African posting as a way to escape the "sameness" of European life. As Marcus put it, "Last year, after two years in West Africa, I went back home to work. At first it was wonderful: movies, ice cream, telephones. I saw my family every day. But after six months, it was *sooo* boring." Marcus sat upright in a rigid position. "Every morning, get in the car. Fight the traffic, work, come home."

As we walked to dinner, we watched the setting sun shoot red streaks across the shallow waters of Lake Chad. "Our Olympic pool," Marcus said. It was not a beautiful scene in any traditional sense—a muddy patch of water surrounded by scrub grass and thorn trees—but it had a quirky, rough appeal.

"I missed this," Marcus said after a moment.

"But not the mosquitoes," a friend laughed. They came off the lake like waves of suicide planes.

It was Fernando who reminded us it was Thanksgiving. He mentioned it in an offhand way while we stood at the head of the long buffet marveling at the pasta, the veal, the pastries. "An untraditional Thanksgiving, no?" he said. Ann and I looked at each other, not understanding what he meant, and then we both looked up at a wall calendar featuring a nude girl riding a tractor. He was right, it was Thanksgiving.

I gorged myself despite a stomach gone queasy for days. Later, I vomited wildly in the bathroom, while Marcus and his friends waited for me in their Toyota Hi-Lux pickups. We drove, whooping and hollering like teenagers heading home from a football game, to a modern ranch-style house not far from the compound. The Italians insisted Ann knock on the door, and when an attractive Italian came to the door and saw her, he gaped and stuttered. Everyone thought this very funny and Marcus and his friends erupted from the shadows in laughter.

The Italian living in the ranch house was a consultant and hence exempt from the communal living of Calabrase Construction. He had a gelato machine, and we sat eating ice cream and talked about the comparable prices of apartments in New York and Rome.

We left Bol the next morning at dawn.

Chapter
Twenty

The German flagged us down. He stood in the middle of the sandy path waving a white cloth. Dressed totally in black, with high boots fitted with glinting silver studs, he was an apocalyptic vision.

"Hello!" The German spoke with a heavy accent in guide-book phrases. "Good day."

We got out of the Cruiser and shook hands. (I was careful not to turn off the engine; despite the Italians' efforts, I was terrified of being stuck with a dead engine in Lake Chad.)

The German was sunburned a deep brown, with blisters on his forehead and nose, but he lacked the swollen lips or black tongue of the seriously dehydrated. Nor did he seem overly desperate. "We have a bit of a problem, actually," he said in a voice that seemed far too chipper for the circumstances.

"We?"

He gestured over a small sand rise. About a hundred yards away, three figures waved weakly. Next to them sat a vehicle unlike any I'd seen.

"What's that?" I asked.

"Ahh." The German nodded. "That's our problem. A bit of a sticky wicker, actually."

He looked quite proud of the phrase.

"Wicker?" Ann asked.

"Tell me," I said, as we trudged over the sand to his friends, "did you learn English in England?"

He had, he explained, while playing guitar for a heavy-metal band in London. "Early Death," he said. "That was the name of our group—Early Death. Perhaps you have heard of us? We made a record."

Further discussion of his career with Early Death was forestalled by our arrival at his vehicle. Closer inspection revealed it to be a Citroen Deux Chevaux; though it was one of the most popular and distinctive cars in France, this particular unit had been altered beyond recognition. Butchered would probably be a better word.

"The engine is buggered, so we push it. To make it lighter, we cut off the roof."

It looked as if some giant had attacked the car with a can opener. The top was sheared off, leaving jagged edges. Other parts were missing as well: the bumpers, the doors.

"How long have you pushed this thing?" Ann asked after we had gaped for an appropriately respectful period.

"Four days."

"Four days?" I thought about that for a while. The temperature was over a hundred degrees, according to the little thermometer I had in the Cruiser.

"Sometimes the engine works, but not so often."

I finally asked the obvious. "Why don't you just leave it?"

"We would like to fix it and continue with our safari." He used the word unironically. "Is there a garage in Bol?"

We told him about the Italians, and left them with refilled water cans. As we walked back to the Cruiser, they argued about whose turn it was to push and whose to drive. We didn't stay to find out.

While passing through England on my way to Africa, I had spent an afternoon on the Land Rover test-driving course with a demonstration driver. We bounced up and down imitation mountains, wallowed through mock jungles and forded a few ferocious drainage ditches. The main skill I was aiming to develop, however, driving through sand, was the one hazard the course lacked.

"Sand?" my jovial instructor had asked. "I'm afraid we don't have a grain of that stuff. But don't worry," he went on to reassure me, "you handle sand just like driving over a big patch of English meadow after a hard rain. Understand?"

I didn't in the least, but after a long discussion over a few pints later that day, I began to get a vague glimpse of what he was implying: sand, like wet turf, is soft; it requires a firm, steady acceleration to avoid bogging down; shifting gears must be done quickly or the car will lose momentum and slow to a wheel-spinning halt.

Of course what made at least a little sense in the warmth and comfort of the Spotted Calf pub became instantly irrelevant in the wilds of Lake Chad. The sand changed in texture and depth at uneven, unannounced intervals. Deep holes full of a fine gray powder jolted the car, the dust exploding like a land mine.

Keeping the windows closed was the obvious way to keep the sand and dust out of the car, but in hundred-plus degrees, that turned the interior into a death zone. Cleverly, Bertrand wrapped a fold of his white robe around his head, turning it into a veil. Ann and I followed suit, tying strips of a tee shirt disintegrating from battery acid around our mouths. The fumes lent a hallucinogenic touch to the afternoon.

Our progress was not improved by the Cruiser's refusal to stay in four-wheel drive. When we hit a stretch of deep sand, the gear knob shuddered forward from four- to two-wheel drive. This instantly threatened all forward motion. I would grab for the stubby gear knob, cursing as the car lunged sideways. This was Bertrand's cue to jump up from the back seat and try to grab either the shifter or the steering wheel. He also cursed, so that a lot of noise bounced around the car. With both of us flailing about, our mutual ineffectiveness was guaranteed. Eventually Ann would intervene, pulling the gear back into four-wheel drive just as the wheels began to spin futilely in the loose sand.

"Can't you just hold that thing in place?" I asked.

"Hold it in place? All day?"

"Well . . ." (Yes! I wanted to scream.)

"It takes two hands to keep it from jumping out."

"Well . . ."

"Are you crazy?!"

Faced with the prospect of fighting a rebellious gearshift across Africa, Ann evolved a better solution. She took a belt and looped it around the gear knob, securing it to the seat post. The tension held the gear in four-wheel drive, though it quivered and groaned as if in seizure.

Had someone told me that driving a vehicle was exhausting, terrifically hard work, I would have scoffed. Race car driving was something I viewed as an endeavor for failed models, and the "sport" of driving jeeps through rough terrain seemed to be the sort of endeavor with special appeal for those athletes who can't touch their toes.

But banging across Lake Chad beat me black and blue. The day we left the Italians at Bol we drove ten hours straight and covered no more than twenty-five miles. The worst stretch was a range of undulating sand hills not large enough to be called dunes but sufficiently steep that driving straight up was impossible. We traversed sideways, the Cruiser slipping downward one foot for every two we moved forward. Momentum was the key: once stopped, the likelihood of moving again without a massive amount of digging or a tow was remote to impossible. I tried to skirt the edge of the bowls formed by the rolling hills, while gravity and loose sand conspired to suck us down as if into a whirlpool.

Our Michelin map showed no villages in Lake Chad. (This made a certain amount of sense, I suppose, as, according to the map, the entire area was underwater.) The lack of information created an aura, however false, of legitimate exploration. Though Bertrand had made the journey before, he was vague in the extreme about directions and gave every impression that he was never quite sure where we were. In truth, I think he had only made the trip once or twice. While the literature of the desert is filled with stories of tribesmen who always know their precise location in a markless world of sand, Bertrand was more of an urban product, clearly homesick for the familiar comforts of his village.

All of this made our arrival at any village, however tiny, an occasion of genuine surprise, mixed with a dose of relief. Our pleasure at the unexpected break in the monotony was tempered by the potential problems and by the inevitable demands of the resident military and/or police. The officials were like the weather in a locale with a more volatile climate: unpredictable, often annoying, but inescapable.

Complicating our dealings with the authorities was our uncertainty over which country we were in, Chad or Niger. Bol was the last official town in Chad, but the actual border lay at some unmarked point in what had been the middle of the lake.

This became a significant difficulty late in the afternoon of the first day we left Bol. As we topped the rise of a hill and began to slip down the other side, we spotted a tiny village. Drawing closer, a figure in shorts and a tattered khaki shirt ran toward us, gesturing wildly. He carried a rifle and waved it up and down as he stepped into our path.

He was clearly excited by our arrival. Panting from his exertions, he stuck his head into the open window of the Cruiser and began to talk rapidly in a French I had no chance of understanding.

"He wants help with something . . . ," Ann pieced together after he had repeated himself several times. He kept using a word that sounded like "milk."

"Milk from the bosom?" Ann asked him. She thought perhaps there was a child in need of milk.

The man blushed. No, no, no, he exclaimed, and motioned for us to drive forward into the village. He sat down on the hood of the Cruiser like a bodyguard. A dozen children ran beside the car.

He signaled us to stop in front of an acacia tree in the center of the town. Twenty yards of sand stretched between two rows of white houses. We followed the short man with the gun into an open shed. "Milk," the man said, and gestured.

Before us was a granary press powered by a donkey. Several burlap sacks of grain lay half-opened in the sand.

"Millet," Ann said. "That's what he's saying."

The man was pleased we finally understood. He motioned for Bertrand to help carry a mammoth sack of grain toward the Land Cruiser. "Let's talk about this," I interrupted.

In the wide expanse of sand that served as the main street for this unnamed town, we conferred with the soldier. (He quickly explained that he was in the army. When we asked him which army—unsure, as we were, whether we were in Chad or Niger—he seemed hurt, as if we had insulted him. We apologized profusely. I have a rule always to apologize to people with guns.)

The soldier wanted us to carry the grain, all four sacks, to the next army outpost near the actual frontier with Niger. He wanted us to take him along as well.

This was a problem. With the extra water and fuel we carried, our poor rear springs looked like inverted U's. I expected them to break at any moment and had been contemplating different ways I might repair the damage. (As an indication of my mechanical expertise, I intended to tie the leaves of the spring together with rope. Later, when I mentioned this repair concept to a Toyota mechanic in England, he literally fell out of his chair laughing.)

Even if we could have fit all the bulging sacks into the Cruiser (which we couldn't), the added weight would have amounted to several hundred pounds. I had no doubt this would have sealed the fate of our springs.

Ann explained to him our concerns about weight. She pointed to the springs. He seemed to understand her French, at least enough to get the point.

He laughed.

I can't blame him, really. Though tired and beat up around the edges, the Cruiser was a technological marvel in a world where camels and donkeys were still the accepted mode of transport.

When the soldier finished laughing, he went back to loading the grain sacks. Bertrand looked at me imploringly as the big sack filled the space where he'd been sitting.

I stepped forward and put my hand on the sack in the soldier's arm. He put the grain down and started to get into the seat. I shook my head and held the door closed.

He stared at me incredulously. I was filled with a sudden sense of guilt. I knew he couldn't understand why I didn't want him along.

The soldier gestured with his gun at the car. Sweat poured off his face.

A crowd began to gather. Surely everyone in the village was watching. I was glad. I wanted witnesses.

Ann asked him where we should take the two sacks of grain, whom we should give them to. The soldier began talking very loudly. Neither Ann nor I could understand him.

Bertrand spoke in a soft voice: We take the grain to the next army post, he said, we give it to the commander.

The soldier yelled louder as we climbed back into the car to leave. Bertrand squeezed in on top of a grain sack, smiling nervously. I slipped the car in gear; for a moment it seemed that we would be stuck, the wheels slipping in the sand. Some of the children hanging on to the car pushed us forward. The soldier waved his gun.

We emerged from Lake Chad on the edges of N'Guigmi, Bertrand's hometown. Wallowing out of a sand pit, we found ourselves unexpectedly on a smooth strip of asphalt. *"Bonne route!"* Bertrand exclaimed proudly.

It was more than a good route, it was extraordinary, a road the likes of which I'd never seen in Africa: smooth and wide and pothole free. Bertrand beamed.

"What's that?" Ann asked, pointing to a tall, squat structure with an unlikely high-tech look. Radar dishes sprouted from the roof.

"What's that noise?" I asked. A roaring sound rose above the usual deafening rumble of the Cruiser's diesel engine.

The roar grew louder. The air quivered. I slammed on the brakes.

A uniformed soldier rushed out of the building waving his arms.

First we saw the shadow, dark and ominous. And then we saw the plane, low enough that we all ducked.

It was about this time that I realized we were on an airstrip!

"Bonne route!" Bertrand confirmed from the crouching position we'd all assumed.

The plane, an old prop trainer painted in desert camouflage, circled back around for another pass as I hurried the Land Cruiser off the tarmac onto the sand streets of N'Guigmi. Ann suggested that I might want to lend my spotlight to the control tower for night landings.

It was a largish town, its size increased in perception, no doubt, by the emptiness of our days crossing Lake Chad. Bertrand appeared to know everyone. He greeted them regally through the back window with a half wave, rather like Queen Elizabeth.

We drove, of course, directly to the gendarmerie. We were conditioned so that it would have felt odd not to report immediately to the higher authorities.

The police station was a large room with signs of less tranquil times. Bullet holes danced across the entranceway; a large whip hung from the wall behind the single desk. The ceilings were high, the roof straw. Persistent flies clogged the air.

Though there was unanimous agreement our passports must be stamped, confusion reigned as to the exact stamp. A row of sundry stamps lined the desktop. The officer behind the desk examined each, pondering their use. Finally he chose not to use any stamp but rather to write a short paragraph in our passports. It read: "This person came from Lake Chad. I do not know where to travel they go. They have done nothing wrong."

I thought the last bit quite an unprompted recommendation.

The officer followed us back to the Cruiser holding Bertrand's hand. It was the tender gesture of a relative (though they were not related) welcoming a young wanderer home from a dangerous journey. N'Guigmi might look like the bleak end of the world, but I could understand why Bertrand missed it when away.

Chapter
Twenty-one

Africa does odd things to one's sense of language, to the very meaning of words. Take a simple declarative sentence like "You must buy insurance."

This is a straightforward statement with little room for ambiguity. I understand the meaning of this phrase. I have bought insurance many times. Buying insurance is a skill I have mastered.

At least, I thought I had. But Africa has a way of rearranging the known and the unknown.

The insurance we'd bought in Yaoundé had long expired. This was cause for little concern bouncing across Lake Chad, but Niger, we were learning, was a strict country. Niger had more cars than Chad. Niger even had a paved road.

It stretched across the bottom of the country from the border of Lake Chad to Niamey, the capital, some 1,200 kilometers away. We wanted to go to Niamey, or, more precisely, we wanted to travel *through* Niamey on our way to Mali and Timbuktu. From Niamey on, the route paralleled the banks of the River Niger, one of the great waterways of the world, a strip of life in a land of sand, the Nile of West Africa. I am not one easily swayed by the romance of place names, but these were destinations to rattle the imagination, ones that even on a hot day full of officials and flies could set one to dreaming.

Niger, though, was a security-mad country with roadblocks and police checks every twenty or thirty miles. The routine of paranoia had been accelerated by a coup a few days earlier in neighboring Burkina Faso. Like virtually every West African leader, the president of Niger had catapulted himself to power in a similar coup and no doubt viewed the events in Burkina Faso as intimations of his own mortality. (The Burkina Faso president, an exceptionally charismatic guitar-playing young leader, was gunned down in his residence, as is the custom.)

All of this meant it was impossible to travel a mile in Niger without immaculately ordered papers, including insurance. There was no insurance office in N'Guigmi but Diffa, fifty miles down the road, was reputed to have one. The lack of a facility to buy insurance did not impress the military officers manning the road-blocks in N'Guigmi. The law was quite clear, they maintained with steadfast logic: Insurance is required to drive any vehicle. Without insurance, one doesn't drive. That there was no opportunity to buy insurance did not affect the law.

For a long time, it appeared we would be forced to leave the Cruiser and hitchhike to Diffa, buy insurance, then hitch back to N'Guigmi. Finally, after a serious bout of tea drinking and numerous toasts to the friendship between the Nigerois and American peoples, we were allowed to drive to Diffa. (Our gifts of a calculator and cassette tapes of Rockin' Dopsie and the Zydeco Twisters, albeit half-melted by the sun, were considered an apt display of this friendship on our part.)

It wasn't until we got to Diffa, still chortling over the smooth black road, that we realized it was Saturday afternoon and all offices were closed until Monday. We were informed of this by the police commissioner when we reported, as required, for the ritual passport stamping. (So far in my one afternoon in Niger, my passport had been stamped four times and the day was far from done.) The commissioner took a particular interest in our situation when we mistakenly drove into his residential compound thinking it was the police station. The guards, who had been asleep, awoke to find a strange Land Cruiser bearing down on their boss's house and assumed, not unreasonably, that white mercenaries had arrived. (Rumors abounded, falsely, that hired guns had aided the rebel forces in Burkina Faso.) Several shots were fired into the air, waking the commissioner, who was asleep on his porch in a hammock. I braked.

Rather than angry, the official, a good-natured sort, acted embarrassed that we had caught him in an unguarded (psychologically, at any rate) moment. We followed him next door to his jail/office. A soldier slept on a metal bedframe in the dirt yard; that he had not wakened at the sound of gunfire was remarkable, though his blaring radio may have masked the noise. His commander reached down and tickled the man's bare foot, laughing softly to himself.

His jail was a truly repulsive place, stinking of human and animal excrement. For some reason, a large number of donkey saddles were stacked in the airless cell. As it was difficult to imagine what fiendish deed the saddles could have perpetrated to merit imprisonment, I concluded that they were of sufficient value to require their locked safekeeping. After writing a short essay in our passports (he had lost his stamp), the commissioner gave us detailed directions to the insurance office. We asked if it was open. He answered that it probably wasn't but we might as well try as there was nothing else to do in town and we couldn't leave without the insurance. He was a most logical man.

Though in a town the size of Diffa it might seem impossible to get lost, we managed it quite nicely. Eventually, the proprietor of the main street's bread stand (thirty cents a loaf for delicious, unrisen loafs) grew tired of watching us drive back and forth and announced he would accompany us to the insurance office. There was a time when I might have demurred, thinking it ridiculous to take a man away from his work simply to locate a business in a town with the population of my high school. I had learned in Africa, however, to welcome aid in any form.

Of course, as always there was the question of communication. The man spoke French but in a style not normally associated with that language. When he directed us down an alley to a small house sitting behind a mud wall, we assumed he had misunderstood. Ann repeated that we needed to buy insurance. He nodded vigorously and motioned for us to follow him.

In the courtyard of the house, a powerfully built African faced east preparing for prayer. He washed his feet and hands three times, then knelt on a flowered prayer rug. We waited.

Some ten minutes later, prayers completed, the man introduced himself as the local insurance agent. Elaborate tribal scars decorated his face. The four of us squeezed into the front seat of the Land Cruiser and drove to the agent's office, stopping for a snack of bread along the way.

The insurance office was a fortresslike affair with metal gates and barred windows. The office was empty save for a bare desk, three chairs and a sign that read, "Our service is the Umbrella of your sleep." We purchased impressive insurance documents decorated with an umbrella logo. The transaction complete, we drove back to the bread stand and had a long conversation about soccer.

It was, I concluded, a most pleasant way to do business.

The Peace Corps workers talked about the big party next weekend. People were coming from all over West Africa. "Man, let me tell you, when PCVs get together, it's wild."

PCVs, they explained, were Peace Corps volunteers, not, as I supposed, a type of plastic pipe.

"We're like an extended family," the girl said.

"A wild extended family?" I asked.

When I thought of extended families I pictured dinner on the ground and ancient aunts who gave tiny socks for Christmas gifts.

The meeting with the PCVs was unexpected. We'd arrived in Zinder looking for fuel. The only gas station had no supplies but, not surprisingly, a man emerged eager to direct us to a cache of black-market diesel. But first, he insisted, we should eat something. (We had, I suspect, taken on a permanently hungry look.) He would take us to Zinder's best restaurant.

In a little courtyard outside a collapsing mud hut, we met the PCVs and enjoyed a feast: mashed potatoes and steak with Fanta orange drink. Consuming the minibanquet was something of a gymnastic challenge: the thick blanket of flies required constantly moving one hand over the plate while eating with the other.

The three Peace Corps workers, one female, two male, had the serious self-involvement of college freshmen. When I asked their opinion of the Peace Corps, they responded with a report on how the organization treated *them:* the pay, the vacations. When I pressed on with questions about the purpose of the Corps and its cost, the girl rose up in defense: "It costs a lot less than a few tanks!"

There was something about this I liked. While they buzzed with clichés, I thought about all the fresh college graduates I knew scrambling for a place on Wall Street or in the big law firms. That was a cliché as well but of a less interesting stripe than the Peace Corps compulsion to Save the Natives.

The history of white influence in Zinder was hardly illustrious. In the nineteenth century it was the southern way station for the trans-Saharan slave caravans. Over three thousand slaves a year tramped through on their way to be exchanged for guns and European goods. But while white traders cashed in on "Africa's black bullion," the institution of slavery was quite indigenous. "It is exceedingly painful to live in a place like Zinder, where almost every householder has a chained slave," wrote a British traveler in 1851. "The poor fellows (men and boys) cannot walk, from the manner in which the irons are put on, and when they move they are obliged to do so in little jumps." John Richardson's conclusion was "that only foreign conquest by a power like Great Britain, or France can really extirpate slavery from Africa."

The French conquered Niger at the turn of the century and made Zinder the capital until 1926, when it was moved to Niamey, a more convenient location on the River Niger. While slavery did fade, the violence of the French conquest rivaled that of the slavers. In one raid in a village near Zinder, a French commander slaughtered 150 women and children in reprisal for the deaths of two of his men. Many of the children were hung from trees, until there were no more trees and the remaining bodies were burned along with the village huts.

It took three days to reach Niamey. We measured distance traveled not in miles but police roadblocks passed. What would have seemed remarkable in our normal lives assumed the regularity of a Holiday Inn. There was always a barrier of sorts and a small hut with mattresses or bedframes out front. Some soldiers slept; others asked for papers. Off to the side, there were prayer rugs of bright plastic laid out next to a little water jug for the ritual washing of the hands and feet. Usually flags hung from a tottering post; the flags never made it all the way to the top, as if they had run out of energy on their climb upward.

The roadblocks created free enterprise zones manned by aggressive peddlers of every description. They swarmed around the car offering canned goods (usually bearing the label of a relief organization; the spaghetti "Donated by the Dutch People" was outstanding), Elephant Power powdered soap, baby formula (also donated), cheap flashlights and Bic pens. By the standards of Chad and Cameroon, the variety of goods, if not the quality, was overwhelming. Like starved refugees (a description that was becoming less metaphor and more reality) Ann and I stocked up on all essentials. The only taste treats we declined were the swarming masses of termite larvae proffered like a holy offering in great bowls. The first time a bowl was stuck under Ann's nose and the peddler reached in for a handful of squirming white creatures, she blanched, a rare reaction from a woman with the admirable ability to eat just about anything.

Each evening we found a campsite in the low hills of dry dirt. It was a highlight of the day, choosing a site, and though there was little variation from one spot to another, we discussed the choices at great length.

"Over there, by that thorn tree—"

"No, too many thorns. How about on top of the hill?"

"Too windy."

"That's good, keeps the flies off . . ."

On the paved road one could feel as if civilization were, if not at hand, certainly lurking nearby; but five hundred yards off the road, it was the same Africa we'd known in Chad and northern Cameroon, a place of a few acacia trees and fewer people, of dirt and sand with sunsets that colored the sky like Mark Rothko paintings.

In the mornings, I rose at first light and, while it was still cool enough to concentrate, read *The Conquest of the Sahara*, Douglas Porch's account of French colonial folly in the deserts of Africa. It is a story full of exaggerated expectations, of careers staked on preposterous expeditions to claim vast areas of sand and scrub that proved worthless to the politicians and accountants back home.

The pattern of the French expeditions was predictable: they began with too many men and too few plans, only to end, a year or two later, with a handful of survivors who held, as their reward, meaningless "title" to unproductive lands. "The vast plain covered with brambles and dwarf palms yielded little except people to butcher," Douglas Porch wrote, describing what awaited an 1898 French expedition along the route we were traveling through southern Niger. The French officers "took out their frustration on the guides: 'We would hang them and most of them, hanged very close to the ground, had their legs devoured by the hyenas, while the rest were left for the vultures,'" a surviving lieutenant later testified at an inquiry.

Whenever Ann and I arrived at a military control point, which was every few minutes, we brandished our *American* passports like a peace offering. "We are not French," I insisted immediately. Often this announcement was met with a puzzled look, followed by, "Yes. That is why you have American passports." Ann found my insistence on proclaiming the obvious embarrassing. I agreed, but the image of guides devoured by hyenas was so vivid, I continued my unsolicited clarifications.

Chapter
Twenty-two

The closer we got to the hippos, the smaller the pirogue felt. This was, I realized, due not only to the size of the creatures, but also to the fact that the pirogue was slowly filling up with water and sinking. When we had left shore and shoved off into the Niger, the straw in the bottom was perfectly dry. Now it floated.

This might have worried me considerably had I not been more concerned with the river's swift current and our lack of progress therein. The problem was our paddles. The bowman had a piece of board nailed to another piece of board; our man in the stern had only a long pole, perfect for maneuvering through the shallows along the bank but useless here in the deep water of midstream.

Kneeling directly behind the bowman, I could see the muscles tighten through his ripped shirt. His partner in the stern urged him on as he flailed helplessly with his pole. Ann let out a sigh and said, "Well."

A loud crack rose above the sound of the current. The boards in the bowman's hands separated, leaving him with two short paddles. I grabbed one and set to work.

The sternman began making odd sounds of belching and hissing, interspersed with crashing slaps at the water. He sounded, I realized, just like the hippos. We laughed and this pleased him, so he did it some more. The hippos, if they heard, chose to ignore the impostor.

"Beaucoup hippos!" the bowman grunted, breathing hard from the short, quick strokes.

The Niger was a fantastic stretch of water, almost a mile across, dotted with islands and false channels of marsh. We broke through the swift current and drifted down to a series of rocky islands. This put us very close to the hippos and the men were no longer laughing. They became respectful, impressed. We stood on the rock and watched the hippos play; they dove and surfaced with insolent power. Never had I seen such big, silly-looking things; they seemed to relish their very hipponess.

The sternman, a wiry fellow with bright, intelligent eyes, whispered to us a story of crossing the river in his pirogue and having a big bull hippo surface underneath his boat, exploding him, his paddle, his load of melons and his wife into the Niger. He acted out the entire scene with great vigor, rolling around on the rock and leaping upward like the hippo.

We enjoyed it so much he repeated the performance back on shore when we shared a lunch of watermelons and canned hash.

I had fallen in love with the River Niger. In the three days since leaving Niamey, our route had paralleled the river, sometimes running along the bank, other times drifting away a mile or two. But one always felt the presence of the river; even when unseen, it dominated the landscape like a mountain range. A river—a huge, wide river—running through the heart of a land so dry it was easy to forget this was still the Sahel and not the Sahara.

We had spent our time in Niamey with two goals in mind: repairing the Land Cruiser and eating. We had more success with the latter than the former.

The Peace Corps workers in Zinder had given us a most valuable tip: the American Recreation Center in Niamey. It was an extraordinarily pleasant compound full of trees and tennis courts and a *snack bar* that served bacon cheeseburgers. Magnificent bacon cheeseburgers. Also thick, rich milk shakes and French fries—all the food I never ate in America. But after weeks of canned hash and ravioli, it tasted wonderful, the stuff of gustatory dreams. And, unlike every restaurant we'd encountered in West Africa, the snack bar was cheap.

That there were enough Americans in Niamey to merit (if that's the right word) a recreation center was, to me, a confounding surprise. Like Chad, though, Niger was an American beachhead in West Africa. A gleaming new embassy sat on the outskirts of town, part of a compound that included a new ambassador's residence. There were sufficient American military advisers and marines to field a potent side in the local rugby league. The Peace Corps training center for Africa (which included 60 percent of the entire Peace Corps) was in Niamey, and the years of drought in the Sahel had created a small army of advisers, World Bank types and UN "experts."

The reality of recurrent droughts so close to the tons of flowing fresh water in the Niger is a paradox that has long taunted Western observers. In 1928, a French professor of geography wrote:

> In spite of existing conditions, there is reason to expect that this region around the elbow of the Niger will have the finest future of any portion of the Sahara, and one out of all proportion to its present wretched state. The future lies naturally in the river itself, a mighty water-course flowing through the midst of the desert and bringing to it tremendous annual floods which overflow and spread across the terrain. It is truly a second Nile, lacking only management to cause it to fertilize a second Egypt. There is not another spot in the whole Sahara where such financial possibilities are indicated.

Since 1928, of course, the "wretched state" of the region has only worsened and it's an open question whether the army of relief professionals has slowed or accelerated the process. As British journalist Patrick Marnham wrote in his superb collection of essays on West Africa, *Fantastic Invasion:* "For all the difference it made to the people of the Sahel, it might not have mattered if the relief planes had flown out over the Atlantic and dumped the grain into the sea. Much of it was never distributed beyond the main reception centres until more than one year after the drought had ended, by which time local food supplies had been restored."

But traveling in 1977, four years after the drought of 1973, Marnham saw "the terrible after-effects of the relief operation. . . . On the promise of free assistance thousands of people abandoned their traditional resources. . . . There is nothing for them to do, their economy has been destroyed, and there are no schemes to rebuild it. They are refugees in their own country."

After Niamey, 450 kilometers later, there was only Gao, Mali. It was the jumping-off point, the last outpost on the edge of the Sahara. That's how it had been since the seventh century, when Gao began its rise as a commercial and political force. In 872, Yaqubi hailed it as "the greatest of the realms of Sudan, the most important and powerful. All other kingdoms obey its king."

Freud wrote that "anatomy is destiny," and surely the same, with a slight variation, is true for places as for people: geography is destiny. Location made Gao. On the banks of the River Niger and the edge of the Sahara, the town became one of the richest trading hubs in Africa. Everything, from slaves to spices, heading in and out of West Africa passed through Gao. In the sixteenth century, Leo Africanus declared of Gao: "Here are exceedingly rich merchants. . . . It is a wonder to see what plenty of merchandise is daily brought hither, and how costly and sumptuous all things be. Horses bought in Europe for ten ducats, are sold again for forty and sometimes for fifty ducats apiece."

I thought about this tradition of traders when negotiating with "Bob" for canned chickens, black-market diesel and a guide across the Sahara. "I control chickens in this town," he asserted threateningly, his eyes hidden behind sunglasses. "You want chicken, you deal with me."

His real name, we learned from his pals, was Muhammad, but, "Bob!" he'd cried when we first met. "Call me Bob!"

Why not Ishmael? I wondered.

He was, at most, thirteen, though he claimed twenty-one.

(Perhaps he didn't appreciate that, were it true, he would have qualified as a midget.) But age was no obstacle for Bob. He was a Master Fixer.

We were eating omelets in a little shack of a restaurant when he pounced on us. "You need chicken?"

Somehow he'd heard that we were on the hunt for supplies and magically appeared: a short, pudgy figure in dark glasses, accompanied by an even younger assistant dressed like the rock singer Michael Jackson.

In the custom of his ancestors, Bob did not *own* anything, but this did not stop him from selling everything. He was not a merchant but a trader, with instincts of the killer shark variety.

"You need guide to Timbuktu? I am guide."

"Yes?"

"I guided a French car from Gao to Niamey last week."

"But it's impossible to get lost from Gao to Niamey. There's only one track, along the river."

Bob laughed. *"You* know that, not the French."

The young Fixer grasped the dominant economic imperative of Gao, a combination of necessity and lack of choices. There were certain things you had to have before crossing the desert, and Gao was the final place for them to be had. It was now or never.

Fortunately, fierce competition among the merchants kept prices down, and *everyone* in Gao sold something. Had a cartel formed to control rice or jerricans, any price could have been successfully demanded.

With Bob in tow, we wound our way through Gao's markets, negotiating for canned gas for our stove, food, additional jerricans for water (we needed, conservatively, one hundred liters), motor oil, extra mantles for the lantern: the necessities of life.

We camped outside town on an empty stretch of riverbank. It was a scene straight out of a tropical fantasy: a white beach (with only a few dead rats), palm trees, a big moon and warm breezes. To prolong the island fantasy, I read Anthony Burgess's

Malayan Trilogy by the lantern and fell asleep in the sand, convinced no scorpions would dare break the serenity.

The next morning, I awoke to find the white sand black with motor oil.

It had happened before, though never so suddenly. Across Niger, we'd left a trail of oil. At first we assumed it was a slow leak in the engine block but the oil level never dropped. That left the gearbox, which on the Land Cruiser is filled with engine oil. We kept the level topped off and tried, unsuccessfully, to find a mechanic who might have a solution. No one could understand why we were concerned. In Niamey my encounter with the local Toyota whiz, a very bright fellow, went like this:

"It's leaking," I explained.

He looked under the car and reemerged nodding. "Yes, it's leaking."

"What do you think is wrong?"

"Does it leak very much?"

"No, I don't think so."

"You have oil to fill it with, yes?"

"Yes."

He looked puzzled. "Do you really want me to take apart the gearbox to try and fix a slow leak? This is not France, my friend. Every car in Africa leaks. You think you have a problem? Look at these cars." He gestured around the dirt parking lot of his tin garage. Typically there were a half dozen Land Cruisers and Rovers in various stages of disembowelment. None looked as if they would roll again.

"These people have problems. You have a leak."

But now we had more than a leak, we had a gusher. Something had to be done.

We had heard that there was a Swiss mechanic on the outskirts of town working with a UN relief organization. Driving back into Gao from our campsite, gears grinding, we stopped

a Land Cruiser with a UN insignia and inquired about the
mechanic.

The driver, a Spaniard, was frantic in his advice. "Don't let
anyone touch that car in Gao except for the Swiss! Everyone else,
they work with knives!" He grabbed a long Tuareg dagger off his
dashboard and brandished it like a district attorney waving a
murder weapon.

The UN compound consisted of several tin buildings and a
small garage surrounded by a mud wall. Like every building in
Gao of even remote value, a Tuareg guarded the entrance. He
emerged from his slouching tent dressed in blue robes, his face
hidden under a sweeping headdress. A long sword hung from his
belt. A Doberman with bloody fangs in full rush would not have
stopped an intruder more quickly.

The Tuaregs are Berber tribesmen who once controlled the
main trade routes of the Sahara. For over a hundred years, until
a final uprising in 1917, the Tuaregs fought the French with a
combination of treachery, ferociousness and indigenous tough-
ness that finally succumbed only to the advanced weapons and
numerical superiority of the Europeans.

Today they carry no passports and still consider themselves
"citizens of the Sahara," but domesticity is destroying their society. The droughts of the last twenty years have decimated their
camels, forcing many Tuaregs down from the desert into the
bordering towns where they capitalize on their one remaining
asset: a reputed love for violence.

The sentry spoke little French but we managed to convey our
purpose. He in turn, with much pointing and drawing in the sand,
explained that this was Sunday. Tomorrow the mechanic would
be at work.

"You mean the Swiss mechanic?" Ann asked.

This was entirely beyond our mutual communication skills.
But the watchman offered to take us to the mechanic's house.

The Tuareg's sword rubbed against my leg as we drove a few
blocks to a neat row of houses that had the look of UN work. A
handsome black man in his mid-twenties came to the door rub-

bing his eyes. He had extravagant sideburns sweeping up into muttonchops.

"I was sleeping," he explained with a shy grin. We told him that we were looking for a UN mechanic. He nodded and asked our problem. When we explained, he went back inside and returned with a toolbox. "I will try to help," he said.

Walking back to the Cruiser, I pulled Ann aside and whispered, "He's Swiss?"

"I don't know."

"Ask him!"

She did. He nodded pleasantly. She looked at me and shrugged.

"I lived in Switzerland for four years," I hissed. "I never saw a black Swiss."

"I lived in Switzerland, too," she reminded me. Actually, it was where we had met. "What do you want me to do? Ask him to name the capital of every canton? Ask him who William Tell was?"

"Yes! That's a great idea. William Tell. Ask him."

"I will not!"

Fuming, I drove back to the UN compound, pondering ways to determine our mechanic's nationality. I thought of offering him Tobler chocolate, in hopes he might say, "Oh, just like home," or something like that. But there was no Tobler to be had in Gao.

Complicating my frustrations was the realization of what a fundamentally decent and kind thing the mechanic, regardless of his nationality, was doing. On a Sunday morning he was coming to work to help a pair of total strangers. And though the undertaking might hold some promise of financial reward, he had made no mention of money nor of an expected *cadeau* or gift. Insomuch as I had grown accustomed to random passersby asking for everything from my hat to my car, this did not go unappreciated.

But I still wondered if he was Swiss.

The tin garage housed a concrete grease pit. That figured. Only a Western relief organization would go to the trouble to construct something as solid and enduring as a concrete grease pit.

The mechanic opened his toolbox and went to work. I noted with some relief that he did not seem to have a single knife.

The first step was the removal of the bottom plate on the gearbox housing. Once off, I suspected, we would discover a failed seal.

The only problem was, we couldn't get the plate off.

Were one looking for a metaphor for why most grand improvement schemes founder on the shoals of Africa, this simple affair in the grease pit of Gao would do nicely. It is always the *little* things mucking everything up in Africa. The lack of trucks to distribute food or the proper stamp on a piece of paper to allow the trucks to leave or a working telephone to call the right person or not enough spare tires or oil filters or wrenches. It was wrenches that did us in. To open the gearbox we needed a long wrench. We couldn't budge the bolts.

Even the right sort of pipe might have worked: say a three- or four-foot pipe that we could have slipped over the small wrench to provide the mechanical advantage required to dislodge years of African grit. We looked all over Gao for a pipe. There wasn't one. A can of Liquid Wrench would have been a godsend; an electric drill fitted with a socket an unequivocal miracle.

But all we had was a hand wrench and, though we tried kicking and pulling, grunting and screaming, nothing worked.

The mechanic, however, was a most ingenious fellow. When we had tried everything, when I was ready to abandon all hope, he had an idea.

"Glue. You have glue?"

We did, in fact. A tube of epoxy glue.

"We make a seal," he said, wiping his brow. We were standing under the car drenched in grease, sand and sweat.

And that is exactly what we did. We cleaned off the gearbox housing and applied a layer of glue around the joint. Then we filled the box with oil and waited. Had Saint Sebastian appeared before us shot full of arrows I could not have been more astonished: the seal held.

"Where are you going now?" the mechanic asked when the delicate operation was complete.

"To Timbuktu and then across the desert."

He looked at the gearbox for a long moment, no doubt thinking to himself that crazy Westerners would do anything. I had thoughts along the same lines.

"Take very much water," he said, smiling. "The desert is dry."

Chapter
Twenty-three

There are two main routes across the Sahara. On the Michelin map they appear as comforting red lines, bisecting the yellow emptiness of the map like superhighways. The most popular, known as the Hoggar (named for the spectacular Hoggar mountain region of Algeria, which it bisects), actually has stretches of pavement, though this only makes the driving more difficult. As the *Sahara Handbook* explains, "Long stretches of once beautiful new asphalt roads have deteriorated rapidly. . . . Traffic soon establishes myriads of pistes on either side of the former road with deep ruts, or ornières, and terrible corrugations. This can turn a two-day journey into a long frustrating ordeal." The Hoggar runs from Algiers south to Tamanrasset and into Niger.

The more direct route from Gao is the Tanezrouft. "It's more rugged than the Route du Hoggar," reads the guidebook from Lonely Planet, "takes considerably longer, and there's far less transport along the way."

We decided not to take either one, at least not for the entire distance. Our plan was to drive first to Timbuktu, then slant northeast across the desert to Tamanrasset and pick up the Hoggar. It was a less direct way to reach the Mediterranean but it was the shortest distance from Timbuktu to Tamanrasset, Algeria. And Tamanrasset was a place I had to be—by the twenty-second of December. That was when my wife was arriving from America. Air Algerie promised—though I was dubious in the extreme—that it was possible to fly to Tamanrasset from Algiers; one flight a week but it could be done. We left Gao on the ninth:

almost two weeks to make it to Tamanrasset, more than enough time if the tires didn't blow (we were down to one spare tube), the four-wheel drive expire (the gearshift still had to be strapped down), the rear springs collapse (the same springs that had been diagnosed terminally ill in Chad), the wheels fall off (the car vibrated so fiercely I had to tighten the lug nuts each evening) or, of course, the gearbox glue dissolve.

There is no road to Timbuktu. One finds it the same way people have for the last ten centuries or so—by following the River Niger. *Africa Overland* reports, "We had to find our way to Timbuctoo through 200 miles of untamed desert, using only the stars and our compass. . . . This was going to be the toughest section of the desert."

The navigation was fairly simple: northwest for 95 kilometers to Bourem (here there was even a sign: "To Timbuktu") then west along the river for 292 more kilometers. Counting the kilometers was essential. Since the river had shifted course leaving Timbuktu inland by a dozen kilometers or so, it was possible to drive right past the town, always expecting to see it over the next rise. Eventually you ran out of gas. (The question of whether or not diesel fuel was available in Timbuktu was an open one. Sometimes there was, truck drivers told us; sometimes there wasn't. Without it, we had problems.)

In *News from Tartary*, Peter Fleming's tale of a journey from Beijing to India in 1935, he describes a Tibetan village as having "more than the usual fairie tale look." I felt the same way about the settlements along the Niger, though these jumbles of black African and Arab cultures made for a very different sort of fairy tale than do the peaked roofs and prayer wheels of Tibet. Here there were mud brick huts, some quite large, and the distinctive lopsided Tuareg tents that always looked as if they were about to fall down. Children and goats played together in the ruins of huts long abandoned and broken walls blown over with sand. It gave one the sense that these were places where civilization had been attempted and then abandoned for lack of interest.

In a final touch of mocking irony, the River Niger gleamed

in the background, with sandy beaches straight out of a tropical vacation brochure.

At night we always tried to camp by the river. If its meandering curves hid it from view, we left the track and bushwhacked south, knowing that eventually we had to hit water. Invariably we waited too late in the day (hoping the river would appear along our route, as it did from time to time), so that we found ourselves driving through the scrub brush and acacia thorns in failing light. The terrain, to my surprise, was rolling, complicating both the navigation and the driving.

Searching for the river the second night after leaving Gao, we were startled to find ourselves suddenly driving not on sand but across black rocks. The light was flat and dim; it was like skiing on a hazy day. We dropped down into a gully, bucked our way across and up the other side. I was thinking about the rocks and how our tires left no imprint on the hard surface. I glanced at the compass hanging from the dash, trying to fix our direction. Tomorrow we wouldn't be able to retrace our tracks—there were no tracks. Something—peripheral vision? mental radar?—made me glance up from the compass.

"There's the river," Ann said.

It hung in front of us, glinting in the muted sunset. But there was an oddness to the way it looked, as if the river were *down* there and we were *up* here.

That was it. I slammed the brakes to the floor.

We got out of the car and walked forward. A few feet in front of us the black pebbles ended in a sudden cliff that plummeted twenty or thirty feet to the level of the river. The cliff was composed of a curious black rock, porous as lava.

Off to the left we spotted a gully running down to the river. We followed it to the water and made camp on the shore.

I woke up at first light and brewed coffee on the little gas stove. The mornings were the best time of day, when it was cool enough to forget, at least for a little while, the strangling heat of the upcoming hours. A pirogue floated through the mist, a graceful craft with bow and stern rising upward like outstretched arms.

There were two teenagers poling the boat. They landed and hoisted out a bulky fish, mouth gaping. It was a capitaine, a breed of giant perch I'd first seen pulled from the Ubangi River in Bangui.

We talked, in the way people do with only a few words of shared language. They wanted to sell the fish and I wanted to eat it in the worst way. But there was nothing I could do with the ten or fifteen pounds of fresh meat that would be left after even the most heroic eating efforts. So we drank coffee and looked at each other, waiting peacefully for the day formally to begin. Tiny red birds darted between the thorn bushes, perfect little things that looked like Christmas tree ornaments.

When Ann rose up from the Cruiser roof wrapped in her sleeping bag, the fishermen—who hadn't realized there was a person inside all that blue nylon on the roof—gasped in surprise and backed protectively toward their pirogue.

She reassured them with a soft laugh. We drank more coffee.

It is customary for Westerners to speak of their disappointment on reaching Timbuktu. René Caillié, the first European to see Timbuktu and return alive, wrote of his visit in 1828:

> I looked around and found that the sight before me did not answer my expectations. I had formed a totally different idea of the grandeur and wealth of Timbuctoo. The city presented, at first view, nothing but a mass of ill-looking houses, built of earth. Nothing was to be seen in all directions but immense plains of sand of a yellowish white color. The sky was a pale red as far as the horizon; all nature wore a dreary aspect, and the most profound silence prevailed; not even the warbling of a bird was to be heard.

The third European to visit Timbuktu, the German explorer Heinrich Barth, wrote a detailed description of the town as he found it in 1853, including a map with descriptions of every major building. Little is changed today. Timbuktu is still "a mass of ill-looking houses," full of "profound silences."

I visited most of those houses searching for a barrel.

Travel has a charmingly sneaky way of making the unexpected terribly important. Never would I have imagined that the acquisition of a barrel—a fifty-gallon drum, more precisely—would be important. But in Timbuktu, thanks to a German we ran into, it was a task bestowed with a compelling imperative.

"Friends, friends, friends," the German announced solemnly as we hovered over the map, "from here"—he pointed to Timbuktu—"to there,"—his finger traced the breadth of the Sahara—"there is no certainty of fuel supplies. You must carry your own stores." He had the vocabulary of a military commander—*fuel supplies, stores*—and the look of a sixties refugee: long black hair, tattered beard sprinkled with gray, shorts and sandals.

"For ten days," he continued, "I once waited here"—his finger stabbed a point in the middle of the desert—"for a truck to pass with fuel. I had water for eleven days. On the tenth a truck came and I bought fifty liters of fuel. It cost me three hundred dollars. But it was better I think than dying." He said the last as if he had truly pondered the question, weighing both sides of the equation.

The German, Hernst Whitney, was one of those perpetual graduate students forever working on their doctorate. His thesis for his anthropology degree was on Tuareg blacksmiths. He knew a great deal about Tuareg blacksmiths, and about crossing the Sahara, a tour (his description) he'd made over a half dozen times.

We met him at our hotel in Timbuktu, though hotel is a grandiose description for that collection of dusty mud brick rooms with collapsing ceilings and walls decorated with slithering lizards. I took one glance at the bed, with its gray sheets and tortured mattress, and decided to sleep on the roof of the Cruiser parked out front in the sand. It was the hotel's shower we were really after, that halfhearted stream of tepid brown liquid where all the fashionable lizards hung out.

Hernst had floated down the Niger from Bamako, the capital

of Mali, to Timbuktu on one of the river steamers that still plied
the trade route. He'd traveled with two French soldiers and a
Tahitian woman; she was the wife of the soldiers' comrade-in-
arms, who had not been able to make the trip. She was also
exceedingly beautiful, a fact not lost on the German or on the
French soldiers, who spoke openly of the anguish imposed upon
them by the obligations of loyalty to their friend. Apparently
they felt no such restrictions toward Ann, though she seemed to
find their charms resistible.

Having completed the drive from Gao to Timbuktu without
disaster, I felt quite sanguine about negotiating the Sahara. But
the German changed all that in a hurry. It started with his question about our maps. "You have good ones?" he asked in his
perfect English.

I beamed confidently and fetched from the Cruiser my bulky
cartographic collection. In Paris before leaving for Africa, I had
discovered a map store that specializes in West Africa and bought
what I assumed was a world-class collection. Ann groaned when
she saw the bundle. All across Africa I had bragged about the
maps and pored over them with a pleasure bordering on the
fetishistic.

"Umm," the German asked, thumbing through the package,
"you have no aircraft charts?" This he said in a deeply disappointed voice.

"Aircraft charts?"

"No? How about topographical maps. Any of those?"

I shook my head in shame.

"Well," he said. "Well."

We were sitting in Timbuktu's only restaurant, the front
room of a two-room mud house next to the market. The location
was significant as the chef took orders then sent his son out to
buy the ingredients. Unfortunately, the child was a ferocious
bargainer who held out to the bitter end for the best price, so the
process—from ordering to eating—took at least two hours. This
is, I would venture, a record for omelets. As the sounds of the
rapacious negotiations—shouts of scorn, laughter—wafted in the

open doorway, the chef put on a proud "That's-my-boy!" grin
and poured rounds of bubbling sweet tea.

Using my woefully inadequate maps, the German went over
our route stage by stage, warning us about stretches of deep sand,
the location and quality of wells, and areas where it was easy to
get lost. (There seemed to be a chilling number of these.)

"How much petrol can you carry?" he asked.

"We have six jerricans." It was understood that all jerricans
held twenty liters.

"And does your Land Cruiser have double petrol tanks?"

"No."

He made calculations in the notebook he carried everywhere.
Anthropologists always carry notebooks. "In the deep sand," he
asked, "you use what, twenty liters per hundred kilometers?"
This was how everyone in Africa talked about fuel consumption,
not "how many liters to the kilometer" but "how many liters per
hundred kilometers."

I nodded. Actually the Cruiser used slightly more fuel but I
remained silent out of loyalty to the vehicle.

"You must travel at least fifteen hundred kilometers to cross
the desert. More if you are lost. It is best to plan for two thousand
kilometers. If you are wrong you die," he observed cheerfully,
"so caution is best. For two thousand kilometers you need . . ."
He divided some figures.

"At least four hundred liters of fuel," Ann spoke up.

The German smiled. "Yes. Math and anthropology do not
mix so well, I think."

I did some figuring of my own. With the six jerricans we
carried and the 90 liters that the Toyota's tank held, we had only
210 liters, about half of what the German estimated we needed.
This was not good.

"I don't know how we could fit ten more jerricans in the car,"
Ann said.

"I don't know how we could afford ten more jerricans," I
said. Each can cost almost fifty dollars at the inflated prices of the
desert oasis.

"What you need," the German observed sagely, "is a barrel."

It made sense. A single 200-liter oil drum would solve our storage problems—if we could fit it in the Cruiser. And if we could find one.

For the better part of a day, we roamed through the sand streets of Timbuktu looking for a barrel. I became a student of the 200-liter metal drum.

It is quite astonishing the number of uses one can invent for the basic oil drum. I saw drums used as stoves, usually with the top half decapitated. I saw water collection drums, mud mortar–mixing drums, grain drums, cooking fuel drums, drum tables, drum lanterns, drum jacks (hoisting ailing Land Rovers), trash drums and even latrine drums. The problem was, most had been altered to suit their converted purpose (ruining their original fuel-toting ability) and were hopelessly contaminated by their new role; this was particularly true of the mud and latrine barrels.

As the word went forth that we were in barrel-buying mode, eager salesmen chased us down the narrow sand alleys rolling their merchandise in hot pursuit. We finally settled on an old Shell oil drum that we located in the courtyard of a house near the great mosque.

A mad scene ensued. With a crowd jamming the alley, we unloaded everything from the Cruiser and struggled to squeeze the drum onto the back seat. After much sweating, swearing and ripping of upholstery (what little was left), we succeeded and then faced the challenge of repacking the car with about a third less available space. The loading process greatly entertained the gathered multitudes and made me question my sanity. Was I really contemplating driving across the Sahara in a vehicle that looked like something out of *The Grapes of Wrath?*

"California or bust," Ann said, sharing my thoughts.

"Right."

Chapter
Twenty-four

We drove from Timbuktu back to Gao.

There was no choice. It was a question of fuel—or a lack of fuel, to be accurate. After the great barrel hunt, we turned up at Timbuktu's only gas pump to discover the diesel tanks were dry. The situation, I had to admit, reeked of the sort of irony that thrives in Africa. Great energy is expended to solve one problem only to discover the basic premise of the effort is flawed. Why find the perfect diesel drum if there is no diesel? Why import relief food if it only rots on the dock because there are no delivery trucks?

In Gao we could fill the two-hundred-liter drum. So we went to Gao. The delay was only a few days.

Only a few days. I thought, bemused, of the times in my pre-Africa life I had fumed and ranted over late planes and traffic jams. An hour—hell, *a half hour*—was intolerably painful. Now I accepted with a shrug a few days' detour just *to buy gas.*

And anyway, it was good to drop by the little omelet shack in Gao and find our pal Bob coolly spinning deals. "You want diesel?" His eyes brightened. "I control diesel in Gao!"

We spent a day and night in Gao, long enough to buy black-market diesel and get arrested for camping in a military zone. (It was a horrible night. While snoozing peacefully in my sleeping bag, I was attacked by dogs, then nearly run over by an armored car on some kind of drunken maneuver and finally, when dawn came at last, arrested before my first cup of coffee. It took five

Polaroid photos and a box of Cameroonian cigars to buy our freedom.)

We also had enough time to hire a guide.

Bob found him for us. Of course.

"You want guide? I control guide!"

He was a tall, skinny teenager with buck teeth and a hipster's nonchalance. "Water for the journey? Oh, you don't need much."

His name was something like Sidramma Muhammad. Ann called him Siddhartha; I called him Sid. He seemed to like both and did not take our inability to pronounce his name as an insult. (Indeed, he called me Stu.)

Sid lived in Tessalit, the last town in Mali before entering Algeria. He claimed to be intimately familiar with the route from Tessalit to Tamanrasset—the *"piste dangereuse,"* as the Michelin map proclaimed—and was anxious to travel to Tamanrasset in the way all country boys want to visit the big city. That he seemed to think of the desert outpost Tamanrasset as a major metropolis should have made me question whether he had ever actually been there, but after being attacked by dogs, almost crushed under a half-track's treads and arrested as a spy, I was not thinking too clearly. Sid said he knew the way, requested a reasonable fee, and that, as it were, seemed to be that.

In retrospect, warnings abounded that Sid might be, well, problematic. Like when we noticed him trying to crawl under the fuel drum on the back seat when we approached the first of three checkpoints leaving Gao.

"Siddhartha," Ann asked levelly, "what are you doing?"

Like the best comedic straight man, Sid asked, "Me?"

"Yes, Siddhartha. Why are you hiding?"

"A little problem . . ."

"Yes, Siddhartha?"

He dug further under the barrel.

"Sid?" I tried to sound friendly but firm. "Oh, Sid?" I could see the first checkpoint a hundred yards ahead. I slowed down.

"Papers," he finally said.

"What about papers?"

"There is a problem. A little problem." He held his thumb and index finger close together to stress just how little a problem. By now the guard at the checkpoint was watching us curiously; his automatic weapon beckoned us forward.

"Well, Siddhartha," Ann said, "explain it to him."

And he did, or he tried to. The sticking point involved some irregularity in Sid's identity papers. Such matters are invariably so complex that I doubt any official, much less a hapless guard on a checkpoint to nowhere, could understand the details. But however perplexing problems with African paperwork may be, there is always one reliable solution: money.

"Patron," Sid began, "this is a great injustice. This is very much wrong. This man says I can not go home to Tessalit and be your guide. Please, we must give him something." Sid had traded his usual sly grin for the pout of a persecuted child.

I groaned, knowing my choices all too well. We could argue, which would only increase the final price, or try to wait the guard out, hoping he would change his mind—but who had more time than a roadblock guard on the edge of the Sahara?—or, yes, pay the bribe.

"How much, Sid?"

"A little money, that is all."

"Sid?"

"Five thousand CFA."

"Fine."

Sid seemed shocked at my ready agreement.

"But it comes out of your fee. Do you understand, Sid? I asked you yesterday. You said all your papers were in order." This was true.

Sid looked horrified but nodded. His ready agreement shocked *me* until I watched him pocket four of the five thousand-CFA notes, the other going to the guard. Clever boy, this Sid.

An hour beyond Gao we hit deep sand and slowed to a few miles per hour. It was windy and uncommonly bright, the sun glaring off the sand as bright as klieg lights at a Hollywood opening. I wore my darkest mountaineering glasses and wished for goggles.

Our slow pace troubled Sid as we neared a Tuareg encampment. "Go faster," he urged, genuinely nervous. "These are bad people. Go faster!"

There was no more speed to be had in the sand. We poked along, a perfect target for a Tuareg lance or a dagger wielded by a courageous hijacker.

But there were only women waving and children running alongside, as kids did everywhere in Africa. Camels and goats wandered among the dark cloth tents. The few men we saw sat in the tents' open doorways, looking as if we had awakened them from long naps. Tuaregs are famed for surprise attacks, but if this was an act, it was a very good one indeed. Ann pointed this out to Sid.

"Yes," he agreed, now not so nervous, "they are very lazy people."

Somehow, coming from Sid this touch of moral indignation was less than convincing.

Late in the afternoon we came to a tiny village called Aguelhok. Because it appeared on our maps, it was a reassuring sight: the first convincing indication since leaving Gao that we were not lost. A bridge over a dry riverbed was destroyed, forcing us to negotiate the stony river bottom strewn with boulders. A tall, skinny man greeted us on the other side, his white gown flapping in the wind. His eagerness oozed into the unctuous. "Come eat with me, please," he kept repeating. "I have a restaurant. Please."

Sitting around the cistern of a dry well next to his one-room restaurant, we ate macaroni mixed with greasy lamb. The man wanted to talk deals. What did we have to trade? Did we want to sell the car?

I was exhausted from the day spent in deep sand; my sun-induced headache was fierce.

"We have a whole car full of stuff to trade," I said, trying to pick up a piece of the lamb. There were no forks or spoons. "The question is, what do *you* have to trade?"

He laughed and, as if to let us know he was not a small-town operator, said confidentially, "I keep cars for Maurice."

"Maurice?"

"From Marseilles."

Oh, *that* Maurice, I thought.

The man gestured toward a mud building on the other side of the restaurant. "There is a Range Rover in there this very minute. He brings the cars down from France and I keep them for a while. Do you want to sell your car?"

It was such an odd question, as if we could sell the car and then catch a bus or plane back to Europe. Short of camels, I hadn't seen *any* transportation since leaving Gao.

"How much would you give me for the Cruiser?"

"Two million CFA," he said instantly.

I laughed. "But I paid more than that in Yaoundé and there are many cars in Yaoundé. Here you can not be so tough."

"But Maurice sells a Range Rover for only two million!"

"Yes, but my car is not stolen."

He nodded. "I know." His voice was sad. "That is not good. It is much better price if stolen. Maurice steals all his cars."

This he said with a certain pride. I felt as if I should apologize for not stealing mine.

"All cars in Africa are stolen." He shrugged. "Do you have shoes like these?" he asked suddenly, thrusting out his feet. From under his white robe jutted tennis shoes with Velcro straps instead of laces.

"No, but they are very nice."

He nodded, pleased that he had something I didn't. "It is much faster with these," he explained, opening and fastening the Velcro several times. It was indeed very fast. "It saves time."

I nodded, wondering what in the world he did with the extra time he saved not having to tie shoelaces. Everyone else in the village was barefoot.

"Two million two hundred!" he shouted, waving his arms at the Land Cruiser. "No more!"

\\\

We spent two nights on the road traveling to Tessalit, Sid's hometown. Both nights Sid expressed extreme displeasure with our choice of camping sites. The first night he thought the ground was too rocky (it was, but so was every spot for a hundred miles in either direction), and the second campsite he feared was too close to a Tuareg encampment. "We die!" he repeated numerous times.

This concerned me at first, but after Sid vetoed several possible sites due to the Tuareg threat, I began to understand there was a hidden agenda at work. Sid did not want to camp at all. He wanted to keep driving until we reached Tessalit so he could sleep at home. Perfectly understandable as this was, driving after dark in this terrain was akin in danger and difficulty to a night landing on a carrier deck.

We were passing through the Tilemsi Valley, following not a *road* but compass bearings, landmarks and tracks from other vehicles, none of which were worth a damn after sunset. The headlights on the Cruiser were sad little beams of yellow light, only slightly brighter than, say, a refrigerator bulb. Surrounded by crumbling hills, our route through the valley floor abounded with dry riverbeds offering an unexpected plunge at any moment and car-crunching boulders strewn about haphazardly.

We camped at dark; Sid insisted he was going to walk the rest of the way to Tessalit. Ann asked to take his photograph so that she would have it as a remembrance when the Tuaregs killed him. He stayed and slept so soundly, I had trouble waking him the next morning. A Tuareg would have found him easy pickings.

We drove to Tessalit for breakfast.

Sid's hometown had the look of a classic French foreign legion outpost: a hilltop fort of brown walls towering above a warren of sandy streets. It took about ten minutes in Tessalit to realize that Sid's guiding days—at least for us—were over. Not only did he not have an identity card, Sid didn't have a passport.

This became clear when we parked at the base of the hill and

hiked up to the fort, which was now the police station. A kindly
official in a cardigan sweater treated Sid like a favorite nephew.
He was short and round, a mix of Arab and black.

He laughed when we explained that Sid was guiding us to
Tamanrasset. "That boy." He shook his head, grinning. "He told
you that?"

"Well, yes. Why?"

"Are you a smuggler?"

"Well, no."

"That boy can't leave Tessalit—but he does. He has no papers! No papers!" He laughed as if this were the greatest joke in
the world.

"No passport?"

"Of course not! Would you give him a passport?" He pulled
Sid to him and squeezed him in a sudden hug. Sid looked appropriately chagrined.

"You go to Tamanrasset?" the official asked.

"Yes."

"Do you know the way?"

"No, that's why we wanted Sid."

"You think that boy has been to Tamanrasset?" He chuckled. "Good luck." He wasn't laughing when he said this last bit.

We walked back down the hill to Tessalit's only restaurant
to think things over. A large van with Dutch plates sat in front,
an emaciated blond figure stretched out on the hood. He was
middle-aged, with long hair, a mustache and a tie-dyed shirt.

"Are you okay?" I asked.

"No. Not really."

His name was Peter Jokal and he had a chilling story to tell.

Two weeks before he had left Tamanrasset. *Two weeks.* Normally it was a three-day trip, possibly shorter. Four at the maximum.

Two weeks.

"On the second day I get very sick. Diarrhea. Dysentery. I
have three hitchhikers with me. Two German boys and a girl.
They drive and I lay in the back.

"It was very bad. The road—there is no road. Up and down. Bumps. Horrible. Finally I say to the Germans, 'We must stop.' But they do not want to stop. They say, 'We will drive, you rest.' But the pain, it is too much. I say to the Germans, 'We must stop!' They keep driving.

"So I get my knife"—he showed us a two-foot bayonet—"and grab the keys and tell these Germans, 'After you kill me, you drive truck. But maybe I kill one or two of you first.' They were true Germans, cowards in the end."

For eight days, Peter Jokal held the Germans at bay.

"Why didn't the Germans hitch a ride with another car?" I asked.

He laughed. "You do not understand. We were not on the autobahn. Out there"—he gestured toward Tamanrasset—"there is nothing there. A car or truck maybe twice a month, no more."

He paused, as if gathering his strength. "Where are you going?"

We drank sweet tea and told him about Sid and our plans to drive to Tamanrasset. For two weeks he had been living on bits of bread and tea. His bones looked as if they might puncture his skin.

"You have a good car," he said, looking over at the Cruiser. "You should have no problems." He shook his head and looked suddenly as tired as anyone I'd ever seen. "But you never know about cars. You never know. And on that route, if you have a problem, you could be there for two or three weeks. Easy."

There were now eight days until my wife flew to Tamanrasset. I thought of her arriving and not finding us. I thought of her sitting in a hotel in Tamanrasset wondering what had happened.

On the small table we unfolded our now-tattered Michelin map. "If you do not go directly to Tamanrasset from Tessalit," the Dutch traveler suggested, "you can go north on the Tanezrouft across the Sahara and then go across and down the Hoggar to Tamanrasset. It is longer but there are more people on this route. If something happens, you can get help very quickly. Maybe just a few days."

A few days. I silently counted our water supplies. One hundred liters. It seemed like a lot but . . .

We decided to take the longer, safer route. Peter Jokal looked at the map wistfully. "I wish I could go with you. Two vehicles is always safer. But I have no strength. I must stay here." He motioned toward the door that led to the public bathroom, a hole in a concrete floor. "In a few days, maybe I can drive to Gao and then Niamey. In Niamey I sell the truck and catch the first plane to Europe."

We gave him diarrhea pills and left him sitting in the sun near the bathroom door.

We tromped back up the hill to the police station to retrieve our passports, which we'd left for stamping. Our favorite uncle who'd explained Sid's problems took me aside. I sighed, expecting a request for a bribe.

"You go to Bordj-Moktar now," he said, naming the Algerian border town due north of Tessalit.

I nodded.

"There is a man. He travels to Bordj-Moktar." The official nodded toward a tall, impressive figure across the room. He wore a green army jacket and had the detached air of a high-ranking officer.

"He needs a ride?" I asked, getting to the inevitable.

"Yes. He could be helpful."

It was not far to Bordj-Moktar, perhaps one day and a night, no more. Traveling with an official could speed our way through the remaining Malian customs posts as well as the upcoming Algerian border, reputed to be among the toughest in Africa. Algeria had very strict currency regulations and fierce searches were routine.

I agreed to take the official. He walked down the hill with us to the Cruiser carrying a small gym bag. I felt almost smug, delighted with the increased status our new passenger imparted.

At the last Malian posts, the officers greeted our passenger with friendly banter and waved us through. This was definitely the way to travel.

A rocky track led north toward Algeria through the low hills surrounding Tessalit. Ann and I were arguing; she had wanted to stay in Tessalit for lunch and I had insisted we needed to depart at once. Our new route would take considerably longer and I was worried about reaching Tamanrasset. We had, I figured, just enough time to make the journey.

The track split off in two directions. We stopped arguing to ask the officer in the back seat which route was correct. He nodded to the right.

A few miles later we came to a large fenced compound containing a cluster of buildings. A few men in green uniforms stared at us. I waved and kept driving. But just beyond the compound the road appeared to end. I circled back to ask directions.

A short uniformed figure strode out of one of the buildings. He stopped and stared at us with a disbelieving look on his face. Ann asked directions.

"What are you doing here?" he barked.

She explained that we were driving to Bordj-Moktar. Could he tell us please if this was the route?

He stared incredulously then blew a long, piercing note on a whistle hanging from his neck. Within seconds five guards rushed out of a nearby building to surround the car. Their automatic weapons pointed directly at us.

"Passports!" the martinet screamed.

I tried to explain.

"Passports!"

Desperately, I turned to our passenger. Surely he could explain or pull rank and end this misunderstanding.

But what I saw in the back seat was hardly a comfort. The expression on our passenger's face was that of a terrified child. He looked as if he were about to burst into tears.

"Tell them something!" I pleaded. He shook his head, his eyes opening even wider.

"Passports!" The martinet took a step forward, placing his

hand on his holstered gun. There was nothing to do. We dug out our passports. In the back seat, our passenger began to sob. I couldn't believe it.

"Return to Tessalit and report to the police. Now!"

"But our passports?" we sputtered.

"We keep them! Leave!"

All the way back to Tessalit, the man in the rear seat sobbed.

Chapter
Twenty-five

"Why did you listen to this boy?" the police captain implored. "Why?"

"We asked him directions, that's all! He lives here, he should know which road goes to Bordj-Moktar and which road goes to an army camp!"

"But why?" The police captain, who still resembled a kindly uncle albeit an annoyed one, stepped closer to me and lowered his voice. We were in the hilltop fort turned police station; voices echoed through the empty room as if in a deep cave. "This boy is . . ." He touched his head.

"Crazy?" I whispered.

He shrugged and gestured with his palms up. "A little."

I looked across the room and saw the figure that only a short while ago I had pegged as an important military official. He was huddled in a chair, his eyes red. A more pathetic figure was difficult to imagine.

"So what do we do now?" Ann asked.

The police officer shrugged, a gesture I was coming to loathe. "You must wait," he said eventually. "Tell me, did you not see the sign that says 'No Entry' on this road?"

"No."

He shifted his eyes between the red-eyed figure slumped across the room and myself, as if trying to judge who was the greater idiot. "It is a large sign," he said softly with an indigenous politeness.

"We were arguing," I explained.

"About what?" He leaned forward, eager to gossip. It was clear he welcomed this break in the routine of Tessalit life.

"Nothing as important as being stuck at the Malian border without a passport," Ann rightly surmised.

"Well," the officer said, disappointed, "we must wait. But do not worry. Let us have tea. The army will bring your passports."

Ann and I relaxed and followed him over to a low table next to a small gas stove. He asked me for a match, lit the stove and pocketed the unused matches. They were hard to find in Tessalit. Like most things.

"When do you think our passports will be returned?" I asked. I was hungry and wondered if we had time to eat at the town's single restaurant.

He shrugged. That gesture.

"An hour, two hours?" I asked.

He laughed now, his voice bouncing off the red walls of the fort.

"Two weeks if we are lucky. Perhaps longer."

Two weeks. Ann and I drank our tea in silence then walked out through the open doorway. Below us, Tessalit in all its grandeur baked under an impossibly hot sun. Two weeks.

There were, of course, no phones in Tessalit. Two weeks. My wife would arrive in Tamanrasset. We would be waiting in Tessalit. Two weeks.

We walked down the hill to the café.

"What happened?" Peter Jokel, emerging from the bathroom, asked. "Change your mind? You like Tessalit too much to leave?"

Solidarity, the Polish labor organization, and a few rock-and-roll cassettes reduced our sentence in Tessalit to two days. This may not seem like very long. It is. There are nice people in Tessalit. We now know every one. We now know a great deal about their families.

Though he welcomed our company, our patron in the police

station was quite willing to help us retrieve our passports. "I would go talk to the commandant," he told us over a delicious pot of couscous our first evening in town.

"But there is a problem. I have no car."

"Take our Land Cruiser," I quickly offered.

He was profuse in his thanks but refused. "If the army sees your car again they will think you have returned and will shoot it very quickly, before they see I am driving. This will not be good."

As much as I hated to, I had to agree with his conclusion.

So we waited until help arrived, and from a most unlikely source: Polish auto smugglers.

They came in two new Peugeot 504s, a punkish, good-looking couple with spiked hair and heavy Eastern European wing tip shoes. They had Polish passports but no visas for Mali, no insurance, and car registration papers of the most flimsy sort. Our friend in the police station sniffed blood from the very start.

"So," he said when they had made the long hike up the hill to pay homage at his station, "you would like to enter my country, yes? With your cars, yes? These are your papers? Really?"

A deal was slowly crafted over many glasses of frothy tea. He would allow their entrance into Mali if they would drive him to the army camp. He also wanted a fair slice of their cassette collection (which mainly consisted of Eastern European heavy-metal bands).

"We sell the cars and give the money to Solidarity!" the couple boasted to Ann and me, expecting all Americans to have a soft spot for Walesa and company.

Passports regained, we left Tessalit for the second time. We did not take any passengers and we did not miss the proper road.

I felt liberated, thrilled to embark on the final stretch. There was just enough time to reach Tamanrasset by the twenty-second.

The next morning, an hour or two before dawn, I woke up in the desert vomiting uncontrollably.

\\\

Ann looked down from the roof of the Cruiser. "Can I ask what you're doing?" she said in a sleepy voice.

I had a needle and syringe in my right hand and with my left I was rubbing a wet towel on my bare thigh. Alcohol is the standard preinjection cleanser but there was none of that to be had.

What I was doing was shooting four milligrams of Compazine into my leg. When a doctor friend had given me the vials and a handful of needles back in the States, he'd laughed at my avowed squeamishness over self-injection. "Don't worry, if you really need this stuff you'll do it in a second."

He was right. "This is the strongest antivomiting medicine I can give you," he told me. "I hope you don't need it."

I did.

We were in the desert somewhere near the Mali-Algerian border. This was the real Sahara, with no road at all but only an odd marker—an old refrigerator, an oil drum—every ten or fifteen kilometers to show the way. It was a flat, exhilarating expanse of open vistas to the horizon and rocky, firm sand.

"I didn't think this was possible," I gasped to Ann between seizures. "I mean, I really didn't."

The Compazine helped, increasing the time between heaves. As the sun bolted upward, Ann drove us toward Algerian customs in Bordj-Moktar.

Ahead was reputedly the worst customs post in West or North Africa. For the first time, we actually had something to hide: cash. French francs and U.S. dollars tucked away to trade on the black market. I had intended to put on one of my usual "Charm the Customs Officials" shows to counter a serious search.

"Maybe you can just vomit all over the customs officers and they'll be too busy to search the car," Ann suggested. "This really could be a lucky break."

I groaned.

In a way she proved to be right. Not that I vomited on

anyone, but the officials quickly realized I was ill in a most unpleasant way and responded with the basic decency and grace that is quintessentially Algerian. The rough-looking, bearded officials in their drab olive uniforms shook their heads like the best Jewish mothers and hurried us through their office.

"There is a doctor here. You must go see him."

"A doctor?" It was hard to believe. A real doctor?

There were two, actually: a doctor and a dentist. They found me asleep on the cot in the one-room medical center. Both were recent med school graduates sent to Bordj-Moktar for their mandatory national service.

They asked me the usual questions, poking and probing. "Have you taken any medication?"

When I told them Compazine, they grew very excited.

"You have Compazine? Really? How much?"

The state of medical facilities in Bordj-Moktar was such that in my little kit of pharmaceutical odds and ends I had more medicine than the army clinic. Too polite to ask, the doctors looked on my unused vials of Compazine with undisguised envy.

But what they did have was a two-bed infirmary and enough kindness to fill a major hospital. We spent a day and night under their care; mostly I slept while the two doctors engaged in intense intellectual discussions with Ann. For several hours they analyzed in detail the differences between the films *Platoon* and *Apocalypse Now*, with a corollary comparison of the Vietnam War to the Algerian battle for independence. Outside the window, the Sahara stretched for over a thousand miles.

The next morning they implored us to stay for another day, a week, a month. They said they'd send a military plane to Tamanrasset to retrieve my wife. Their final words were, "Be very careful. Crossing the Sahara, people still die. Every week a corpse is brought here. People get careless."

Late that afternoon, hours into the desert, the Cruiser died. We were stranded.

\\\

The demise of the Cruiser was quite undramatic: no flames, no grinding, just a quiet rolling to a halt. One minute we were chugging over the stony sand at thirty kilometers an hour and then there was nothing. The engine still roared mightily but no power reached the wheels.

We got out and walked around, staring in disbelief. The Cruiser had served us well. We loved the Cruiser. The Cruiser would not abandon us.

Particularly not in the middle of the Sahara Desert. This was uncalled for.

My feeble powers of automotive deduction pointed me toward a transmission problem. I thought about the epoxy sealing the gearbox.

All afternoon we tried to revive the Cruiser. We added oil to the gearbox, fluid to the clutch. We topped off the fuel tank. Nothing worked.

As the sun slipped away, a hot wind kicked up from the north; the blowing sand made cooking impossible. We laid our sleeping bags behind a wheel and fell asleep.

To be stuck in the Sahara with a dead car is never a pleasant prospect. But our situation was far from desperate. We had one hundred liters of water and food; we were traveling on or close to one of the major north-south routes of the desert. As these things go, we were in good shape. Someone, we figured, would pass us. It had to happen.

And it did: two Italians in a strange dune buggy vehicle bombing over the sand. Two Italian *mechanics.*

It was a stroke of extraordinary luck. In all of North and West Africa there were perhaps ten people capable of fixing the Land Cruiser—at least without spare parts. The problem was a dead clutch and the obvious solution was a replacement clutch. We didn't have one, nor did the Italians.

The two, Giancarlo and Marco, were the picture of Italian chic. Young and good-looking, they wore fashionable jeans and Polo shirts that would have done them proud in Milano. They approached the Cruiser's sad state as a great challenge, a puzzle plunked down in the Sahara for their amusement. For hours they worked under the car while I handed them cigars and coffee.

At first they feared it was hopeless. The clutch plate was completely worn. We discussed what to do: Ann would ride with them back to Bordj-Moktar and I would stay with the Cruiser.

But Giancarlo refused to accept defeat. After a cup of coffee and a discussion of Italian rugby tournaments (we discovered we had both played in the same tournament near Venice), he charged under the Cruiser and, after much cursing and banging of wrenches, proposed a solution.

"I think I can jam the car into gear. One gear, no clutch. You would have one gear. It might work."

Marco was dubious. "It is not easy to drive in the desert with *four* gears. With one . . ." He shrugged and threw up his hands.

But the alternatives were bleak. Even if Ann mustered a tow truck in Bordj-Moktar, it was doubtful there was a clutch to be had. We would have to leave the Cruiser there and catch a ride across the Sahara with a truck driver, buy a clutch then return. It was also questionable whether there was a mechanic in Bordj-Moktar who could install the clutch. It was, after all, a town of nine buildings.

And there was the question of my wife's arrival in Tamanrasset. I had concluded that we could never reach there in time, but I held hopes of finding a phone on the other side of the Sahara. There were, of course, no phones in Bordj-Moktar.

So we decided to risk the single gear. We debated for a long time the proper gear: should it be second or third? Marco and Giancarlo disagreed, each presenting eloquent arguments for his favorite gear.

In the end, third gear won. Marco did the deed. We restarted the Cruiser and it lumbered immediately forward, shuddering at the work of starting in third gear.

"Don't stop!" Marco and Giancarlo shouted, jumping up and

down in glee. I drove around them in a tight circle so we could talk. "Drive straight. Drive fast! Do not stop!!"

We left them puffing on the last of my Dannemann cigars, waving furiously.

Hundreds of kilometers lay between us and Reggane, the Algerian town on the northern edge of the Sahara.

The ride was the wildest of my life. With no gears to shift, speed was our only hope of making it through the soft stretches of sand. The Cruiser bucked and snorted like a wild mustang. As we flew over the sand ridges, all four wheels often left the ground, landing with a shuddering crash that felt as if a giant were beating on the roof with a sledgehammer. I tried not to think about the rear springs.

The wind continued to build into a sandstorm. We drove by compass directions, praying we wouldn't happen onto a parked truck convoy or a string of camels.

We drove all through the night, aided by a full moon. The wind died and we could see for miles in the pale light. It was strangely peaceful: the screech of the motor protesting its third-gear imprisonment, the white light spilling over the desert, the simplicity of our goal. Don't stop. Reach Reggane.

Just before dawn exploded on the desert, we saw the faint lights of a town hovering on the horizon.

Chapter
Twenty-six

I t was watching the engine lift out that really scared me. I felt a deep, wrenching sensation as Yusuf and I hung from the chain pulley, raising the diesel heart of the Cruiser toward the tin roof of his garage. Wires and hoses dangled like arteries. One thought ran through my head: *What have I done? My God, what have I done?*

"Ahhh!" Yusuf screeched triumphantly. He released the chain and climbed into the hood cavity where the pistons once throbbed so powerfully. This left me holding the chain supporting the engine.

"Now we can begin!" he crowed.

I wondered if he intended for me to stay attached to the chain for the duration.

Cheik-ben wandered into the garage with Ann, followed by Habib, the Palestinian. They gathered around the disemboweled Cruiser offering advice to Yusuf. No one seemed to notice me holding on to the chain.

"I had no idea," Ann said in an academic tone I found all too aloof, "that the entire engine had to come out so the clutch can be replaced. How interesting."

"Would somebody please tie off this chain!" I finally shouted.

We were in Adrar, the first sizable town north of Reggane. Still in third gear, the cruiser had limped into town on a Thursday afternoon. This proved unfortunate timing as it coincided with the beginning of the Muslim weekend. All of this was explained by the policeman who stopped us as soon as we entered the town.

The sand ladders mounted on the front—my beloved battering ram—had caught his eye.

"You don't need that here," he insisted with some indignation, as if we had insulted the progressive state of his hometown. "We have roads here. Good roads."

He warmed up to us when he realized we weren't French. (Adrar had been very close to the site of the French atomic bomb tests in the 1950s—*aboveground* tests. The leukemia rate was exceptional.) When we explained our predicament, he directed us to the town's best garage: Yusuf's.

"He is gone now," the policeman explained, "but I will go look for him." So we waited.

That's how Cheik-ben Bou Djemaa found us: waiting, parked in front of the big metal doors to Yusuf's garage. A gregarious fellow in his mid-thirties, Cheik-ben was short with a big belly and a scraggly black beard. His jewelry store adjoined the closed garage.

Immediately Cheik-ben expressed outrage that his town had treated us so poorly. "It is terrible you must wait here," he said. "What is happening that two visitors all the way from America must wait in the street!"

When we told him that the policeman had departed in search of Yusuf, he scoffed. "I know Yusuf. I take you to him."

His insistence was irresistible, as was his suggestion that Ann accompany him. "You must wait with the car," he explained to me, "so that if Yusuf returns you can tell him what is wrong."

"Of course," I agreed. It wasn't until a few minutes after Cheik-ben and Ann departed in his tiny Toyota that I wondered why it was necessary for Ann to accompany him. This I thought about more when two hours had passed and there was no sight of anyone: Ann, Yusuf or Cheik-ben.

Well, now, I thought, this is just great. Ann is probably headed for the auction block in Tangiers, I'm here with a dead car in a closed town, and my wife arrives in forty-eight hours. This is just swell.

But in truth I found it pleasant to lie back on the hood of the

Cruiser with nothing to do. My body still tingled with the jolts of the desert crossing. In a vague way I thought about what I would need to do if Ann did not return shortly: make inquires in Cheik-ben's store, look for Yusuf (if Yusuf really existed), find a policeman. I drifted to sleep.

Habib woke me up. "Can I help you?" he asked politely, like the steward on a cruise ship at teatime. He was a portly fellow wearing a tweed jacket and rep tie with a scarf thrown over his neck. His accent was English, his manner that of an amiable Oxford don.

"I'm waiting for a friend," I explained, trying to sound as casually elegant as he looked.

"I see." He peered at me through thick glasses. "You have friends in Adrar. How nice."

I told him the whole story. He chuckled when I expressed concern over Ann and Cheik-ben's lengthy absence. "They probably take coffee at Yusuf's home. It would be impossible for Yusuf not to insist that a foreign visitor take refreshment in his home. It would be a great insult."

I thought about Ann's fondness for refreshments and our lack thereof for quite some time. I was certain it would require little insistence on Yusuf's part.

Habib was a Palestinian, a teacher by profession, forced to Algeria with his family after 1948. With little prompting, he launched into an astoundingly intricate analysis of the Israeli-Palestinian situation. At regular intervals he interrupted the erudite lecture to grasp my arm, encrusted with a grimy layer of oil and sand, imploring, "You see? You must help us!"

Eventually I realized that he meant the United States government, rather than myself. I nodded vaguely, trying to come up with words befitting my new diplomatic status. It had been so long, however, since I had discussed anything more elaborate than a dead clutch or a flat tire that the best I could muster was a gravely, if ludicrously, uttered, "I see."

In fact this was probably not a bad start for a diplomat.

Just as Habib was demanding I explain the true relevance of

UN Resolution 242, Ann and Cheik-ben returned with Yusuf in tow.

"You have problem?" Yusuf asked.

"We had tea," Ann spoke up before I could answer. "And cakes. Wonderful sweet cakes."

Yusuf wanted French francs, not Algerian dinars. "Our money," he said cheerfully, "it is no good."

This was true. Algeria, unlike the former French colonies of West Africa, had strict currency regulations. Travelers declared all foreign funds upon entering the country and Algerian citizens were strictly limited in the amount of money they could take with them when leaving the country. As Algerians were a sophisticated lot with a keen interest in international travel and trade, they evolved numerous ingenious schemes to circumvent these annoying currency restrictions.

"There is a thriving black market both inside and outside the country," explains the Lonely Planet guide. "French francs are the preferred currency. The Algerian authorities are well aware of these rates, so they're very keen on preventing you from using the black market and, as a result, there are heavy baggage and body searches (shoes off, a quick look in your underpants, etc.). If you're taking in black market money, you'll need to hide it very well. If they find the money it will be confiscated."

Ever the good student, I followed this advice with great enthusiasm. Convinced my cleverness would win me a place in the Smuggler's Hall of Fame, I secreted a small fortune in French francs inside the hollow aluminum poles of my mountain tent.

But what had seemed so brilliant on conception had one resounding difficulty: I couldn't get the money out.

I discovered this after Yusuf and I negotiated a price for the new clutch, payment to be made in francs. While he worked in the empty cavity of the engine compartment, I unfolded the tent on the garage floor and set about to retrieve my artfully hidden funds.

Like Robinson Crusoe constructing his first canoe too far from the water, my clever planning had a rather basic flaw. I had assumed, to the degree I had considered the question, that the francs would simply slide out of the hollow poles. This proved inaccurate.

Habib and Cheik-ben watched while I whipped the tent poles through the air, trying to force the francs out of the open end.

"My people have suffered like no American can imagine," Habib droned.

"Please, Habib," I begged. "I am suffering. Believe me."

"But you are an American. Americans have no problems!"

I flailed the tent poles against the cinder-block floor.

"Habib, please. I am in Adrar with a car that has no clutch—"

"Yusuf replaces your clutch! No problem!"

"With all my money stuffed down these damn tent tubes."

"I believe that is Yusuf's problem," Cheik-ben chuckled.

"And my wife arrives in Algiers in two days."

"Algiers is a beautiful city. A city more greater than Paris!"

"And once she is in Algiers, she will get on a plane to Tamanrasset expecting to meet Ann and me and I will be sitting here in Yusuf's garage still trying to get my money out of these tent poles!"

"It was a very smart hiding place," Cheik-ben said thoughtfully. "I must remember it the next time I go to France."

"But why would you take a tent to France?" Habib, the scholar, asked. "The hotels in France are excellent. After the 1986 PLO council meeting in Tangiers, the old man and I traveled to Saint-Tropez."

I had one end of the pole in my mouth, alternately blowing and sucking. This caused the francs to ruffle teasingly but they remained firmly lodged.

"You should call your wife," Yusuf shouted from the depths of the Cruiser. "It is not good to keep your wife waiting!"

It was, of course, good advice. But telephoning from Adrar to America was a daunting challenge.

Complicating the procedure was Cheik-ben's fervent insistence that we use the telephone in his house, not the post office. "It is logical," he asserted, "because you must stay at my home."

I demurred. Adrar actually had a hotel, a rather decent-looking one. It was such a rarity, I was looking forward to a night between real sheets.

"For you to stay in the hotel and not my home would be a terrible, terrible insult. We cannot even talk about this." He scowled, and then broke into a huge grin when we accepted with thanks, embracing each of us in a crushing bear hug.

"You will like my mother," he promised.

Cheik-ben was the only man in a houseful of women: his mother, two sisters and a young black woman who seemed part servant, part family member. "She is very poor," Cheik-ben explained. "We take care of her since birth."

"She's a slave," Ann whispered. "A slave!"

This may have been true but then the same could have been said for Cheik-ben's mother and sisters. They hovered in the background of the four-room house, awaiting Cheik-ben's commands. These came with decided regularity.

Cheik-ben held court in the largest room in the house, decorated with thick pillows and rugs; the centerpiece of the room was a television resting on an orange crate. It was a comfortable, cozy space. Cheik-ben's life greatly resembled that of a stereotypical American teenage girl: he spent all spare moments watching television and talking on the telephone to his friends. The phone rang constantly. His callers apparently were situated in similar circumstances, as the favorite topic of conversation was a running commentary on the television show of the moment and what their mothers and sisters had just brought them to eat.

Cheik-ben and his pals were all Muslims; they also drank prodigious quantities of scotch. Friday night was the highlight of their week, not for religious but rather entertainment reasons. "Disco on television!" Cheik-ben shouted happily. "Tonight! Every Friday!"

A half dozen of his friends dropped by during the long American dance show dubbed in Arabic. They squatted around the delicious couscous prepared by the household's female contingent and debated fiercely the relative appeal of the dancing girls on television.

"If I come to America, she will marry me, yes?" Cheik-ben frequently inquired.

While the music blared, I tried continually to telephone my wife in America or the Air France office in Algiers to leave a message. The operators were gracious in the extreme but our efforts were futile. "Do you like disco?" my favorite female operator asked, hearing the music in the background. "I love to dance! I would love to dance this minute! I'm sorry, there are no circuits. I feel sadness for your wife."

It was that same operator who telephoned near dawn. "Have you heard?" she asked excitedly.

"Heard?"

"There is a strike in Algiers! That is why we could not get a circuit. A big strike!"

"I see." I started to fall asleep.

"But this is very good news for your wife!"

"It is?"

"The airport is closed! Her flight from America will be delayed. You will have time to finish your car repairs and drive to Algiers. Everything will be happy!"

I thanked her and hung up the phone. The disco show was over, replaced by a red and green test pattern. Cheik-ben and two of his friends snored loudly, wrapped in each other's arms like kittens. Scotch bottles and plates of dried couscous littered the floor.

"Is there any food left?" Ann asked sleepily. She was across the room, as far from Cheik-ben and his friends as possible. Toward the end of the evening they had been very interested in trying some of the American dances with a real American girl.

"In the kitchen," I said. "A big pot of couscous."

"I'm starved."

"Let's eat some couscous and then walk over to the hotel for coffee." We were still enthralled by the novelty of the hotel.

"And then we have to work on the poles," Ann reminded me. There were still several hundred dollars in francs stuck in the tent poles.

"I've got a new idea," she said. "What if we poured motor oil down the tubes and—"

"Oil?"

That afternoon, Yusuf finished the clutch repair. I paid him in francs, as agreed.

"But these francs, they are sticky! What has happened?" he cried, but slipped them into his pocket with alacrity.

As we were leaving, he handed me a large box of motor parts.

"What's this?" I asked.

"We had these parts left over after we put the engine back in."

I stared at the heavy box. "All these parts?"

He nodded happily. "It is much better. The car is lighter now and runs better. You can sell these in Algiers."

I started to stay something but didn't. I put the box in the car.

"How much do you think we can get for the parts?" Ann asked as we drove out of town.

We talked about it all the way to Algiers.

Abacus now offers an exciting range of quality titles by both established and new authors. All of the books in this series are available from:
    Sphere Books,
    Cash Sales Department,
    P.O. Box 11,
    Falmouth,
    Cornwall TR10 9EN.

Alternatively you may fax your order to the above address. Fax No. 0326 376423.

Payments can be made as follows: Cheque, postal order (payable to Macdonald & Co (Publishers) Ltd) or by credit cards, Visa/Access. Do not send cash or currency. UK customers and B.F.P.O.: please send a cheque or postal order (no currency) and allow £1.00 for postage and packing for the first book, plus 50p for the second book, plus 30p for each additional book up to a maximum charge of £3.00 (7 books plus).

Overseas customers including Ireland, please allow £2.00 for postage and packing for the first book, plus £1.00 for the second book, plus 50p for each additional book.

NAME (Block Letters) ....

ADDRESS ....

....

☐ I enclose my remittance for _____

☐ I wish to pay by Access/Visa Card

Number ☐☐☐☐☐☐☐☐☐☐☐☐☐☐☐☐

Card Expiry Date ☐☐☐☐

"There's an evil resistance out there searching for the immortal. It's only a matter of time before they find it."

Clivo looked at the bag of fur. Was it possible? Was the Otterman really the immortal? Lana was right, though. Even if it wasn't, it was another cryptid crossed off his list. But if it was, he had to get there before someone from the evil resistance found it. Especially the person who had killed his father. "Come back tomorrow afternoon. I'll try to find out where the Otterman is by then."

"How will you do that?" Lana asked, her eyes once again probing him, as if trying to read his mind.

"Like I said, once the immortal is in safe hands, I'll be happy to tell you."

Clivo waited until Lana and Thomas's rental car was far down the driveway before Skyping Stephanie. With the time change it was probably close to her bedtime, but he hoped she was still awake. It took a few moments, but eventually Stephanie's face appeared on the screen. Clivo knew she was in her room, as evidenced by the large bed behind her and the poster of Stephen Hawking on the wall. She was wearing flannel pajamas, her hair was sloppily pulled back, and she was munching on takeout Chinese food with chopsticks.

"Hi, Stephanie," Clivo said, relieved that she had picked up.

"Anyway, the Order has been digging through legends and folklore for decades, figuring out which creatures are just stories and which actually exist. But we didn't try to find the cryptids themselves, just things they left behind."

"Like what?" Clivo asked, his interest causing him to take a seat.

"What we all leave behind," Thomas said, picking at his teeth with a fingernail. "Strands of hair. Flakes of skin. Droppings."

"Is that what the lab coat is for? To analyze poop samples?" Clivo asked, not attempting to hide the mockery in his voice.

"Don't knock it, chief, everyone's poop tells a very interesting story." Thomas pulled a bag of nuts from the lab coat's pocket and popped one in his mouth.

Clivo was about to respond but stopped when he saw Lana's eyes shooting daggers at him, so he sank in his seat and motioned for her to continue, which she promptly did.

"Over the years, we haven't found an actual cryptid because we didn't need to waste our time finding every single one. We just needed to find the one that mattered, the immortal. So we examined what they left behind, figuring that if the cryptid was the immortal one, something in its hair or nail samples would indicate so."

Clivo considered that. It all made sense, that was for sure. "So, who's the immortal?"

Thomas kicked his legs off the table and, with a

flourish, laid the briefcase on top, like a magician preparing for his final trick. Lana pulled a key from her pocket and opened the sturdy locks. Clivo tried to peer inside, but Thomas moved the case so he couldn't see anything. Clivo sighed and waited as Thomas slowly pulled out a plastic bag and laid it on the table. Clivo instantly reached for it, but Thomas slapped his hand away.

"No touching, please," Thomas chided.

Clivo rolled his eyes and leaned in for a closer look. Inside the plastic bag was a ball of what looked to be brown fur. "What's that?" Clivo asked.

"A sample." Thomas grinned. "The immortal is none other than the Otterman, otherwise known as the Kooshdakhaa."

"I still have no idea what that is," Clivo replied.

"It's a mythical creature, half man and half otter. Legend says it either saves people from freezing to death or eats small children," Lana explained, applying a fresh coat of red lipstick. "We found that sample in a southeastern Alaska rain forest. It tested as fur belonging to no known animal and—"

"Let me! Let me!" Thomas said, snatching the bag. He carefully pulled out a sample of fur and held it in front of Clivo's face. "Watch this." He grabbed a lighter from his pocket and set fire to the fur, which promptly turned a bright silver and flashed like a sparkling firework. Thomas lowered his voice to a whisper. "All creatures, one blood.

Some remain hidden, others come fore. In one who is hidden, the blood is gone, replaced by the spring of life. A silver lightning drop of eternity."

Clivo let out a laugh of disbelief. "That's your proof? A bit of sparkling fur?"

Thomas threw the fur on the floor in frustration and stomped on it with his foot, leaving a burned spot on the carpet. "What more do you want, chief? We can't drag the Otterman in here and have him confirm it to you personally!"

"The proof is good, Clivo," Lana said, leaning toward him with a glint in her eye. "But even if we've made some kind of mistake, which we haven't, the worst that will happen is you'll cross another cryptid off your list."

"Or it'll eat my face off," Clivo mumbled. He ran a hand through his hair and let out a heavy exhale. "So, I guess you've come to me with this information because you want me to find it?"

Lana smiled. "We're here to help each other. We discovered the immortal; now you need to catch it."

"With our protection of course," Thomas added.

"How are *you* going to protect me?" Clivo asked him. "What skills do you have, besides an unhealthy interest in fur collecting?"

Thomas cracked his knuckles. "That's for me to know and you to find out."

"Time is of the essence, Clivo," Lana continued.

Stephanie's eyes suddenly snapped to the screen. With all the noodles dangling out of her mouth, she looked like a walrus.

"Clivo? Hey! Everything okay?" she mumbled as she quickly swallowed her food.

"Yeah, everything is fine. I think." Clivo told her everything Lana and Thomas had told him about the Otterman. He left out the part about his dad being murdered because he didn't want to scare her. As long as he didn't tell anybody about the Myth Blasters, they should be safe.

"Oh, boy, I may have to sedate Charles when he finds out. He *loves* the Otterman," she said, wiping her face with a napkin.

"What do you think about that? Do you think it's possible this creature is the immortal one?" Clivo asked.

The sun was setting, casting long shadows in the forest outside. His house creaked and groaned, like ghosts were dragging their chains across the floor upstairs—a horrible reminder of the gathering storm of evil.

Stephanie scratched her head. "Honestly, we've spent all of our time discovering which cryptids exist and how to find them. We haven't even begun to consider which one might be the immortal."

"I'm in a rush, Stephanie. Do you have any information on the Otterman?"

"We've researched it a bit. When do you need the intel by?"

Clivo winced. "Tomorrow?"

Stephanie began typing on her computer. "Okay, we know it's not in southeast Alaska anymore—"

Clivo raised his eyebrows in surprise. "Where did it go?"

Stephanie squinted at her computer screen. "Let's see. At one point the Otterman accidentally wound up in an airplane—don't worry, I'll explain that more later; we know approximately where that plane crashed but not the exact spot, so we could triangulate the last known flight path, but that would take too much time. Drat! I wish I still had access to my satellite, but that company is on to me and kicks me off the second I start poking around."

They sat in silence for a moment until a thought struck Clivo. "What if I could get you access to a satellite?"

Stephanie looked up. "*You* have satellite access?"

"I might. I'll call you back in an hour and let you know."

Stephanie scrambled for her phone. "Amazing. I'll rally the troops to come back over. Tomorrow's Saturday, so we can work here all night. We may just be able to pull this off, Clivo."

"Thanks, Stephanie. It's really great having your help on this."

"You're on our team now, remember? Helping is what we do." She looked down for a moment, a question forming on her face. "What are you going to do with the immortal when you find it? We haven't even talked about that."

Clivo played with the beaded bracelet around his wrist that his father had given him. Memories of his dad flashed through his head and his stomach knotted with grief. He thought about what his father would have done had he actually found the immortal, and suddenly he felt enormous sadness that Russell wasn't around to answer that question. "Honestly, I haven't really thought that far ahead yet."

"Don't worry, you'll figure it out. You're a smart kid, Clivo. You'll know what to do."

A look of confusion crossed Clivo's face.

"What? What is it?" Stephanie asked, concerned.

"It's just, well, nobody's ever accused me of being smart before," Clivo said with a slight laugh. "You're kinda the first in that department."

Stephanie looked at him with surprise. "Wait, but don't you speak, like, forty languages?"

"Only five," Clivo said, shrugging his shoulders. "I still ended up in remedial math."

Stephanie creased her forehead in deep thought. "Well, do *you* feel you're smart?"

Now it was Clivo's turn to think. After a moment he lifted his head and said with certainty, "Actually, I do. I mean, I can't hack satellites or identify a fake photograph, but I know I'm good at some things."

"There are many different ways to be smart, Clivo. I may be good at computers, but put me on a volleyball court and I'm dumb as a stump. Sometimes it just takes time to find out what you're good at."

Clivo smiled—as much as he could under the circumstances, anyway. "Are you going to follow that up with a joke?"

Stephanie laughed. "No way! It took me, like, a week to come up with the last one. Yet another area I stink at."

Clivo laughed, too. Even with everything going on, it suddenly felt like a huge weight had been lifted off his shoulders. "I'll let it slide. Call you in an hour."

"We'll be ready, smarty-pants."

XVII

Clivo hopped on his bike and sped down the mountain toward town, flipping on his handlebar light to beat back the lengthening shadows of the coming night. He had sent Jerry an e-mail telling him he was on his way with a severe math problem. It was evening already, so hopefully Jerry was home and not stuck at SETL with some monumental alien discovery.

He arrived forty-five minutes later, panting from exertion, and was relieved to see the lights on in his friend's bedroom.

He was about to knock on the front door when Jerry flung it open, Hercules the dog cradled in his arms. "You're doing *what*?" he exclaimed.

"Honey, keep it down," Mrs. Cooper yelled from the kitchen, where she was stirring a steaming pot. "Hi, Clivo, baby!"

"Hi, Mrs. Cooper." Clivo waved and then did his best not to wince as he caught a smell drifting from the kitchen that reminded him of dirty feet wrapped in cabbage.

Jerry pulled Clivo upstairs into his bedroom, which was filled with posters of football players and reeked of a smell suspiciously like aftershave. It was in stark contrast to Clivo's bedroom, which held tribal dream catchers and smelled like incense. "You're doing *what*?"

Clivo filled Jerry in on everything that had happened in the past few days—although once again he left out the part about his father being murdered; he just wasn't ready to talk about it, even with his best friend.

"Hang on, hold up," Jerry said. "You're going to *Alaska*?"

"I have to, Coops. The Otterman took a plane somewhere that crashed; I'm just not sure exactly where."

Jerry's eyes widened and his voice rose a few octaves. "The Otterman took a plane somewhere? Of course he did, probably coach too, since they don't allow HAIRY OTTER MONSTERS IN FIRST CLASS!"

Clivo held his hands up and tried to shush his friend. "I know it sounds crazy, Coops, and I don't have the whole story, but I'm pretty sure this is the immortal one and I need to find it fast. All I need you to do is steal SETL's computer codes so this girl I met can break into one of your satellites."

Jerry's eyes snapped from wide to narrow. Even Hercules looked at Clivo with a whine. "That's all, huh?"

There was a tapping at the door and Mrs. Cooper

yelled, "Clivo, hon, you need a snack? I can juice you some greens."

"No, thank you, Mrs. Cooper, I'm fine."

Jerry went to the door. "Ma! Privacy! We talked about this. When I have guests over you need to give me a wide berth for man time."

"Just showing interest in your social life," she said, her voice sounding like her lips were pressed right up against the door.

"Which is exactly what I don't need you to do! I'm a teenage man now! Scootch." Jerry eventually opened the door a crack to make sure she had gone. "Anyway, where were we? Oh yeah, the part where I tell you there's no way I'm passing over our satellite codes."

"Why, 'cause you don't know how to steal them?"

"No! I stole them a long time ago! And if I give them to you my dad will know and send me to a military academy because I keep stealing stuff!"

"Come on, Coops. It's not for anything bad. She just needs to get a closer look at something," Clivo pleaded.

"Wren, our satellites look into space to find aliens. Not down at Earth to find large, angry otters. The operators will know in a second someone's hacked in, and my dad will come looking my way first. I can't risk it, Wren; Dad would kill me."

Clivo was amazed. "You put blue dye in your dad's

shampoo last month! How is *this* suddenly taking things too far?"

"It just is, okay!" Jerry yelled back. "Messing with my parents and teachers and the people at the grocery store deli counter is one thing. But my dad's work is off-limits. No trespassing—got it?"

Clivo looked at his best friend and spoke the next part softly. "If the evil resistance finds the immortal, none of that stuff will matter, Coops."

Jerry let out a long sigh of exasperation and plopped down on the edge of his bed. He sat in silence, scratching Hercules behind the ears as Clivo stared at the floor. When the dog began to snore, Jerry finally spoke.

"All right. I'll do it. Even though my parents will probably kick me out of the house and I'll have to come live with you and the furballs," Jerry said morosely.

"Thanks, Coops. And if your dad finds out and comes after you, I'll tell him it was all my idea. I'll take the fall."

"Nah, I can handle the heat," Jerry said. "Just look out for yourself and don't get killed, okay? That newspaper picture may have made you look like some kind of beast slayer, but you're still a softie in my book."

Clivo remembered beating Blirgenbach in the fight after taking a branch to the head, but he didn't think now was the time to tell his friend about it.

Jerry put Hercules on the floor and stood up, letting

out a dramatic sigh as he did. "Okay, might as well get on throwing my future down the toilet. Who am I giving the information to?"

Another knock sounded on Jerry's door.

"For the love of Moses! I said a wide berth!" Jerry yelled before yanking open the door. Mrs. Cooper quickly stepped forward.

"Sorry to interrupt you boys again. You're staying for dinner, right, Clivo? We're having a special brussels sprout stew."

Clivo had completely forgotten about their Friday-night dinner plans. "Shoot, I'm really sorry, Mrs. Cooper, but I just can't stay tonight. Can I take a rain check for next week?" He always enjoyed their dinners together, but he was so distracted by everything going on, there was no way he could pretend to have a regular conversation.

"Of course, hon," Mrs. Cooper replied. "I'll pack some stew for you when you're ready to go."

Jerry slowly closed the door on his mom, who was still hovering in the doorway.

"Out! This is my private space! I am a man now and demand my own private space!" Jerry stomped his foot in frustration.

As soon as the door was closed, Clivo pulled his laptop out of his backpack and Skyped Stephanie. She answered quickly, and the other Blasters were standing happily behind her, their faces crammed into the camera's view.

"DUDE!" Charles said, his face bright red with joy. "The Otterman is the immortal?! I may have to be sedated because I am literally about to have an out-of-body experience!"

"That's intense stuff, man," Adam agreed. "In-flipping-tense. Gotta give mad respect to whoever figured that out."

"Mad respect," Hernando agreed.

"Who are these nerds?" Jerry whispered to Clivo. "That one guy has a rad set of single-forever glasses."

"Guys, this is my best friend, Jerry. He'd like to be part of your team, if that's okay," Clivo said.

"What's up?" Jerry said.

"'Sup," Adam responded, puffing his chest out in an attempt to look more muscular.

Charles eyed Jerry suspiciously. "We'll give him a one-day emergency team membership. After that, he's gonna have to earn it."

"One day only," Hernando concurred.

Clivo nodded in acceptance. "That's all we need. Stephanie, Jerry's going to give you access to his dad's work computers and from there you can steer their satellite."

"Got it. Jerry, what company does your father work for?" Stephanie's fingers hovered over her keyboard.

Jerry looked at Clivo uncertainly.

"The fate of mankind is determined by this, Coops. Please?"

Jerry grunted. "This Earth-saving crusader stuff better not cramp my style, Wren. Fine, he works for the SETL Institute."

The Myth Blasters stared at Jerry as if he had suddenly turned into the tooth fairy.

"You're giving us access to a *SETL satellite*?" Amelia asked in awe.

"Have you guys found any aliens yet?" Charles interjected.

Adam cheered. "That's, like, deep-space stuff, man. We could spin that baby around and check out the Andromeda Galaxy! That's totally an alien playground, I know it!"

"Hang on, hang on!" Jerry said, pointing his finger at the screen. "I am giving you access to this satellite only for terrestrial research, not *extra*terrestrial research. If you take one peek into space, I'm cutting off your access, got it?"

"He's a spicy one," Adam muttered.

Stephanie focused the computer's camera onto herself, blocking out the others. "Don't worry, Jerry, I'll do a quick Earth scan and be right off, okay?"

Jerry relaxed a bit. "Okay. This can get me in serious trouble, so just try and be fast."

Stephanie cracked her knuckles. "I'll be in and out quick as a whisper."

"She's kinda adorkable," Jerry whispered to Clivo. "Okay, Stephanie, let's make some magic."

As Stephanie was gaining access to the satellite, the rest of the Myth Blasters went to work in the background.

"Okay, Blasters," Amelia began, rubbing her hands together. "It's showtime. Hernando—"

"Present," Hernando said, raising his hand.

"I want you to dig up the plane's flight path and last known coordinates so Stephanie has a smaller search area. Charles—"

"Locked and loaded," Charles said, cracking open a Moxie.

"I want you to do the same for the last known radio call from the plane. Adam—"

"Yup."

"See if you can find any information on this International Secret Order of Mythological Beasts, Legends, and Cryptid Catchers. First of all, it's a stupid name, and second of all, I've never heard of them and that bothers me." Amelia was playing with her nose ring, her face wrinkled in concentration. "As for me, I'll research whatever clues I can find in the literature regarding the Otterman while Stephanie hacks. Clivo, might as well get some rest; we'll be at this all night."

"All right, thanks, guys. I'll talk to you in the morning," Clivo replied.

When Jerry had finished with Stephanie, Clivo closed his computer. Jerry was shaking his head. "That's a very interesting team you've got there, Wren. I just hope you know what you're doing."

"I don't, but *they* do."

Saturday

XVIII

The next morning Clivo paced around his house,
glancing at the grandfather clock in the dining room every
few minutes. To say he hadn't slept the night before was
putting it lightly. He had tossed and turned and finally
gotten up at three A.M. to stare out the window, watching
the light rain that was now falling as if it could somehow
take his mind off of what lay in front of him. No matter
how many lights he turned on, he still felt like he was being
swallowed in darkness.

He finally went into the hallway and looked at pictures
of his mom hanging on the wall, hoping they would bring
him comfort. There was one of them sledding together;
another one showed her smiling as she rubbed noses with
him as a baby. Clivo suddenly doubted his ability to do
the right thing if he actually found the immortal. If he
had found it before his mom died, he would have given
her the gift of immortality, just so he wouldn't have to lose
her. But who got to decide who lived forever and who
didn't? Did Douglas get to make that choice, too? Clivo

shuddered at the thought of Douglas yelling at him for all eternity.

Clivo took a deep breath and realized that before figuring out any of these questions, he first had to face the Otterman, who might enjoy eating kids for a snack. If he survived that, then he could deal with the question of living forever.

The clock chimed seven and Clivo turned away from his mom's photos, wishing that she were there to shake the Egyptian rattle over him. He needed all the protection he could get right now.

Finally his computer dinged and he raced to it.

"Good morning," Stephanie yawned.

"Hey! How'd it go? Did you guys find out where the Otterman is?" Clivo asked, eager to know what his next step was. He was hoping his nerves would subside once he had something to focus his mind on.

"Yeah, we did!" Charles yelled, his hair puffed out like a cotton ball and his eyes wild.

"Sorry, he's been chugging energy drinks all night and is about to have a stroke," Stephanie explained.

Adam ushered Stephanie out of her seat, jelly from a powdered doughnut covering his face. "Hey, dude. So we've compiled our data, but we didn't have time to put a formal presentation together so we're going to have to wing it."

"I'm going to give you a shortened version of the

Otterman's origin tale," Charles interrupted, pushing Adam's face out of the way.

"Dude! Out of my face and chill! Origin stories are my territory!" Adam yelled, engaging in a quick hand-slapping war with Charles.

"Dude! We talked about this! The Otterman tale is all mine!" Charles yelled back.

"Oh, right. Sorry, man. Take a seat."

"Thanks, dude," Charles said, taking Adam's seat. Charles took a deep breath, closed his eyes, and steepled his fingers under his chin, as if this was something he had been waiting for his whole life and he wanted to savor every moment of it. He finally opened his eyes and spoke in a slow, reverent tone. "The Otterman. That beast of the Alaskan wilderness. Similar to the infamous Alaskan Hairy Man but way cooler, since the Hairy Man is pretty peaceful and doesn't feast on human flesh for dinner."

Adam poked his head in and yelled in Charles's ear: "Today, frizzhead, before the evil resistance finds the otter dude!"

Charles waved Adam away and continued, though he did speak a little faster. "In the folklore of the Tlingit Indian tribe, *kushtaka* means 'land otter man.' Some say the Otterman saves lost people by turning them into other Ottermen. But our evidence shows that the existence of many of these cryptids is highly unlikely. Which means the other legend must be true—there's only one Otterman, and it sends out a high-pitched whistle to lure sailors and children into its clutches, whereupon it eats them using its razor-sharp teeth. That makes the Otterman one of the most malicious cryptids out there, perhaps due to its existence in sad yet manly isolation in the desolate rain forests of southernmost Alaska—"

Adam popped his head into the screen again. "We said no poetry, dude, stick to the facts."

Charles paused for a moment and took a sip of water, letting out a long exhale before again steepling his fingers and continuing on. "As for its origin tale, it's a cool one. Many people claim the O-man is a shape-shifter, an otter that turns into a man—a wereotter, if you will. We already know of creatures on Earth that shape-shift, such as the chameleon, puffer fish, and rain frog, but their shifting is pretty small compared to a tiny otter busting into an eight-foot-tall man. But what if something happened that did allow for such a crazy transformation? Let Hernando demonstrate."

Hernando stood behind Charles holding a rock and a stuffed animal far apart from each other. Then he slowly brought them toward each other while making loud jet-engine noises. At the last second he slammed them together with an explosive sound, a bit of spittle shooting from his lips.

Charles applauded. "As Hernando just demonstrated, this is where astrobiology and cryptozoology intersect. We believe that a massive meteor discovered in southeast Alaska in the 1800s delivered a space organism that affected the DNA of an otter, allowing it to shape-shift into a wereotter."

Clivo tried to picture a cute furry creature turning into a flesh-eating beast. "And how does it camouflage itself?"

"As far as we know, it just turns back into an otter," Charles said, scratching his nose. "But we are still researching other options that would be more awesome."

"And where is it? Stephanie mentioned something about it no longer being in southeast Alaska," Clivo said, feeling like he was talking to some kind of nerdy oracle.

"Now, listen to this little awesome-sauce piece of adventure," Charles began, his eyes opening even wider with excitement.

"No way, dude, my turn. Move it," Adam said, pushing Charles out of his seat. "Okay, so get this: the Otterman is still in Alaska, just in a different part. Fifteen years ago there was a big project to relocate some otters out of southeastern Alaska by airplane because there were just too many of them. The plane crashed en route to its destination, and since then there's been no sightings whatsoever of the Otterman."

Adam took a bite of a jelly doughnut and stared at the screen in silence as he chewed.

"Today, Adam," Amelia's annoyed voice said from off-camera.

"Dramatic pause completed. Moving on," Adam continued. "We believe the Otterman ended up on this plane in otter form and shape-shifted to the man beast when the plane was in flight, thus scaring the bejesus out of everyone on board and causing the plane to crash. More proof for this theory is that close to a year after the plane crash, sightings of the Alaskan Hairy Man began to pop up in the Revelation Mountains, where the plane crash happened. But the Alaskan Hairy Man is in the southwest part of the state, which is nowhere near the Revelation Mountains."

Clivo took a moment to absorb all the information. "And do you think it's possible the Otterman is the immortal cryptid?"

"YES!" Charles yelled from the back of the room, where he was pacing back and forth in excitement.

Amelia pulled up a chair and sat next to Adam. "Honestly, we don't know, Clivo, but it's possible. If the Otterman was created by an extraterrestrial organism, who knows what other special powers it has? What proof do you have?"

Clivo looked at the carpet where Thomas had stamped out the flaming fur. He found a little bit that wasn't singed and grabbed some matches from a drawer in a cabinet. "Apparently this is some Otterman fur. Watch." Clivo lit the fur with a match, silver sparks instantly springing from it. All five Myth Blasters looked at him with blank stares.

"That's your proof?" Amelia asked. "Sparkling fur?"

"Don't ever become a scientist, dude," Adam said, shaking his head. "That's the weakest proof I've ever seen."

"I thought it was pretty," Hernando said quietly.

"Guys, I'm just the messenger here," Clivo said defensively. "The Order says they've run other tests on this fur, too, and it doesn't come up as any known animal."

"Speaking of which, Clivo," Amelia said, "we couldn't find any information on this International Secret Order of Mythological Beasts, Legends, and Cryptid Catchers. They're either off the grid or this Lana and Thomas are not who they say they are."

"They're British. Maybe that's why you can't find stuff about them," Clivo offered.

The Blasters all rolled their eyes and murmured, "Oh, they're *British* cryptozoologists."

"Still," Amelia chimed in, "crypto folk love talking to each other and sharing their ideas. It's part of what we do—mainly to try and one-up each other. If they're for real, we should have heard of them. Just be careful."

"And watch out for bears and wolves in Alaska. That's wild country up there," Adam added.

Clivo swallowed. "Does *anything* live there that doesn't want to eat me?"

Stephanie tapped Adam on the shoulder and took his place in front of the camera. "I e-mailed you a map with coordinates and satellite photos that show the plane crash site. There are a couple of lakes and streams around there where the Otterman should be."

"I summoned Nessie with food; maybe I'll try the same thing with the Otterman. Any idea what it eats?" Clivo asked.

Stephanie pursed her mouth shut and looked worried. Charles once again yelled from the back of the room, "It's a man-eater, dude! You're the food!"

Clivo gulped.

Stephanie gave Clivo an encouraging smile. "Remember, an animal shape-shifts to protect itself when it's in danger. You may have to provoke whatever otters are up there to find the right one. You got this."

"Right, I just need to encourage a man-eating beast to attack me," Clivo said, attempting to return the smile. "Talk to you guys soon. I hope."

Clivo hung up with the Myth Blasters and grabbed his phone to call Douglas.

"Are you dying?" Douglas's gruff voice asked.

"No," Clivo replied, already wincing in anticipation of Douglas yelling at him.

"Then why are you calling me?" It sounded like Douglas was chewing on some very crunchy chips.

"Well, I just wanted to let you know that I think I've found the immortal," Clivo said excitedly.

"You *think*, or you *have*?" Douglas replied, giving a little belch.

"I think I have. I mean, I'm pretty sure. I just have to go find it." Clivo's excitement was slowly leaking out of him like a deflating balloon. Douglas tended to have that effect on him.

"Good. Go find it, *then* you can call me and I'll be sure to shower you with congratulations. Otherwise, you're just a pest. Anything else?"

Clivo took a deep breath. "Well, I'm going to find the Otterman."

There was a long pause on the other end of the line. "Oh, I'm sorry, am I supposed to say something here?"

"It's just . . . well, it's pretty dangerous, and if for some reason I don't, you know, make it back, I just wanted to make sure you'll tell Aunt Pearl. I mean, not that I was killed by the Otterman, obviously, but just let her know *nicely* that I won't be coming home. And that I love her."

"I'll do all of that, except telling her you love her. Too mushy for my taste. Good luck, kid, and try not to get killed," Douglas said.

"Wait, wait! I have one question!" Clivo quickly said.

Douglas moaned heavily in exasperation but didn't say anything.

"Do you know who killed my dad? I know it wasn't the chupacabra."

"How do you know that?" Douglas growled.

"Well, to be honest, I've met—"

"Bah, doesn't matter," Douglas interrupted. He let out

a long sigh, and for the first time his voice sounded comforting. "I don't know who killed him, kid. And I'm sorry about that, but believe me, I'm looking for them. I told you it was the chupacabra because it was far better than the truth. And it made for a good story, your dad going down fighting a fearsome beast. Instead, his death was senseless, a huge loss, and I'll be honest, I miss the man. And if I ever find out who did it, you can be sure they'll be answering to me. You probably haven't noticed, but if I put my mind to it I can be a very nasty person."

The last part almost made Clivo laugh, which was good because it tamped down the lump that had been growing in his throat. "Okay, thank you, Mr. Chancery."

"You're welcome, kid. Now, this heartfelt conversation is about to make me throw up on my shoes, so I'm going to rudely hang up on you. Good luck. Go and save the world."

XIX

A few hours later, Thomas and Lana came knocking.
Clivo opened the door to a hailstorm that was blanketing
the ground with icy pebbles.

"Good afternoon, sunshine!" Thomas said, clapping
him on the back and sauntering in, tracking water all over
the hardwood floors.

"Good afternoon," Lana said, climbing up the stairs
with a smile. Her hair was pulled up in a ponytail and she
was wearing a cozy, oversized sweater. But she still wore her
vampire-red lipstick.

"So, give us the update on your progress, chief," Thomas
said, helping himself to a ginger ale from the fridge.

Lana looked at Clivo's backpack resting by the door,
all packed and ready for the trip.

"You found the Otterman already," Lana said. It wasn't
a question, and once again she looked like she was trying
to read his mind.

"I did," Clivo said, averting his gaze. If she could read

minds, he wasn't taking any chances. Amelia had said not to trust these guys, so he didn't.

"You found the Otterman already?" Thomas sputtered, dripping soda on his lab coat. "How did you do that?"

"Does it matter?" Clivo challenged. "The point is, we need to leave immediately. I have to be back by Monday or my aunt Pearl will send the whole U.S. Army after me. We might have time to find the immortal and be back by then."

"Your aunt Pearl is the least of our worries right now. If you know where the Otterman is, I'm sure other catchers do as well," Lana said distractedly, her eyes still on him. Clivo thought she should have a staring contest with Blirgenbach to see whose eyes shot laser beams first. "But really, how did you do this so quickly? Did you have help?"

Clivo glanced at her. Her expression was innocent, but she was waiting eagerly, her fingernails clicking together. Even her nail polish was blood-red. Clivo made a mental note to ask the Myth Blasters if they had evidence that witches exist.

He grabbed his things and ignored her probing question. "Do you guys have winter gear?"

"We came prepared for anything; we're fine," Lana said. She looked outside at the storm that was whipping into a windy frenzy. "But I don't know about getting a flight out. They're all probably canceled with this hail."

Clivo had a thought. "I might know someone who can help us."

Thomas's rental car practically slid to the airport in the ferocious storm. The roads were flooded and visibility was nearly zero. Spun-out cars littered the sides of the road like some apocalyptic wasteland. Finding a plane to take them in this weather would be a miracle.

They ran into the terminal, which was packed with stranded passengers dragging their luggage, looks of defeat on their faces. Clivo wove his way through the throng to the Pangaea Air counter, and his heart sank when he saw the long line of angry passengers.

He glanced frantically at the ticketing agents and was relieved to see the woman with heavy makeup who had helped him a few days earlier. She was calmly talking to a red-faced man who was screaming at her, her disheveled hair showing the strain she was under. Clivo pushed to the front of the line, much to the shouted indignation of those around him.

"Sir, as I've stated, Pangaea Air does not control the weather," she said with a weary smile.

"Well, who does?" the red-faced man retorted.

"That would be Mother Nature, sir."

"Well, get her out here. Immediately. I have some strong words for her."

The woman sighed, but her face brightened when she saw Clivo waving his Diamond Card.

"Mr. Wren! Welcome back, young man. How can I help you?"

The red-faced man was so flustered by being dismissed that he huffed and puffed as he tried to get some strong words out.

"Hi," Clivo gasped, chest heaving from his run through the airport. "Is Serge here? It's an emergency."

The woman slammed her hand on the red button without another word, and Serge practically broke down the door behind her.

"Mr. Wren! You okay?" Serge asked, his high voice rising even higher.

Clivo spoke softly. "Serge, can you help me and a couple friends fly out of here?"

"Come on back. I've gotcha covered."

Clivo motioned to Lana and Thomas and they all hurried through the door behind the counter. The red-faced man picked up his things and attempted to follow, but Serge slammed the door in his face.

"Come on, folks, head to the back," Serge said, hustling them along with his tree-trunk arms.

They ran through the inner workings of the airport, past empty luggage conveyor belts that were squeaking and shuddering. Bored airport workers sat on crates, playing cards underneath flickering fluorescent bulbs.

"Are you in danger, Mr. Wren?" Serge asked, his caterpillar brow doubling up in worry.

"I'm going to be if I don't get to the Revelation Mountains in Alaska as soon as possible. Can you help us?"

"Of course. Take the hallway to your right."

They turned down a hallway that was filled with cardboard boxes on wooden pallets stamped with the words SPEEDY STAMP!: WHEN YOU NEED A PACKAGE TODAY, WE'LL GET IT THERE YESTERDAY. An open freight door stood in front of them, ushering in the pelting ice.

As they approached the door, Clivo heard the welcome sound of an airplane engine. Standing in the storm was an older guy decked out like an English barnstormer in a leather jacket, brown cap, and long white scarf. He was loading some of the packages into an old but sturdy-looking propeller airplane.

"Alex!" Serge yelled, though it sounded like a baby squeaking.

Alex turned around and smiled broadly.

"Serge! My man! How's it shakin'?"

Serge gestured to Clivo, Lana, and Thomas. "I have some very precious cargo for you. You still heading to Alaska?"

"Does a beaver chew on wood? It'd take more than a few raindrops to ground me and Bertha." Alex patted the airplane, which was covered with scratches and corrosion. A fleck of paint came loose and landed on the ground.

Thomas turned to Serge, craning his neck to look up at him. "You want this very precious cargo to fly in *that*?"

"Trust me, Alex is the best. He flew dogfight missions in Vietnam. Rumor has it he landed a fighter jet on a carrier after its wings were half blown off. If anyone can get you good folks through this storm, it's him."

They looked at Alex, who was rubbing his hands furiously and cackling with glee. "All aboard! I hope you don't get airsick!"

Alex took off into the storm, the plane dipping and dodging as if trying to avoid every pellet of hail. Clivo cinched his seat belt tight and looked out the window into nothing but gray clouds. He did his best to shut out the sound of Thomas losing his lunch in one airsickness bag after another behind him.

After the plane had traveled through the worst of the storm and leveled off above the clouds, Alex called back to them over the roar of the propellers.

"Okay, folks, someone want to tell me where you're going?"

Clivo unbuckled his seat belt, grabbed the printed map from Stephanie's e-mail, and took the seat next to Alex. He looked out the front window into the dark sky and felt like he was flying into a black hole. "We're heading to the Revelation Mountains."

Alex whistled. "Can't get any more remote than that. Just plug the coordinates into my GPS there."

Clivo moved to type the coordinates on an ancient keyboard attached to a small screen with dangling wires. On his first tap of a key, a small spark shot out, causing him to withdraw his hand with a yelp.

Alex cackled. "Ha! Does that every time! Should be fine now; go ahead."

Clivo delicately typed in the rest of the coordinates, grateful that he wasn't electrocuted again. As soon as he was done, a red dot emerged on a radar screen. Alex let out another whistle.

"Going right into the belly of the beast, aren't you?"

"What do you mean?" Clivo asked.

"That's where the beast lives. You going monster hunting?" Alex gave him a wink.

"No, no monster hunting for us. We're just doing some camping," Clivo lied.

"It's okay to admit it," Alex continued. "Lots of folk go up there looking to find a creature. And there's plenty of 'em. Alaska is filled to the brim with superstitions and lore. My guess is you're looking for the Hairy Man. Can't be the Otterman, he's only been seen farther south."

"You know the stories about the Hairy Man?" Clivo asked, turning toward him.

"Sure do," Alex said, taking his hands off the steering

271

yoke and giving his arms a good stretch over his head, causing the plane to go into a sharp dive. Clivo resisted the urge to reach over and pull the plane up. After a good yawn, Alex grabbed the yoke's handles again and leveled them off. "I fly up there a lot to deliver packages. The locals who work at the airport talk about this stuff all the time. Howls heard in the night, large footprints in the snow. The Dena'ina Indians have plenty of stories about seeing the Hairy Man, always from a distance, though. Some natives claim the Hairy Man ran off with their children, but those are just stories to keep their kids from misbehaving."

"How do you know they're just stories?" Clivo asked, intrigued.

"Most monster folklore is just stories to scare people into doing the right thing. The 'Don't lie or the bogeyman will get you' sort of thing. But the real monsters, the real legends? They exist all right, but they'll never be found."

"Why not?" Clivo asked, picturing his father and the twelve cryptids he had caught.

Alex was scanning the horizon. "Well, creatures become legends when they exist but are never discovered. That's because although they walk the same earth as us, they exist in a different dimension, a magical one, if you will, that's just slightly out of time from us. We may catch glimpses of them occasionally, if our two worlds intersect, but only for a second."

Clivo considered that. He supposed it was possible, although he wondered what the Myth Blasters thought about the existence of magic. "But what about Nessie? She's a legend and someone found her."

Alex's face fell and for a moment his hands slipped from the steering yoke again, causing the plane to drift to the right. "By golly, you're right." Alex stared blankly ahead for so long Clivo thought the plane might do a somersault until Alex finally righted them again. "Something's happening then, kid. Either our world is growing stronger, or the magical one is growing weaker. Either way, the worlds of legend and reality are colliding."

"In that case, I may just have a shot at finding the Hairy Man," Clivo said with a joking laugh.

Alex looked at him, his grizzled face sad. "You just might. And that won't be a good thing."

"Why not?" Clivo asked, disturbed by the worry in Alex's face.

"People need their myths, son. They need to believe in something greater than themselves. They need to believe there is still some mystery in the world. If you take that away from them, the world could be plunged into chaos. Just do me a favor—if you do find the Hairy Man, don't ever tell anyone. Ever. The world needs its magic, and you have no business taking it away."

Clivo looked out into the night, into the darkness that stretched before him. His dad had always said that, too—that some things needed to stay hidden. Was that why his dad had never told him that cryptids existed? Was it simply to preserve some kind of magic? To keep some sort of mystery alive in the world? Once again Clivo felt the burning frustration that he would never know the answer.

"Feel free to get some rest, folks," Alex said, settling into his seat. "We'll be flying through the night, so now is a good time to get some shut-eye."

Clivo went back to his seat and tried to sleep, although all he could think about was how he couldn't imagine a good enough reason for his father to have lied to him for his whole life, and wishing with all his might that his father hadn't.

Sunday

XX

After a fitful night's sleep in the cargo plane, Clivo woke just as daylight was cracking. He'd dreamed about his father and mother, about all of them traveling the world together as a family to search for cryptids. They'd eventually found what looked to be a small, harmless dragon, but it immediately attacked them, tearing at them with long claws and sharp teeth, an inferno of fire spewing from its mouth. His mom tried to escape the flame and ended up toppling over a cliff, his dad managing to grab her arm just before she fell into a chasm filled with lava.

Clivo's father turned to him, his face red and sweaty from the exertion of holding Clivo's mom, and yelled, "Why did you insist on coming, Clivo? I tried to keep you away from all this!"

The dragon exhaled another burst of fire and his mom and dad fell over the cliff, Clivo screaming as he ran forward. He scrambled to grasp his parents' hands as they slipped away, but was unable to reach them before they disappeared into the river of lava. He was jerked awake with the sound of his scream still in his ears.

Clivo rubbed his eyes and looked over at Lana and Thomas. Thomas was soundly asleep, his open mouth emitting snores loud enough to drown out the hum of the propellers. Lana was awake, her fingers typing away on a phone. She glanced up and saw Clivo looking at her, so she smiled, but Clivo noticed that she slid the phone quickly into her pocket.

Ahead, the sky was just brightening over the tallest mountains Clivo had ever seen. They rose up like a field of granite towers from the snow-covered landscape. He thought about his task—to find the immortal and keep its secret safe from the evil resistance. He thought about Lana and Thomas. Something about them was still making Clivo's hair stand on end. He trusted the Myth Blasters; he even trusted nasty Douglas. But there was something about Lana and Thomas that still seemed off.

Clivo shook the doubts from his head. There wasn't anything he could do about it now. He needed their protection, and if having them along helped him find the Otterman first, then so be it.

Alex lowered his goggles to his eyes and shouted over his shoulder, "Okay, folks, hold on to your seats! Getting to this landing strip can be a bit tricky!"

Clivo cinched his seat belt tight just as Alex dove straight down, barely missing the peak of a mountain.

Thomas awoke with a snort and immediately began screaming. Clivo closed his eyes and gripped his armrests, willing himself not to do the same. He peeked over at Lana, who was calmly putting on a fresh coat of red lipstick while humming to herself.

After what felt like a long free fall toward certain death, the plane leveled out and landed with a hard bounce on a frozen runway. They taxied for a few minutes before arriving at a small building that must have been the terminal, although it was no bigger than a shack.

Clivo climbed out of the airplane and was instantly hit by the coldest air he had ever felt. The airport was in a small valley surrounded by towering, snow-covered mountains on all sides. "Remote" didn't even begin to describe the place.

Alex climbed out behind him, wrapping his arms around himself for warmth. "Welcome to the end of the world. This airport serves as the last outpost before the Revelation Mountains. You can get some food inside and rent snowmobiles. But if you get lost, don't expect any help to come for you. Once you leave this place, you're on your own."

"Thanks, Alex," Clivo said, shaking his hand. "I really appreciate your help in getting us here."

"Oh, I didn't do it for charity," Alex said. "This junket cost you an arm and a leg, believe me."

"That's fine," Clivo said, knowing that Douglas would blow a gasket at the cost. "I'm still grateful."

"Good luck, kid. Just remember—some things aren't meant to be found. But if you do find anything, I hope you're smart enough to know what to do with it."

"Me, too," Clivo replied.

Clivo, Lana, and Thomas rented snowmobiles, packed up some food and water, and headed into the Revelation Mountains. It was a sunny day, but the air was so cold it felt like Clivo's nostrils froze with each inhale. He had changed into his puffy down jacket and snow pants, and was relieved to see Lana and Thomas were equally well-equipped. Facing the Otterman would be challenging enough, but dealing with Mother Nature was even more dangerous. And the last thing he needed was to hear Thomas complaining about the cold all day.

"Whew," Thomas said, pulling his huge pom-pom hat over his ears. "I am going to be complaining about this cold *all* day."

"How far do we have to go?" Lana asked, jumping on her snowmobile and revving it like an expert. Her snowsuit was bright pink and clashed with her shiny red lipstick.

Clivo checked the local map and compared it to the map Stephanie had given him. He looked at the terrain, seeing that they would be traveling through a glacial valley surrounded by granite spires. "Hang on, I'm calculating the distance."

"Before I freeze to death, please," Thomas whined.

Lana gazed at the majestic mountains and took a deep breath. "It's rather fitting that we'll find the immortal in the Revelation Mountains."

"Why is that?" Clivo asked, glancing up from the map.

"They're both named after the Book of Revelation in the Bible," Lana said, her eyes flashing with excitement. "My favorite quote is in there: 'Come! Let those who are thirsty come; and let all who wish take the free gift of the water of life.'"

"That's a good one," Thomas said, rubbing his hands together eagerly.

"But it's not a free gift," Clivo corrected. "Our job is to find the immortal and keep it a secret, keep it safe from those who want to use it recklessly to dominate the world."

Lana's face flushed with an angry fire before she quickly smoothed her expression over. "Of course, Clivo. Don't worry, we'll keep it safe."

"Very safe," Thomas agreed with a grin. "Now onward! I'm becoming a popsicle."

Once again the hairs on Clivo's neck stood up. What was it about Lana and Thomas that didn't feel right? He grunted and looked down at the map, making a quick decision. "We're about two hours away. There's an opening in the basin just up the valley from here. We should be there by midmorning."

Lana revved her snowmobile. "Let's go, boys. Our journey for the ultimate is about to come to an end!"

They headed into the mountains, the cold air threatening to creep through Clivo's layers of clothes. He was desperately trying to plan for what was ahead, but it felt like his brain was freezing. The cold pit of dread in his stomach wasn't helping matters, either.

After two hours of traveling through the ice-crusted basin, they finally arrived at a large plateau that had a forest on one side and a short but sheer drop-off to the rocks below on the other. Clivo stopped his snowmobile near the cliff and almost lost his leg as he stepped off next to a steel-claw bear trap.

"Whoa!" Clivo said, jumping back. He studied the spring-loaded contraption designed to snap shut around a poor animal's leg.

Thomas ran over and whistled at the trap. "Close call, chief. Looks like someone else is also eager to trap the Otterman!"

"Or is doing some illegal bear trapping," Clivo said, glancing around to make sure there weren't any other traps in the area. He looked at the rusted contraption and saw a long chain attached to a nearby tree. He walked around the tree, but didn't see any other chains that would have indicated more traps. "I think this is the only one, but just be careful where you step."

"Don't worry; hopefully we won't be here long," Thomas said, pulling a rectangular black box that looked like a DVD player from his backpack. "It's time to let the master do his work!"

"What is that?" Clivo asked as he pulled out his tranquilizer gun and fitted it with a dart.

"Well, you asked me earlier what my skill was, and here it is!" Thomas piled up a pyramid of snow and laid the black box on top of it. "What do you think?"

"For a black box, it's totally fascinating," Clivo replied.

"You forgot to turn it on, Thomas," Lana pointed out.

"Oh, right." Thomas flicked a switch on the box and a sheet of green laser shot out over the basin, into the trees, and halfway up the mountain. "Not too bad, if I do say so myself."

Clivo had to admit it was very impressive. "What is it?"

Thomas stood proudly, his hands on his hips. "It's a Reader of Cryptid Movement sensor. If the Otterman is anywhere within two miles of us, the laser will stun it into submission. Speaking of which, don't let the light hit you or you'll be unconscious for a week."

Clivo wrinkled his face in confusion. "What if it hits a bear or a wolf?"

"They'll be knocked unconscious, too. What does it matter?" Thomas asked in a huff.

"Well, it's not really a sensor of cryptid movement, then, it's just a device that stuns whatever it hits," Clivo said, stating the obvious.

"What's your point, smart guy?" Thomas asked, poking Clivo in the chest with his finger.

"My point is that you don't really know how to find cryptids, and neither does this device," Clivo said, poking Thomas right back.

"Boys, calm down!" Lana said, stepping between the two of them. "We're on the same team, remember, Clivo? To save the world from those who seek to use the gift of eternal life for evil. Maybe this device can help with that."

As Clivo was about to respond, several deer ambled out of the trees, right into the laser's path. They frolicked and jumped through the light, trying to rub it with their noses and paw it with their hooves. After a few moments of play, they bounded off.

Thomas scratched his head. "That didn't work very well, did it?"

Lana sighed heavily and faced Clivo. "Look, without you we can't find cryptids. But without us, you have no protection. We told you who the immortal is because we trust you. Can you trust us?"

Lana's face was filled with such innocence that Clivo's doubts about her wavered. At some point he had taken a leap of faith in trusting the Myth Blasters; it was time for him to do the same with Lana and Thomas. "Okay, I'll show you how to catch it."

"Yes! What do we do, chief?" Thomas asked excitedly. "How did you find Nessie? How did your dad find twelve cryptids? What's the secret, mate?"

"That doesn't matter," Lana said, swatting him away. "How do we find the Otterman? How do we find the immortal?"

Clivo looked out over the frozen tundra, his eyes behind his goggles blinking from the sunlight. He had to trust Lana and Thomas without reservation. If the Myth Blasters were right, they were close to the Otterman. He either accepted Lana and Thomas as part of his team, or he walked away. He finally made a decision.

"Here, Thomas," Clivo said, handing Thomas his loaded tranquilizer gun. "The Otterman responds to food. Unfortunately, *we're* the food. I'll walk toward the trees as bait, and when it approaches, please shoot it before it makes a meal out of me."

"No problem, chief," Thomas said, hoisting the gun to his shoulder.

"And when you get it, there's a blood sampler in my bag," Clivo continued, walking toward the open meadow. "Just put some of its blood in there and it will confirm whether or not it's the immortal."

Lana looked hungrily at Clivo's open backpack, where

the blood sampler stuck up past the zipper. "Thanks, Clivo. Is there anything else?"

Clivo watched Lana carefully. "That's it. I've told you everything."

"Thank you, Clivo. Unfortunately, now that we have the tranquilizer gun and blood sampler, we don't really have use for you anymore."

Clivo's stomach did flip-flops. "But I volunteered to be the bait," he said desperately. "You need me for that!"

Thomas raised the tranquilizer gun. "I hate to tell you this, chief, but you've been the bait all along."

Thomas fired the gun into Clivo's leg. The dart wasn't a big one, so it didn't pierce too deeply, but it still hurt more than Clivo had anticipated. He doubled over in pain and held his leg in anguish.

"Oh, I'm sorry," Lana cooed, walking over and stroking Clivo's head. "Did you really believe we were the good guys? Maybe if you were a bit smarter, you would have realized that your dad didn't want to work with us because he figured out *ages* ago that we're the bad guys."

Clivo grimaced in pain. He stumbled a bit and dropped to one knee, his leg throbbing. Then he fell onto his back, and let his limbs go limp. He had taken a leap of faith and it had backfired. He should never have trusted Lana and Thomas, not even for a second. At least he knew that now, without a doubt; he just wished he had trusted his instincts earlier. In a weak voice he asked, "What are you going to do with the immortal?"

"That's an easy one, sport," Thomas said, still gripping the tranquilizer gun. "We're going to turn ourselves and a few close friends into immortals and form a small yet formidable power that will slowly and carefully work toward complete and total world domination. Oh, and I plan to use my ample time to study filmmaking, because what I really want to be is a director. It's important to have a hobby, or else living for eternity is going to feel like *forever*."

Lana tilted her face toward the sky, closing her eyes to the sun as she considered the question. "Definitely world domination, of course. And I'd love to learn how to figure skate. I should be able to get a gold medal in the Olympics at some point over the next thousands of millennia."

"Or you could just enslave the Olympic Committee and force them to give you a medal," Thomas suggested.

Lana laughed. "I could, couldn't I? Oh, immortality is really going to be great fun."

"That all sounds wonderful," Clivo said through gritted teeth. "There's only one problem." He grabbed the tranquilizer dart and pulled it out, wincing as blood flowed down his leg and instantly froze. He slowly stood up and held the dart in front of him, a smile of satisfaction spreading across his face. "I loaded it with an empty tranquilizer dart. If *you* were a bit smarter, you would have figured out that I was testing my suspicions that you were the bad guys."

Lana kicked at the snow in a huff and Thomas's jaw went slack with disbelief.

"Oh, *man*! What gave us away! Our accents? I told you not to use a British accent, Lana! All bad guys use British accents!" Thomas stomped his feet on the ice.

Lana grabbed the dart from Clivo's hand and threw it into the snow. "Okay, you discovered our little secret. But I have a feeling we're not all that far from the immortal. So, what do you suggest we do now?"

"We're close all right," Clivo said, backing away. "But I'm going to insist that I find it alone."

Lana laughed. "And how are you going to do that?"

Clivo launched himself into a fighting pose and smiled. "Looks like it's time to fight."

Thomas ran and hid behind a tree, calling out, "Oh, boy!"

Lana observed Clivo, her head tilted to one side. "Wouldn't it just be easier to give me the map? I don't want to kill you for it, but I will. But you can make this easy on yourself—you can leave here and go back home. Back to Aunt Pearl and your cozy little house. Because let's be honest, Clivo—you are in way over your head here. You always have been."

"Just give her the map, chief!" Thomas begged, peeking out from behind the tree. "Or she will karate chop you into next Tuesday, and blood makes me queasy!"

"Come on, Clivo," Lana said, taking a step forward. "Do the smart thing. Don't end up like your dad."

A seething anger boiled in Clivo's chest. "Did you kill my father?" he asked through clenched teeth.

Thomas held up his hands. "No way, sport! That was NOT us! We may be malicious and want the gift of immortality so we can rule the world and enslave others, but we don't go around *murdering* people. At least up until this moment, when Lana might do just that if you don't GIVE HER THE MAP!"

"Your father was too smart to be tracked by anyone, Clivo," Lana continued. "We tried, believe me. We tried to find him, but he was good. Very good. Too slippery to be tracked. No home address, no phone number. He lived off the grid. We have no idea how someone was able to find him and kill him. It's a shame, too. A lot of cryptid secrets died with him."

"Speaking of which, do you want to tell us any secrets he passed down to you?" Thomas said, darting his head out from behind the tree.

"Not a chance," Clivo said.

"Fair enough." Thomas shrugged.

"So how did you track me?" Clivo asked. "How did I mess up?"

"May I?" Lana asked, pointing to Clivo's backpack. Clivo nodded. She walked over to his pack, unzipped a pocket, and pulled out what looked to be a small coin about the size of a dime. "It's a rather simple tracking device. Nothing fancy. Someone just had to get close enough to plant this and, voilà! We found your hidden lair."

Clivo looked at the device, his mind clicking through who could have planted it. Who had been close enough to him to have put it in his bag? His stomach lurched when he wondered if he had led them to the Myth Blasters. He'd never forgive himself if he had.

But his heartbeat settled when he realized the obvious. The person who had planted that device was someone he had met *after* visiting the Myth Blasters.

"Blirgenbach Schnauss," Clivo growled, picturing the small, mustached Luxembourger.

"Yes?" Thomas said, poking his head out from behind the tree.

Lana groaned. "Thomas! You just blew it!"

"Huh?" Thomas asked, confused. "Oh, shoot! Sorry, Lana, but I warned you that disguising myself as different people was bound to confuse me!"

Now it was Clivo's turn to be totally confused. He looked at Thomas, all bundled up in his snow gear, the goggles obscuring his face. He pictured Thomas with slicked-back hair, a pencil-thin mustache, and no glasses. It suddenly hit Clivo why Thomas had felt so familiar to him. "Wait, you're Blirgenbach Schnauss?"

Thomas stepped out from behind the tree and took a fighting stance that Clivo immediately recognized. "Yes, but you can call me Thomas. Blirgenbach was my alter ego meant to terrify and intimidate you into giving us all your information."

"Obviously that didn't work very well," Clivo said, angry with himself for not picking up on Thomas's disguise. The man's petite size should have given him away. "How's your face after I made you eat that tree?"

Thomas's expression melted into a scowl, but Lana put out a hand to stop him from charging forward. "It really doesn't matter who we are, Clivo," she said, her British accent morphing into a Luxembourgian one. "We're still the bad guys, and we're still going to get the immortal."

"So, you Luxembourgers are the terrible evil resistance I'm supposed to be so frightened of?" Clivo asked, his hands shaking with anger at how he had been duped so easily.

"We're *one* of the evil resistances," Lana said with a smile. "There are many out there, but we're the only ones good enough to find you."

"High-five, Lana!" Thomas said.

Clivo's eyes scanned his surroundings for some means of escape. "From what I heard, you guys were tipped off about my whereabouts to test me, to make sure I didn't crack under pressure. You were chosen because in the cryptid-catching world you're seen as a joke."

"There's no need to be insulting, chief!" Thomas complained.

Lana narrowed her eyes. "Last chance, Clivo. Either give us the map, or we'll be forced to take it from you."

Lana and Thomas spread out in front of him. Clivo exhaled slowly, focusing his mind on the dual threat about to attack. "Like I said, looks like it's time to fight."

XXI

Clivo dropped into a fighting crouch, and Lana and Thomas did the same.

The Luxembourgers looked like they were getting ready to coordinate their attack, which gave Clivo the split second he needed to charge first. His dad had always taught him that the best way to win a fight was not through strength, but through smarts, and attacking first was something they obviously weren't expecting.

Lana and Thomas froze in shock when they saw Clivo barreling toward them. Clivo leaped into the air and pushed himself off Lana's chest with one foot, propelling himself toward Thomas, whom he tackled. They did a somersault in the snow and Clivo ripped off Thomas's goggles, leaving him half blind in the piercingly bright air.

With Thomas temporarily disabled, Clivo turned his attention to Lana, who was picking herself up off the snow. "Well, now that that little element of surprise is over, shall we get down to it?" she asked, straightening the hat on her head.

"Ladies first," Clivo responded.

Lana smirked and ran at him, unleashing a flurry of kicks and punches. But this time Clivo was ready for her. He blocked and deflected her blows and was even able to grab a high-kicked foot and throw her into the snow.

"Oh, so all of a sudden you think you know my moves," Lana said, once again dragging herself to standing.

"Yep, it's taijutsu," Clivo said, catching his breath. "I didn't recognize it when you attacked me at my house. Too bad you showed me your skills when it didn't matter, because it gave me time to figure out exactly which technique you were using."

"It doesn't really matter what technique it is," Lana replied with a taunting smile. "I'm a better fighter than you and you know it."

"That may be true, but why don't we test it anyway?"

Lana and Clivo went at it again, but this time Clivo was able to deliver some kicks and strikes of his own. Lana expertly blocked them, but bit by bit she fell back. She stopped striking and just focused on blocking the kicks and punches that Clivo delivered. He was able to identify her weaknesses and exploit them, slowly moving her back even more.

In his peripheral vision, he saw Thomas running at him, the Luxembourger's eyes squinting with the cold. Clivo turned to face him and immediately stepped aside, once again throwing Thomas headfirst into a tree.

Lana doubled her kicks and punches, her breath coming in gasps and grunts. But Clivo knew her pattern now. She was strong and had good technique, but she repeated the same moves with predictable precision. If Clivo could get ahead of her pattern, he could throw her off just a little bit and take advantage of an opening.

After a few more punches, Clivo found his opportunity. He ducked a high kick and got behind Lana, then grabbed her jacket and pulled it over her head, trapping her arms and face inside. He tied up her coat sleeves, leaving her helplessly bundled as her muffled shouts pierced through the jacket.

Clivo was about to grab his stuff and jump on a snowmobile when he heard an ominous click. He whirled around to find Thomas sitting with his back against the tree and his nose bloody, aiming a silver handgun at him.

"The map, please," Thomas said, wobbling to his feet.

Clivo looked at the gun and knew he was sunk. Even if he could somehow destroy the map, they could still force him to lead them to the Otterman. He looked around, once again searching for a way to escape, but no good options presented themselves.

Clivo held his hands up and exhaled in defeat. He looked behind himself at the cliff; it dropped into a narrow valley, but it was too far down to jump.

"Fine, you guys win," Clivo said. "The map is in my backpack. I'll just grab it."

"Don't do anything stupid," Thomas warned. "I hate violence, but I will shoot you in a hot second."

"Do you want the map or not?" Clivo asked.

Thomas motioned with his gun for Clivo to go ahead and open his backpack.

"Hang on, I need to take my gloves off to open the zipper," Clivo said. He made a show of trying to take off his gloves and getting them stuck in the sleeves of his jacket. "Ugh, hang on."

Clivo took off his jacket and immediately shivered from the cold. His plan had better work, or he'd be in danger of freezing to death—or shot. Neither one sounded very pleasant.

He took a deep breath and grabbed his backpack with one hand, his jacket with the other. Just to his left was the steel-claw bear trap. He hoped the spring wasn't totally rusted over, or his plan would turn out to be a very bad idea. But seeing as he was out of options, even a bad idea was better than nothing.

Clivo looked up and pretended to see something off in the distance. He furrowed his brow as if trying to understand what he was seeing, then opened his eyes wide. "OTTERMAN!"

Thomas whirled around, giving Clivo the opening he needed. He shoved a heavy water bottle into his jacket pocket, sprang up, and swung the jacket downward as hard as he could onto the steel trap. The trap burst to life and snapped its jaws around the jacket's sleeve, snow and ice spraying with its force. Clivo gripped his jacket in one hand and his backpack in the other, and as fast as he could, he ran toward the edge of the cliff.

"Whoa, chief!" Thomas yelled, spinning back around. "I think jumping off a cliff qualifies as being stupid!"

Before Clivo's rational mind could take over, he hurled himself over the cliff, his hand desperately holding on to the jacket, which was still clamped tightly in the bear trap. He fell, listening to the trap chain as it quickly unfurled. He realized a moment too late that he didn't know how long the chain was, and that he could very well hit the ground before it stopped his descent. But there was nothing he could do about it now. He barreled toward the ground, the cold air slicing through him like sharp icicles.

Just when he thought he was a goner, the chain pulled tight, and he jerked to a stop right above the ground, his arm almost yanking out of its socket as he dangled from the jacket clutched tightly in his hand.

With a glorious tearing sound, a chunk of his sleeve ripped off, and he dropped harmlessly to the ground. Clivo quickly put his jacket on before he froze into a block of ice. He tried to take a moment to gather himself, but the snowy ground next to him shot up in a spray as a bullet ricocheted off it.

Clivo grabbed his backpack and ran along the wall of ice, bullets narrowly missing him as he sprinted toward a cluster of trees.

Clivo traveled for an hour, trudging his way up a steep slope in knee-deep snow. He had heard the Luxembourgers revving their snowmobile engines, but there was no way they could take them through the thick forest. Clivo did his best to cover his tracks as his dad had taught him, but found it impossible with how deep the snow was. His only hope was that the Luxembourgers took off hiking in the wrong direction. But if they were on his trail and he did find the immortal, what then? He had lost them for the moment, but maybe not forever. Clivo pulled out his satellite phone and began talking as soon as Douglas answered.

"Mr. Chancery, I'm close to the immortal!" Clivo said, his breath coming in gasps as he trudged up the hill. His lungs were burning so much they felt like they were about to explode. "But two evil Luxembourgers are on my trail!"

"Luxembourgers?" Douglas roared, turning down the sitar music that had been playing loudly in the background. "Why did you allow those fools to follow you?"

"I didn't! You're the one who told them I was at Loch Ness, and they've been tracking me ever since!"

Douglas's voice got low and angry. "Well, that wasn't very smart of me, now was it?"

"No, sir."

"Don't agree with me!"

"Yes, sir." Clivo gulped a deep breath, the steam from his exhale freezing in mid-air. "So can you send reinforcements or something? If I find the immortal and they find me, we could be in a lot of trouble."

"No problem, kid, I've got a Navy SEAL team on standby."

Clivo stopped in his tracks. "You do?"

"NO!" Douglas yelled, making Clivo wince. "Just hold them off as long as you can; I'll see what I can pull together. Was there anything else?"

Clivo sputtered, "Apart from being close to the elixir of life while being in mortal danger? Nope, that about covers it."

"Drama, drama, all the time with you kids. Just put a little bit of effort into not being killed by those morons and I'll see what I can do."

"Thank you, Mr. Chancery—" But Douglas had already hung up.

Clivo grunted in exasperation and was tempted to throw the phone in a snowbank. He should have known Douglas wouldn't be much help in an emergency.

After another half hour of constantly checking his map and compass to make sure he was going the right way, Clivo came to a large, snowy meadow with thick forest on all sides. In the center was what looked to be a huge, ice-covered rock.

Clivo ran toward the structure, scraped away some ice, and looked straight into an airplane's cockpit. The Myth Blasters' map had been exactly right about where the plane carrying the Otterman had crashed.

Clivo circled the plane and found many small cages lying in the snow—obviously the ones used to relocate the otters. Their doors were open and the inhabitants long gone. But one stood out among the rest. Its bars were bent and snapped, as if the creature inside had torn them open like a tin can. Clivo shuddered at the thought of how strong the Otterman must have been to do that.

Clivo looked at the map again and noticed a lake nearby, so he trudged even farther into the forest. After a short time the trees opened to a majestic sight: a frozen mountain lake nestled against a towering range of snow-covered peaks. A small stream emptied out of the lake, gurgling water bursting through the ice in spots. Scurrying over the tundra and snow were hundreds of otters playing in the sun.

"Well, this should be easy," Clivo mumbled, his heart sinking at the number of critters splashing about.

He put down his backpack and grabbed some pinecones from a tree. He sat on a rock and observed the otters, looking for one that might be different from the others. He figured that if one of them was able to morph into a were-otter, it must be distinct somehow.

But after a good half hour where he couldn't tell one from the other, he gave up and decided to do it the hard way.

"I'm really sorry about this, guys."

He had to threaten the otters, to make them feel like they were in danger so the one he was looking for would shape-shift to protect itself. He picked out the closest otter and tossed a pinecone directly at it. The pinecone splashed harmlessly in the water and the otter looked at him curiously, then went on with its playing.

Clivo tossed more and more pinecones, even bonking a few critters right on the head, but they still just went about their activities.

The sun was beginning to set and the temperature was dropping. Clivo decided he needed to hurry up and get out of there before he froze to death, so he opted for a more direct approach.

He took a deep breath and began running at the otters with a yell, feeling rather silly as he waved his arms in a menacing fashion. The otters squeaked and ran off, hiding in the brush or diving into the water.

He splashed sticks around, threw rocks in the water, and in general did his best to frighten the poor creatures. They seemed scared all right, but none of them turned into a furry man and ran after him.

Clivo stopped and caught his breath. Maybe the Otterman had fled the area. There must be loads of lakes and streams in the mountain range; perhaps it had roamed about, trying to find its way back home.

A memory flashed through Clivo's mind.

"It's not here, Russell," Clivo said, *peering through the trees, looking for the deer he had been tracking for well over an hour.*

"The deer caught your scent, C, so it's hiding. Now it's watching you. Don't look for where it was, look for where it retreated to." His dad's hand was on his shoulder, covered in a bandage that supposedly concealed a scratch from an archaeological digging tool. But Clivo had no idea what kind of tool would leave such a large wound.

Clivo turned his eyes from where the deer had been heading and focused on the areas off to the side, where the trees were thicker. He looked for something out of place. A movement, a different color, a shape. Within seconds he spotted the deer, kneeling behind a bush, staring directly at him.

"There it is, Dad!" Clivo whispered, pointing to the deer. He was so excited he had completely forgotten to call his dad Russell, something he had started doing out of anger and hurt because he didn't understand why his dad traveled away from home so much.

His dad patted him on the shoulder, a joyful smile lighting his face at being called Dad, which meant that Clivo's anger toward him was thawing. "Good job, C. Remember, don't look for where they should be, look for where they go to hide."

Clivo turned his attention from the stream, where the otter should be, and slowly walked toward the trees. He squatted by a rock and used his senses to locate something out of place. He listened, he watched, he even smelled the air. He figured something called the Otterman must have a distinctive smell to it.

Where would I go to watch me? Clivo wondered. He glanced up toward the lake, which sat on a slight hill. In terms of attack positions—and he assumed the Otterman would be preparing to attack—being uphill would offer the greatest advantage.

He pivoted slightly to get a better view of the scene and instantly saw it. Crouching by a tree was the biggest otter he had ever seen, with a gray, furry body and a white face, its black eyes staring right at him with a look that was unnervingly human.

"Okay, it's showtime," Clivo said, willing his legs to move even though they suddenly didn't want to. He picked up a rock and rose to standing. His intention was to toss the rock just to the side of the creature to scare it, but his shaking hand threw it off target and it bounced right off the otter's nose. "Yikes! I totally didn't mean to do that!" he yelled.

The otter shook its head and glared menacingly at Clivo. Its weasel-like body instantly began to shape-shift, the fat otter growing even wider and taller. The limbs stretched out and became arms and legs, the body ballooned into a huge mass, and the tiny face expanded into a large, hairy head. Bones groaned as they morphed and elongated until a creature that indeed looked like a man-shaped otter, down to the triangular black nose, took form. But this was no cuddly creature; this was a huge beast that, judging by the look on its scowling face, was very, very angry.

Clivo reached for his backpack to grab his tranquilizer gun, but found nothing but air. He whirled his head around and saw the backpack lying by the stream, where he had left it. He gave the Otterman a sheepish smile. "Wanna give me a head start?"

The Otterman opened its tiny mouth, which was unfortunately filled with razor-sharp teeth, and let out a high-pitched scream. Clivo took that as his cue to run, and he *ran*.

He grabbed his backpack and kept running, opening the zipper as he went. He ran into the forest, not bothering to look behind him. He could tell by the thrashing of branches that the Otterman was close behind.

His hand fumbled for his tranquilizer gun, but it wasn't there. His stomach dropped as he realized he had left it with the Luxembourgers. Great, now he had an angry wereotter chasing after him, and he had forgotten his gun. His hand closed around a tranquilizer dart that was going to have to be delivered up close and personal.

Clivo ran until he reached a clearing. He glanced over his shoulder to make sure the Otterman was still following him, which it was, its fat legs and clawed feet stumbling through the snow.

"Okay, Wren, you've got one shot at this," Clivo said.

He planted his feet and came to a stop, quickly pivoting and running back toward the Otterman. A high-pitched scream came from the Otterman's mouth, and Clivo found a shout of attack coming from his. The beast bounded through the snow, its long arms and pointed claws reaching out as Clivo held the dart in front of him like a sword.

The second before the claws grabbed him, Clivo dropped to his knees and slid under the grasping arms. The massive hands sought to wrap him up, but were too clumsy to reach him; at the last moment he twisted his body and stabbed the Otterman in the leg with the dart.

The Otterman screamed even louder, its hands grasping at the dart protruding from its chubby thigh. It pulled out the dart, its roar turning into a pitiful whimper, and it stumbled a bit as the tranquilizer took effect.

Clivo crouched on his heels ten feet away, ready in case the creature tried for one last attack. But the beast didn't turn toward him; instead, it lifted its nose in the air and sniffed as it stumbled toward Clivo's backpack, which Clivo had dropped in the snow. The Otterman fell to its knees and rummaged through the pack, finally pulling out a chocolate bar that had been shoved to the bottom. With a sigh of joy, it unwrapped the chocolate and took two large bites before sliding into unconsciousness.

Clivo blinked in amazement. Apparently space-made Ottermen had a taste for candy bars.

Clivo shook himself out of his thoughts and grabbed the blood sampler from his backpack. He placed the needle on the Otterman's arm and was about to press it in when he paused. Was he really ready for this? He had faced death several times over the past week, and if this was the immortal, all he had to do was inject some of its blood into his own body and he would never have to face death again. He'd live forever, like a superhero. He could observe centuries passing, witness kingdoms rising and falling, but he would continue on, watching the world change while he lived forever, never becoming a part of history.

Then he thought of Aunt Pearl. And Jerry. Would he really want to live forever without them? Mr. and Mrs. Cooper flashed through his mind; even the Myth Blasters. Who would he go to when he needed someone to talk to? Sure, he could make them immortal, too. But then who would they want to turn immortal to comfort them during the long days and nights of their eternal future?

Clivo realized there would be no end to it. Nobody wanted to travel through eternity alone. The most important thing was the friends and family people traveled through their time on Earth with.

Clivo's fleeting desire for immortality suddenly faded. All he wanted was to be back at home with his friends, with Aunt Pearl, even with the cats. He wanted to hear Jerry's laugh and have his cheeks pinched by Mrs. Cooper. He wanted to feel the warmth of Mr. Cooper's hand as he shook it, and smell the incense in his home in the mountains. He even missed the clinking of wind-bells on his front porch.

Clivo thought of his parents. Living forever without them suddenly seemed very, very lonely. He pictured his mom's smile and felt his dad's hand ruffling his hair. He realized that he would gladly give up the gift of immortality for just one more day with them. Time was nothing; it was the amount of love packed into it that mattered.

With a deep exhale, Clivo pressed the needle into the Otterman's arm, knowing that he would stay true to his task of keeping its secret safe because he had no use for immortality. The scanner blinked and blinked while the blood slowly traveled up the chamber. With each second, Clivo came closer to possessing the greatest power known to man, and also the most dangerous. He knew there were others who didn't fear living alone forever. They desired power over friendship, craved riches over family. Those were the people who found immortality to be the greatest gift, and Clivo knew it was those people he had to keep it away from.

The blood finally slid up the chamber and the scanner quit blinking, revealing two words that both disappointed Clivo and made him sigh with enormous relief.

NOT IMMORTAL.

XXII

Clivo leaned against the snow, all the energy leaving his body. He was exhausted from the sprint and sudden loss of adrenaline. He looked at the Otterman, its razor-sharp teeth covered with chocolate.

"You're not such a dangerous guy after all, are you?" Clivo said, marveling at the mysterious creature in front of him. He held the Otterman's paw. "And don't worry, I'm not going to let anything bad happen to you. You're safe with me."

He took a photo and sent it to Douglas, cringing as he texted that it was not the immortal. Then he took a selfie to share with Jerry later, of course.

He was just beginning to figure out how he was going to get back to the airport without a snowmobile when he saw some movement in the trees.

"Fabulous," Clivo muttered to himself.

Lana and Thomas came running from the forest, their eager eyes locked on the Otterman.

"What does it feel like, chief?" Thomas asked, grabbing

Clivo and squeezing his limbs as if checking for an injury. "Do you feel stronger? Did your heart stop beating like a vampire's? Are you hungry? I'd be *starving* if I became immortal!"

"It's not the immortal," Clivo said, shoving Thomas away.

"It has to be," Lana said, pushing her way toward the Otterman. "Our research was flawless."

"Obviously not," Clivo said. He grabbed a box of wilderness matches from his pack and pulled a bit of fur from the creature's head. He struck the match and lit the fur on fire. It didn't burst into silver sparkles, it simply simmered and emitted a horrible smell like rotten onions.

Thomas screamed with frustration and went into a massive temper tantrum, kicking and punching the snow like a child having a meltdown.

"Well, all is not lost," Lana said with a sigh. "We still have a cryptid. A very popular one, at that. I'm sure we could sell it to science for research, or to a zoo. We'd make millions."

"Excuse me," Clivo said, raising his hand. "I caught the Otterman, and he's not going anywhere. Not to a zoo and *definitely* not to a laboratory to be experimented on."

"I didn't realize you thought you had some say in the matter," Lana spat.

Clivo took a protective stance in front of the beast. "I guess I'll just have to fight you for him, then."

"That won't be necessary," Lana said with a condescending smile. "Shoot him, Thomas."

"With pleasure," Thomas said. He raised his gun and took aim.

Clivo threw his satellite phone like a Frisbee. It hit the Luxembourger squarely in the face with a crunch and he dropped the gun with a yelp, both hands holding his nose, which was once again dripping blood.

Clivo grabbed the weapon and threw it as far into the forest as he could. "I'm *really* getting tired of you shooting at me."

Thomas took off running with a yelp and Clivo was about to follow when Lana surprised him with a solid punch to the face, sending him sprawling, dazed, onto his back.

Lana sighed. "I wish you had let him shoot you. Freezing to death is going to be so much less pleasant. But I'll be sure to say a few words in your memory when we come back for the Otterman." She punctuated the statement with an evil laugh.

Lana took off running, as well. Clivo tried to stand, but he stumbled back to his knees, his head still ringing from Lana's punch. He watched them head for the trees and instantly knew Lana was right: without a snowmobile to carry him out of there, there'd be no way he'd survive the night. He hadn't brought a tent or sleeping bag, and with part of a jacket sleeve gone, the dropping temperature was already cutting through to his bones.

Clivo heard a thumping and for a moment thought it must be the pounding in his head. Then he looked up and saw a magnificent sight—a huge helicopter flying low over the trees. It hovered over the Luxembourgers, who shielded their faces from the ice and snow kicked up by the rotating blades. A large net fell and landed on them, followed by sparks as clamps were injected into the snow, pinning the net to the ground.

The helicopter came in for a landing and when the engines were cut, the sound of Thomas's wails replaced the whirring of the blades.

A door slid open and Douglas's unmistakable head of unruly gray hair peeked out. Clivo had never thought he'd feel so happy to see the old man.

"Ugh, I hate nature," Douglas spat. He hobbled out of the helicopter and immediately lit a cigar. He limped over to Clivo and gave him a hand up. "You okay, kid?"

"I am, Mr. Chancery, thank you," Clivo said, resisting the urge to give the old crankypants a hug. "How did you get here so quickly?"

"Bah," Douglas said, puffing away on his cigar. "When you said you were going after the immortal, I figured I better hover close in case the excitement made you go all catawampus."

"I'm glad you did," Clivo said gratefully. He backed up a few steps as he said the next part, readying himself for Douglas's anger. "It's not the immortal."

"Yeah, I got your text," Douglas said with a sigh. "Did the dummies tell you it was?"

"Yeah," Clivo said, surprised that Douglas wasn't furious.

"Well, good to know they're still dummies," Douglas said with a raspy laugh. "In the future, kid, be careful who you believe, about anything. When you're dealing with the elixir of life, there aren't that many of us good guys out there. Or smart ones."

"I will, Mr. Chancery. Thanks for coming to rescue me."

Douglas patted Clivo on the shoulder. "Don't get used to it, kid. I just happened to be in a good mood today due to a lack of indigestion. Now, come on, let's load the otter thingie into the helicopter."

"What are you going to do with it?" Clivo asked, suddenly concerned that Douglas was going to sell it to a zoo or loan it to science.

"Don't freak out, kid. I'm taking it home," Douglas said. "I think it'd prefer to be back in the rain forest, don't you?"

"I definitely think so," Clivo said, relieved. "And people need their Otterman sightings, too, to keep the sense of magic alive."

"Yeah, whatever." Douglas looked at the creature and wrinkled his face. "I'm not even going to ask why it's covered in chocolate. As long as you keep catching cryptids, that's your business."

Clivo heard Thomas's wails and looked toward the Luxembourgers, who were still struggling in the net. "What are you going to do with them? You're not going to let them freeze out here, are you?"

"Don't worry about them," Douglas said, heading back to the helicopter, where he pulled out another net to wrap the creature in. "I've got a call in to the Forest Service about some foreigners doing illegal bear trapping. They'll pick them up shortly and deport them back to their embarrassingly small country. Their passports should be flagged due to criminal activity, so they'll be banned from our majestic nation. You won't be hearing from them for a while."

"Good," Clivo said, his shoulders finally relaxing. "I think I've had enough of Luxembourgers for a while."

"They really are absolutely the worst, aren't they?" Douglas snarled.

Clivo and Douglas loaded the unconscious wereotter into the helicopter and took off just as a Forest Service helicopter was swooping in to pick up Lana and Thomas.

Seven hours later, Douglas landed the helicopter in a field near Clivo's house. It was dark out, save for the moon shining brightly in the night sky. Clivo exited the aircraft, the comforting pine smell of the forest greeting him.

"I'm going to say this once, and only once," Douglas

said, turning around in the pilot's seat. "You did a good job, kid. Your dad was right; you turned out to be a good catcher, even though I thought it was highly unlikely."

"But I didn't find the immortal," Clivo said, hoisting his backpack onto his shoulders.

"There's always tomorrow," Douglas replied, "unless getting shot at a few times and knowing there's multiple heinous groups of people out there who want you dead has scared you off?"

Clivo laughed. He *was* scared of the evil resistance, especially if the Luxembourgers were the *least* dangerous of them. But he was more scared of what would happen if one of them found the immortal first.

"I'll let you know when I've found the next cryptid," Clivo said.

"Good," Douglas said with a warm nod. "Now, get out of here. I got sick of your company about five hours ago."

"Okay," Clivo said, letting out another laugh. He was actually beginning to feel a slight bit of affection for the cranky man. "Oh, wait." He pulled some chocolate bars out of his backpack and handed them to the Otterman, who was still tied securely in the net. The creature sniffed the chocolate happily and looked up with what Clivo swore was a grateful smile. "Take good care of him."

"Always, kid."

XXIII

Clivo ran inside his house, taking a moment to enjoy the comforting incense smell of the place.

"Hey, Bernie," he said, knocking on the suit of armor.

He pulled out his laptop, figuring that even though it was late, the Myth Blasters would still be awake waiting for word of what had happened with the Otterman.

"Clivo! Oh my gosh, are you okay?" Stephanie asked, the other Blasters crowding in behind her.

"Dude! We're awake waiting for word of what happened to the Otterman!" Adam said, eagerly peeling an orange.

"Otterman! Otterman!" Charles chanted.

"Once again, you guys were right," Clivo said, pulling out his phone and showing them the photo of the Otterman.

"AAAAAYIYAAAAA!" Charles yelled, punching the air in extreme exultation. "Wait a second. Is that a *chocolate* bar? I'm sorry, the Otterman eats flesh, not chocolate, dude."

"It wasn't the immortal, though, was it?" Amelia asked with a sly grin.

"How did you know that?" Clivo asked.

"Pay up, Charles," Amelia said, holding out her hand. Charles slapped a five-dollar bill into it with a moan of defeat.

"It hurts so much losing a dream," he muttered, shuffling to the back of the room.

"While you were gone, we did some research on the Otterman fur you had, as well as this International Secret Order. We'll start with the fur and a little demonstration by Hernando." Amelia gestured to Hernando, who was standing back from the group. "Whenever you're ready, Hernando."

Hernando nodded and held up a clump of fur that looked exactly like what Lana and Thomas had presented. He flicked a lighter and the fur went up in an enormous ball of silver flame.

"Yipe!" Hernando yelped, dropping the flaming fur.

"Fire in the hole!" Adam yelled, running in with a bucket and dousing Hernando with a splash of water.

As the chaotic scene unfurled behind her, Amelia continued undeterred. "We looked into past Otterman fur hoaxes, and there were a lot. Most fur samples were deemed to be from modern-day animals—dogs, bears, even porcupines."

Stephanie chimed in. "But of course your sample wasn't, since no animal that we know of goes up in silver flames like that."

"So where is the fur from?" Clivo asked, intrigued. "The Order also said they did DNA testing on the fur, and it didn't match any known animal."

Stephanie began to giggle. "That's because it's kind of hard to pull DNA from this."

From under the table she pulled out a large brown teddy bear. Clivo raised his eyebrows in disbelief. "*That* was the fur sample that made the Order believe the Otterman was the immortal?"

"We actually had to do quite a bit of research to find this particular hoax, because it's hard to call something so obvious a hoax," Stephanie continued. "It was only mentioned once, years ago, on one of the chat rooms. Apparently some tour guides got a kick out of fooling people with this stuffed-animal fur. It was a very short-lived hoax, and it was easily debunked. The Order was obviously too blinded by their excitement to check it out thoroughly."

"Or they were stupid," Charles said, still sulking in the back.

"It's actually not that uncommon of a phenomenon," Amelia said. "Sometimes our desire for something can be so great that we believe what we want to, and no amount of science can get us to see otherwise. It's called 'hope.' "

Stephanie leaned in and whispered, "Which is why we finally had to temporarily remove Charles from the research team. His hope that the Otterman was the immortal kept messing up our data."

A sob of despair emanated from Charles.

"So, back to this International Secret Order of Mythological Beasts, Legends, and Cryptid Catchers," Amelia continued.

"I'm sure you've already figured out they were from Luxembourg," Clivo said, accepting the fact that the Myth Blasters would always be one step ahead of him.

"Sure did," Amelia said proudly. "And I'm sure you figured out that they are *not* the good guys."

"Eventually," Clivo responded, a shiver going up his spine as he pictured Thomas trying to shoot him.

"They're actually with the Luxembourgian government," Amelia went on. "They're part of a burgeoning secret program to train cryptid catchers. Apparently the new grand duke, a slight man with horrible teeth and breath that smells like burned bacon, wants to secure his legacy as the most powerful monarch to ever hold the grand duchy by giving his people the gift of immortality. He doesn't really trust anyone outside of his family, however, so he recruited two of his cousins to become part of the Order. Fortunately for us, they were chosen based on their blood ties, not their smarts, so they're not a huge threat in terms of finding the immortal first, as evidenced by them mistaking teddy-bear fur for the Otterman."

"Yeah, I feel kind of stupid myself for buying into their theory," Clivo said, blushing.

"Which brings us to something we wanted to discuss," Stephanie said, her eyes downcast and thoughtful. "The fact that governments are involved in the search for the immortal takes this thing to a whole other level."

"Big level," a soaking-wet Hernando said from behind her.

"From this point forward, we have no idea who we can trust. So we've simplified it: trust no one." Stephanie's face was more serious than Clivo had ever seen it. "You need to work with us, and us alone. We can't risk sharing our information if you give it to people like the Order again. It's just too dangerous."

"I totally agree," Clivo said, nodding. "You guys are the ones I want to work with, anyway. You're the best. I don't need anyone else."

Amelia picked at her fingernails and casually glanced at him. "You don't need anyone else except, perhaps . . . Douglas Chancery?"

Clivo's eyebrows shot up in surprise. "Is there anything you guys *don't* figure out?"

Stephanie smiled at him sympathetically, as if he should have known better than to ask that. "It was really simple. We just traced the Diamond Card that you were using to Douglas Chancery—"

"What do you mean, you traced it? I never gave you the number."

Stephanie smiled. "You showed it to Charles at the museum and he memorized the number."

"I showed it to him for, like, a second, and he barely looked at it."

"His memory is like a steel trap, especially when it comes to numbers. When he turns twenty-one he's going to try his hand at counting cards in Vegas." Stephanie said it as if that were the most natural thing in the world. She looked down again, and her voice sounded hurt when she continued. "How come you never told us about him?"

Clivo squirmed uncomfortably. "I'm sorry, I should have. He's the person who funded my dad's catches and now funds mine. I would have told you about him; it's just that my dad never did, and I thought I should do the same. He's also not a very nice person, so I guess I was kinda protecting you from him."

"Do you trust him?" Amelia asked with a pointed glare.

Clivo thought about it. "I do. And more importantly, my dad did, too."

"Okay, we'll let it ride since he's Mr. Moneybags, but from now on, no more secrets," Amelia said. "We're obviously dealing with stuff way bigger than we thought, and if we're a team, we need to be one all the way."

"Absolutely." Clivo nodded. "I'm sorry, guys, I was just trying to do what I thought was right."

"What's right is what we tell you to do," Adam said, handing Hernando a towel to dry himself off with. "It's best if you don't think too much for yourself from here on out."

"Got it," Clivo agreed, stifling a laugh. "I'll keep my thinking to a minimum."

"All right, Clivo," Stephanie said with a smile. "We're going to get some rest, but we'll be in touch when we've got your next catch."

"Thanks, guys. Talk soon," Clivo said.

"Oh, and Clivo?" Stephanie added quickly. "Good job. Catching two cryptids in one week is pretty amazing. Be sure to take some time to celebrate that."

"I will, thank you, Stephanie. Not bad for a remedial kid, huh?" Clivo said.

"Not bad at all," Stephanie agreed. "Looks like you've found what you're good at."

Clivo turned off his computer and was considering how he would mark such an accomplishment when he immediately fell into a deep sleep right at the table.

Epilogue

Clivo sat in his father's study the next evening after school, quietly doing his math homework. The front door creaked open and two cats came running in and jumped on his lap.

"Hi, guys," Clivo said, rubbing the purring cats. "It's good to see you."

Aunt Pearl tentatively poked her head into the room, trying to hide a giant trophy behind her back.

"Hi, sweetheart," Aunt Pearl said slowly. Her eyes swung around, obviously looking for some kind of destruction. "It doesn't look like you set anything ablaze while I was gone. Or pawned our belongings for snack money."

"Nah, Aunt Pearl, no rotten teenage behavior for me," Clivo assured her. "How was your week?"

Aunt Pearl quit looking around and glanced at Clivo, a distinct sparkle in her eye. "Oh, you know, nothing too exciting, either." She seemed to consider something for a moment, and then, with a happy sigh, she pulled the trophy out from behind her back. "Actually, I've been bad. I wasn't at church camp. I was at a salsa competition. Don't laugh at your auntie! I won first place!"

Clivo covered his grinning face with his hand. "I'm sorry, I'm not laughing at you, Aunt Pearl. It's just—I knew that. And I think it's great, and I think you should salsa dance as much as you want."

Aunt Pearl's face melted in relief. "You do? You don't think I'm naughty for leaving you alone so I can mambo my cha-cha?"

"It's totally fine. And I hope you don't feel like you have to lie to me about it anymore."

Aunt Pearl leaned over and kissed his head. "You're right, sweetie. It's better if there are no secrets between us, don't you think?"

Clivo pictured Nessie and the Otterman and decided that for now, some secrets needed to be kept. "Absolutely, Aunt Pearl, no secrets."

"That's a sweet boy. Have a good night, okay?"

"Good night, Aunt Pearl. I love you."

"Aw. Love you too, sweetie." Aunt Pearl began to exit the room.

"Aunt Pearl?" Clivo asked.

"Yes, sweetie?"

Clivo wasn't even sure what he wanted to ask; there was just something that was still bothering him. He understood the world of cryptid catching, as much as he could, anyway. He understood the necessity of finding the immortal before anyone in the evil resistance did. He just still didn't under-stand why his dad had kept everything a secret from him. "Did my dad enjoy being away from me as much as he was?"

"Enjoy?" Aunt Pearl asked, her beak nose twitching with surprise. "Oh, sweetie, he hated it. Every second of it. Before he left on each trip, he would tell me that he was hoping this would be the last time. That he would find whatever treasure it was he was searching for so he could just stay home with you." She let out a long sigh. "Unfortunately, he never found it."

"It must have been something pretty important," Clivo said, looking down at the desk.

"I guess." Aunt Pearl sighed again. "I do know he was always concerned about keeping you safe, though. He would tell me, 'Make sure to keep C safe.' He wanted me to shake that rattle thing over your head, but I always thought it was rather silly."

Maybe that was it, then, Clivo thought. Maybe his dad hadn't told him anything simply to protect him. It didn't seem like the whole answer, but at least it was something.

"Thanks, Aunt Pearl. I was just curious," Clivo said.

"See you in the morning, sweetie."

Clivo went upstairs to his bedroom and shut the door, petting the cats as they huddled happily on his bed. He went to his closet and pulled out the leather-bound photo album of his dad's cryptid catches. He flipped through the pictures, pausing longer on the one where he and his parents were all together with the gunni. He smiled and allowed himself the wish that they could still have been together as a family.

He took some photos from under his mattress—the ones of him with Nessie and the Otterman—and noticed that his smile in each picture was exactly like his father's. Smiles of wonder, joy, and knowing, one hand always resting comfortably on the beast.

Clivo placed his photos in the album, recognizing how well they fit in with the rest. The legacy of the cryptid catcher was continuing with him. Whether he was ready or not, it was what he had inherited from his father. And he realized that he willingly embraced the journey ahead.

"I don't understand everything, Dad, but I understand what I need to do. And I promise you, I'll do it. You trained me well and I'm proud to follow in your footsteps. Thank you for being one of the good guys."

Clivo slowly closed the photo album, gave it a tight squeeze to his chest, and returned it to its hiding place in the closet.

He collapsed in his bed, the cats snuggling up around him, and fell into a deep sleep as his father's words whispered in his head: *"Some things are meant to be hidden. It's much better for the world to have its myths and its magic."*

Acknowledgments

As a debut author, I'd love to thank everyone who has ever lived or ever will live, and also specifically these people: Maura Malloy, who was the first person to read my writing and who told me to keep going, which meant everything. Joe Spieler and Krista Ingebretson for being the next people who read my work and who also told me to keep going. Annie and Chris Parnell for supporting me in so many ways so that I *could* keep going. Thank you to Juliana and Sean Crouch, Rachel Fowler, and Elena Momich for taking the time to read my stuff when it really wasn't any good at all. Matt Love, because hand-sword-hand forever. To my bb for always cooking dinner as I sat with my head in the laptop. To my youngest readers—Maggie and Lilah Hayes and Patrick Stupearceski—who always gave me the best notes. Thank you Mom, Dad, Wayne, and Joel for always encouraging my flights of fancy. Thank you to Aspen Words and the Catto Shaw Foundation for a dreamy writing residency. Big, huge, eternal thanks to my agent, Jason Anthony, for believing that my original story about a Delta

Force soldier hunting a dragon had potential. So many thank yous to Loren Coleman and the International Cryptozoology Museum for being my inspiration. And last but most definitely not least, to Angie Chen for acquiring me, and to all the wonderful magicians at FSG BYR and Macmillan Children's Publishing Group—including editorial staffers Wes Adams, Jennifer Sale, Megan Abbate, and Melissa Warten, copy editor Nancy Elgin, designer Aimee Fleck, production manager Jie Yang, and publicist Heather Job—for waving their wands and turning my words into this book.

Also, to Richard.

Hi, guys!

Clivo Wren here. I hope you'll keep rooting for me and my mission to save the world in my next adventure, *The Cryptid Keeper!* As you've probably noticed, finding cryptids is hard work, and, to be honest, I could use your help. Douglas Chancery will probably take away my Diamond Card if I mess up again——he's kinda cranky like that. So check out LijaFisher.com for information on special cryptozoologist recruitment events so the Myth Blasters can add you to their team. Lija's one of our members (yes, Adam, she went through the initiation!), and she'll also be posting about super neat stuff, like prizes you can win by learning about cryptids yourself. The evil resistance is growing, and we need good guys like you to help us find the immortal. Will you join us?

Clivo Wren

GOFISH

LIJA FISHER

What did you want to be when you grew up?
I wanted to be an actress! I got my degree in theatre and lived in London, Los Angeles, and New York City for many years acting on stage.

When did you realize you wanted to be a writer?
Honestly, not until I was thirty-five! I was on a trip to New Zealand, touring where the *Lord of the Rings* movies were filmed, and the idea for a story just popped into my head. I wrote it down and haven't stopped writing since!

What's your most embarrassing childhood memory?
In kindergarten, we had a pet guinea pig in class and one student was tasked with taking it home for the summer and caring for it. I took it home, but I kept it outside in a cage. Well, a coyote broke into the cage and ate the poor guinea pig, and I had to tell the teacher that I lost our class pet.

What's your favorite childhood memory?
I grew up in the mountains, and in the summertime I would wander around the forest and search for pirates and fairies and other mysterious things!

As a young person, who did you look up to most?

I always looked up to my mom. She grew up during World War II and immigrated to America from Latvia, where she was born. She overcame a lot of hardship early in life and became very successful, both as a businesswoman and as a mom!

What was your favorite thing about school?

I loved school! I always had the best friends (many of whom I'm still friends with today!) and got involved with the theatre crowd early, so I was always surrounded by really fun, creative kids.

What were your hobbies as a kid? What are your hobbies now?

As a kid, I loved reading, doing theatre, and outdoor stuff like hiking. Those are all my favorite hobbies now, too!

Did you play sports as a kid?

I played softball, volleyball, and basketball as a kid, but I kept breaking my fingers in every sport I played! So I ended up doing theatre, which was safer on my fingers.

What was your first job, and what was your "worst" job?

My first job was working at the local farmers market selling freshly picked vegetables. My worst job was delivering sandwiches by bicycle when I lived in London because I could never remember which side of the road to pedal on!

What book is on your nightstand now?

A whole bunch of really funny middle-grade adventures that I wish I had more time to read!

How did you celebrate publishing your first book?
I took two of my best friends out for a really nice, scrumptious dinner!

Where do you write your books?
I either write at my kitchen table with a window that overlooks the mountains, or at coffee shops.

What sparked your imagination for *The Cryptid Catcher*?
I read an article about people searching for something called the Otterman in Alaska, and I had no idea what that was. So I researched the Otterman and discovered this rich world of legendary creatures that people believe still exist!

What challenges do you face in the writing process, and how do you overcome them?
I don't plot my books out ahead of time; I just make them up as I go along. So sometimes I get stuck and don't know what happens next. When that happens, I go hiking in the mountains where I can daydream, and usually the answer comes to me that way.

What is your favorite word?
"Sword."

If you could live in any fictional world, what would it be?
I'd live in a medieval castle where magic still existed and where mythical creatures roamed the land.

In the concluding book of this monstrously funny middle-grade adventure, Clivo Wren continues searching for the immortal cryptid as the evil resistance gets more dangerous . . .

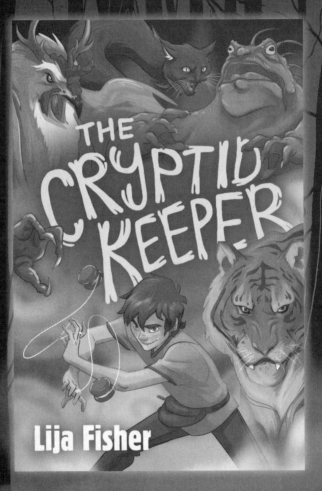

THE CRYPTID KEEPER

Lija Fisher

Keep reading for an excerpt.

I

Clivo Wren sat crouched in the dry yellow grass, a tranquilizer gun on his lap, peering through binoculars at the stream meandering through the boreal forest. A frigid breeze blew, and he wrapped his fur parka tighter around him. *Dang, it's freezing,* he thought. It was the beginning of summer, but apparently the warmth wouldn't hit northern Russia until much later. Why did every legendary creature he stalked have to live in the cold? There must be one by a beach somewhere that he could track in comfort from under a palm tree while drinking from coconuts.

Clivo gagged as he nibbled on some fish he'd caught and cooked the night before, then reminded himself to pack more food for his future quests. He'd been camping along the river for five days now, and his food had already run out, leaving him to survive on the plentiful trout from the river. He had considered snaring a hare for some variety, but had forgotten to bring anything to build a trap with, and he certainly didn't want to waste another of his tranquilizer darts. He'd already used one on a black bear who'd wandered near his tent two nights before, leaving him with just two darts. He would have hated to ruin this catch because he'd wasted all his darts on other wandering wildlife.

He pulled a notebook from his backpack and made a list of things he needed to improve his hunts in the future: More food, more darts, more beaches.

Clivo sighed and looked through his binoculars again at the dam of sticks and twigs blocking the river. It was the third one he'd built to bait his prey, and if he didn't find the creature soon, he knew he'd have to move to a different spot and build another one, which sounded like a miserable prospect. He was ready to go home and eat a hearty meal of something that didn't have scales. A hot bath didn't sound so bad, either, since he was freezing and beginning to stink like fish.

A loud crackle suddenly sounded from his ham radio and broke the stillness of the scene. "Dude! What's taking you so long?!"

Clivo scrambled for the radio in his pocket as other voices also shouted through it.

"Charles! Be quiet! We're not supposed to bother him unless it's an emergency!"

"But this is taking *forever*, Amelia! How hard can it be to find the Ugly Merman?"

"Dude, it's called the Vodyanoy. Use its proper Russian name and give it some respect!"

"Whatever, Adam. 'Ugly Merman' is so much cooler!"

"It so isn't!"

"Yes it is! No! Give me back the radio! I'm the one talking!"

Clivo finally managed to pull the radio out of his thick parka and spoke in a harsh whisper. "Do you guys mind being a little quieter?"

"Oh, hey, dude!" Charles replied chirpily. "How's the Arctic?"

"It's freezing! And I'm tired of chopping down pine trees to build dams with. You sure they're supposed to attract the Merman?" Clivo ran a gloved hand under his nose, which was dripping like a faucet.

"Pretty sure, Clivo." Now it was Stephanie's voice coming through the radio. "It hates anything that obstructs the flow of water. Satellite images show no dams along that stretch of river, whereas the rest of the river is covered with them."

"You sure you're in the right place, dude?" Adam piped in. "You do know how to read a compass, right?"

Clivo rolled his eyes. "Yeah, I know how to read a compass. I'm in the right spot, but you gave me, like, five miles of river to cover, so it took a little while."

"Hi, Clivo," Hernando's meek voice whispered through the radio.

"Well, hurry up, dude!" Charles whined. "I wanna see what the Ugly Merman really looks like!"

"It's called the Vodyanoy, man!" Adam yelled.

"Okay, guys, can you only contact me in case of emergencies, please? I'm kinda trying to stay hidden here," Clivo begged.

"Sorry, dude," Adam said.

"Dude, sorry," Charles agreed.

The radio thankfully went silent, and Clivo pocketed it. The Myth Blasters were an amazing team to work with, and they were always right on with their research on where exactly to find legendary creatures—cryptids—that shouldn't exist. But they were still new to the idea that cryptids actually *did* exist, as he was, so their excitement often got the best of them.

Clivo peered through the binoculars again and scanned the river. The sun was beginning to set, and soon it'd be time to return to his tent and build a fire. He was already dreading his evening meal of more cooked fish.

He tried not to be too hard on himself for coming totally unprepared, seeing as how it was only his fifth catch. Becoming an orphan and then discovering his dad was a cryptid catcher who was searching for the one special beast that could make humans immortal would have been a lot for any kid to handle. Finding out that his dad had secretly been training Clivo all his life to take over as the world's best catcher—which also included fighting off the bad guys—had almost sent him over the edge.

But Clivo eventually discovered that he was more than willing to face the dangers posed by the evil ones to find the immortal. After battling with two Luxembourgers who were dangerous but quite dumb, he knew he had to protect the world from the evil resistance, which sought to use the gift of eternal life for its own gain. He also wanted to protect the cryptids, which were beautiful, mysterious creatures that others sought to lock up in zoos or sell to science if they were ever found.

Clivo thought of Nessie, the Loch Ness Monster, and the Otterman—his first two catches. Neither had turned out to be the immortal, but he'd gotten to see them up close and even touch them, which had been like stepping into a wonderland. Nessie had been very sweet for a massive dinosaur that had been frozen for over sixty-five million years. The Otterman had seemed dangerous at first, with its razor-sharp teeth and claws, but ended up being rather polite and enjoyed eating chocolate much more than human flesh. The horrible thought of these majestic animals being experimented on in labs made Clivo's task of protecting them feel that much more pressing.

Clivo focused his thoughts back on the present and tried to think through the details in the crypto-research manual Adam had prepared for him on the Ugly Merman. The Vodyanoy was a water creature from Russia who'd been sighted since the 1800s. Local folklorists claimed it was a frog-faced naked man who enjoyed playing a game of cards while smoking a wooden pipe, and who occasionally partook in drowning the locals. But Adam's origin theory was that the Merman was actually a harmless Siberian salamander that had undergone a genetic mutation during a particularly strong solar flare and grown to humongous proportions.

Clivo had been relieved by the "harmless" part. Being chased by the Otterman had made him realize that he much preferred catching cryptids that didn't want to rip his face off.

He was just about to call it a night when a loud *crack* sounded. He raised his binoculars and instantly saw the source of the noise—a wart-covered frog the size of a baby elephant was wading in the river and powerfully tearing apart the dam.

One thing was for sure—the Ugly Merman sure was ugly.

"Wow, you really do hate dams, don't you?" Clivo whispered, excited that his time in the Arctic was finally coming to an end.

He grabbed his tranquilizer gun, figuring it should only take one dart to hit the creature since it was so round and bloated. He moved as silently as possible through the tall, dry grass, knowing that if he spooked the Merman it could disappear for days in the freezing-cold water.

When he was finally close enough, he raised his gun and took careful aim, feeling confident that he could easily hit his target. But just as his finger began pressing against the trigger, his radio crackled back to life, disturbing his focus.

"Charles! Give me the radio! Let him do his job!" Amelia yelled.

"I just want to ask him something!" Charles replied.

Clivo flicked his eyes back to the Ugly Merman, which had lifted its head and was staring directly at him, its frog-like face looking very angry.

Clivo fired.

The dart was on target, but suddenly a red tongue at least six feet long whipped out of the monster's mouth and knocked the dart harmlessly into the water.

"Come on!" Clivo mumbled.

His cover blown, he quickly stood up from his place of camouflage and fitted another dart into the gun just as a large log went flying past his head. "What the—?"

He looked up as the creature's enormous and extremely powerful tongue wrapped around a boulder and flung it with ease straight toward him. Clivo barely had enough time to duck and roll before the rock smashed into the ground right where he had just been standing.

"I thought you were supposed to be harmless!" Clivo yelled.

The creature kept attacking Clivo with a constant barrage of projectiles, croaking like a frog all the while. Clivo was so busy scurrying away from the logs and rocks flying at him that he didn't have time to raise his gun.

"All right, buddy, this is getting ridiculous!" Clivo complained as a fish whacked him right in the forehead.

He gripped his gun and rolled down the hill just as the Ugly Merman wrapped its tongue around another rock. Clivo sprang to one knee and fired.

The dart made a smacking sound as it hit the giant frog right in its blubbery belly. The creature let out a mournful croak, its short limbs pawing at the air, before slipping into unconsciousness with its gigantic tongue splayed out on the ground.

Clivo waited a good few minutes before approaching the creature to make sure it was completely passed out. He was pretty sure the lasso-like tongue could easily pick him up and throw him halfway to the North Pole.

When he was certain he wasn't in any danger, he knelt by the creature and pressed the blood sampler to its skin, keeping his eyes on the tongue the whole time.

As the blood traveled up the sampler's chamber, Clivo admired the creature with fascination, as he always did with the cryptids he caught. It looked nothing like a merman, but it sure was unique. It had a bulbous, slimy green body with a broad, flat face and large, protruding eyes. It snored loudly, and its breath smelled like the inside of a sardine can that's been left out in the sun for a few hours.

There was really nothing beautiful about this creature, except for the fact that it was a two-hundred-year-old mysterious animal that was supposed to exist only in imagination and folklore. Clivo patted the slimy skin and smiled. He would do everything in his power to keep it safe from nefarious people who sought to capture and cage it.

The blood sampler finally beeped and Clivo blew air through his lips in disappointment.

NOT IMMORTAL.

Well, apparently this wasn't going to be his last catch after all.

He took a selfie with the creature to show to the Myth Blasters and gathered his things to leave. A hot shower sure was going to feel good.

To be sure some wayward fisherman didn't come across the beast while it was still unconscious, Clivo waited at a distance on the hill until the creature woke up and slid into the water. Then, as Clivo was about to leave, something in the distance caught his eye—a glint of light he hadn't seen before. He knew there was nothing in that direction except more expansive wilderness of yellow grass and pine trees, so who was out there?

It was too late in the day for someone to be out hunting—unless, Clivo realized with a shudder, he was the prey. There were evil groups out there who were not only after the immortal, but also after *him*. He was known as the best catcher in the world, thanks to his father's training and help from the Myth Blasters, and the bad guys were eager to know his secrets. So he stayed on his toes, always making sure he wasn't followed or tracked. He had no desire to be thrown into a dungeon and tortured for information.

Clivo quickly packed up his camp and made the long trek back to the small nearby village, constantly glancing behind him for some sign that he was being followed. His dad had been killed by a fellow cryptid catcher, though which one, Clivo didn't know.

But the one thing he knew for certain was that that person was coming for him next.